DEPARTMENT OF THE ENVIRONMENT

Digest of Environmental Protection and Water Statistics

London: HMSO

Introduction

This publication is the 13th in an annual series which highlights UK trends in some of the main aspects of environmental protection and water supply. The Digest attempts, by abstracting figures from many different reports and papers and bringing them together in standardised form, to make national statistics on environmental protection available on a regular basis.

This issue of the Digest contains chapters on air quality and global atmospheric change, water quality, radioactivity, noise, waste and recycling, land and nature conservation, and water supply and use. A supplementary chapter is included providing background trend data (population, rainfall and temperature, retail prices, national income measures, vehicle usage and energy consumption) which, where relevant, the reader may wish to set alongside the environmental trends in the main chapters. A calendar of events is also included. Further statistics are available in a statistical bulletin (see page 113). The topics to be covered by separate sections are decided each year in accordance with the availability of new data.

The Digest itself aims to provide an extensive and understandable set of statistics and to describe broad environmental trends. Readers wishing to follow up any of the topics covered in the Digest are invited to consult the source documents quoted in footnotes and to purchase the statistical bulletin listed on pages 113.

A special feature of the Digest is the commentary appearing alongside each statistical table. The text emphasises trends, gives information on some of the factors likely to influence them and, where appropriate, links series together.

Presentation

Tables and figures are for the United Kingdom unless otherwise stated; regional figures relate to the standard regions as defined after local government reorganisation in 1974. The data included are generally the latest available in December 1990.

Attempts have been made by the use of footnotes and accompanying text to ensure that each figure or table is self-standing and is as comprehensive as possible, but readers are advised to refer to source documents for a full discussion of the methods of obtaining data and possible interpretations of them. The explanatory text is meant to be used to complement the footnotes and as an aid to the interpretation of the data. A glossary of some of the more technical terms is provided on page xi.

Sources

The tables and figures have been compiled by the Department of the Environment with the help of other Government Departments and non-governmental bodies. The Department is grateful to these organisations for their help in providing data and, in some cases, for information required for the commentary. Many of the data presented have been published elsewhere. Information on sources of the data is given under each table, both in the Digest and in the statistical bulletin. In January 1991 the Scottish Development Department was renamed The Scottish Office Environment Department.

Statistical bulletins

In previous years, a number of separate statistical bulletins were published and updated annually, providing more detailed information on particular topics. Last year, four such bulletins were published covering air quality, water quality, radioactivity and miscellaneous items. This year, much of this information has been published in the Digest itself. A single statistical bulletin has been prepared this year providing additional data that, in general, are too detailed for publication in the Digest. This bulletin may be purchased from the Department; full details are given on page 113.

OECD reports

Two new environmental reports containing information on environmental trends in OECD countries were published by the Organisation for Economic Co-operation and Development (OECD) in January 1991, namely the third OECD *State of the Environment* report with an *Environmental Indicators* supplement. Further details about these two reports and where they can be purchased are given on page 117.

Environmental Protection
Statistics Division
Department of the Environment

Standard regions, National Rivers Authority regions and River Purification Boards

United Kingdom

National Rivers Authority
regions — Anglian

River Purification Board (Scotland)

Standard Region — — Northern

Highland

North East

Scotland

Tay

Forth

Clyde

Tweed

Solway

Northumbria

Northern

Northern Ireland
Northern Ireland

Yorkshire

North West

Yorkshire and Humberside

North West

East Midlands

Severn Trent

Wales

West Midlands

Anglian

East Anglia

Welsh

Thames

South East

Wessex

South West

Southern

South West

Kilometres
0   80

0   50
Miles

The standard regions of England are those adopted on 1 April 1974 following the Local Government Act 1972. The National Rivers Authority was established on 10 July 1989 under the Water Act 1989. The river purification boards of Scotland came into being on 16 May 1975 following the Local Government (Scotland Act 1973. The Department of the Environment (Northern Ireland) is the sole water authority for Northern Ireland.

Contents

List of tables

Tables cover the United Kingdom and the year 1989 unless otherwise stated.

Chapter 4 Noise

Chapter 5 Waste and recycling

Chapter 6 Land and nature conservation

Chapter 7 Water supply

Chapter 8 Supplementary tables

List of figures

Chapter 1 Air quality and global atmospheric change

Chapter 2 Water quality

Chapter 3 Radioactivity

Chapter 4 Noise

Chapter 5 Waste and recycling

Chapter 6 Land and nature conservation

Chapter 7 Water supply

Symbols and conventions used

In tables where figures have been rounded to the nearest final digit, there may be an apparent slight discrepancy between the sum of the constituent items and the total as shown.

Percentages.   Percentage figures are shown in italics.

Symbols.   The following symbols have been used throughout the Digest and statistical bulletins.

..	=	not available
-	=	nil or negligible (less than half the final digit shown)
r	=	revised since last publication
p	=	provisional
$\geq$	=	greater than or equal to
$>$	=	greater than
$\leq$	=	less than or equal to
$<$	=	less than
ppm/b	=	parts per million/billion
pphm	=	parts per hundred million
kg	=	kilogram
g	=	gram
mg	=	milligram
μg	=	microgram
km	=	kilometre
m	=	metre
cm	=	centimetre
μm	=	micrometre
km^2	=	square kilometre
ha	=	hectare
m^2	=	square metre
m^3	=	cubic metre
l	=	litre
ml	=	millilitre
pH	=	measure of acidity/alkalinity
TBq	=	terabecquerel
GBq	=	gigabecquerel
MBq	=	megabecquerel
Bq	=	becquerel
Gy	=	gray
Sv	=	sievert
mSv	=	millisievert
μSv	=	microsievert
μS	=	microsiemen

Conversion factors

1 tonne = 1,000 kilograms
1 international nautical mile = 1,852 metres
1 mile = 1,609.344 metres
1 hectare = 10,000 square metres
1 square kilometre = 100 hectares
1 gallon = 0.00454609 cubic metres
1 litre = 0.001 cubic metres
1 curie = 3.7 x 10^{10} becquerels
1 becquerel = 1 nuclear disintegration per second
1 terabecquerel = 10^{12} becquerels
1 gigabecquerel = 10^9 becquerels
1 megabecquerel = 10^6 becquerels
All the above conversion factors are exact.

Definitions

Some of the scientific and technical terms used in the Digest are defined below.

Air quality and global atmospheric change

Acidity: is expressed on pH scale which indicates acidity/alkalinity: a neutral substance has a pH of 7.0 and the lower the pH the greater the acidity.

Black smoke: fine suspended particulate air pollutants arising from incomplete combustion of fossil fuels. Concentrations of smoke in the air are measured by determining their soiling capacity; a calibration curve is then used to give concentrations in terms of "equivalent standard smoke" per cubic metre of air.

Carbon dioxide: a "greenhouse" gas.

Carbon monoxide: a colourless odourless gas produced by the incomplete combustion of carbon. It can accumulate in the blood with toxic effects though the effect produced depends on the length of exposure.

CFCs: compounds of carbon, fluorine, chlorine and hydrogen widely used in aerosols and as refrigerants.

Lead: a metallic element which, in the form of its compounds, can be retained in the human body with clinical and sub-clinical effects. Lead in the air arises mainly from anit-knock additives to petrol.

Methane: a gaseous hydrocarbon (CH_4), and a "greenhouse" gas.

Nitrogen oxides: there are a number of nitrogen oxides of different composition, emissions normally being expressed in terms of nitrogen dioxide equivalent. Nitrogen dioxide is a brown toxic gas which is involved in photochemical reactions with other air pollutants to give irritant products.

Ozone: a blue pungent strong gas, which is an irritant to eyes, nose and throat and toxic by inhalation. It is produced by photochemical reactions involving volatile organic compounds and nitrogen oxides. It contributes to photochemical smog.

Sulphur dioxide: a colourless gas with a choking smell, the main product of the combustion of sulphur contained in fuels. Globally, much of the sulphur dioxide in the atmosphere comes from natural sources, but in highly developed and heavily populated regions the greater part comes from combustion of sulphur containing fossil fuels (coal and oil).

Troposphere and stratosphere: The atmosphere is divided into layers that are defined approximately by the distance above the surface of the earth. The troposphere 0-15 km, the stratosphere 15-50 km. Each of the layers has distinct physical and chemical properties.

Volatile organic compounds: consist of a large number of compounds including hydrocarbons and oxygenated and halogenated organics.

Water quality

Biochemical oxygen demand or BOD: a standard water-treatment test for the presence of organic pollutants, and is a measure of the oxygen required by the microbes which reduce the wastes to simple compounds.

Biochemical oxygen demand (ATU): a form of the standard BOD test which suppresses the oxidation of ammonia and indicates more accurately the biodegradable matter in a sample.

Heavy metals: generally cover mercury, lead, cadmium, selenium, arsenic and nickel. Accumulate in selective organs of the body, eg, brain and liver, with possible clinical effects.

PCBs: polychlorinated biphenyls. Mainly used as plasticizers and to enhance flame retardance and insulating properties. Highly active biologically, they have been restricted by voluntary agreements.

Pesticides: a product or substance used in the control of pests which may affect public health or attack resources of use to man (eg, DDT, the "Drins" and lindane).

Radioactivity

ATOMIC STRUCTURE

Atom: (nucleus + electrons) the smallest portion of an element that can combine chemically with other atoms.

Electron: an elementary particle with low mass, 1/1836 that of a proton, and unit negative electric charge. Positively charged electrons, called positrons, also exist.

Isotope: nuclides with the same number of protons but different numbers of neutrons.

Neutron: an elementary particle with unit atomic mass approximately and no electric charge.

Nucleus: (protons + neutrons) the core of an atom, occupying little of the volume, containing most of the mass, and bearing positive electric charge.

Nuclide: a species of atom characterised by the number of protons and neutrons and, in some cases, by the energy state of the nucleus.

Proton: an elementary particle with unit atomic mass approximately and unit positive electric charge.

RADIATION

Activity: attribute of an amount of a radionuclide. Describes the rate at which transformations occur in it. Unit becquerel (Bq). 1Bq = 1 nuclear disintegration per second.

Decay: the process of spontaneous transformation of a radionuclide. The decrease in the activity of a radioactive substance.

Decay product: a nuclide or radionuclide produced by decay.

Half-life: the time taken for the activity of a radionuclide to lose half its value by decay.

Ion: electrically charged atom or grouping of atoms.

Ionisation: the process by which a neutral atom or molecule acquires or loses an electric charge. The production of ions.

Ionising radiation: radiation that produces ionisation in matter. Examples are alpha particles, beta particles, gamma rays, x-rays, and neutrons.

Radioactive: possessing the property of radioactivity.

Radioactivity: the property of radionuclides of spontaneously emitting ionising radiation.

Radiation: the process of emitting energy as waves or particles. The energy thus radiated.

Radionuclide: an unstable nuclide that emits ionising radiation.

TYPES OF RAYS

Alpha particle: a particle consisting of two protons plus two neutrons. Emitted by a radionuclide.

Beta particle: an electron emitted by the nucleus of a radionuclide. The electric charge may be positive (positron).

Gamma ray: a discrete quantity of electromagnatic energy, without mass or charge. Emitted by a radionuclide. See x-ray.

X-ray: a discrete quantity of elctromagnetic energy without mass or charge. Emitted by an x-ray machine. See gamma-ray.

DOSES

Absorbed dose: quantity of energy imparted by ionising radiation to unit mass of matter such as tissue. Unit gray (Gy). 1 Gy = 1 joule per kilogram.

Collective effective dose equivalent (collective dose): effective dose equivalent to a group from a source of radiation.

Dose equivalent: absorbed dose weighted for harmfulness of different radiations. Unit sievert (Sv). Usually the factor for gamma-rays, x-rays and beta particles is 1 but for alpha particles 20.

Effective dose equivalent: dose equivalent weighted for susceptibility to harm of different tissues (risk weighting factors). Unit sievert (Sv).

SPECIFIC RADIONUCLIDES

Argon-41: radioactive isotope of Argon, which has a half-life of only 110 minutes, is produced mainly from the activation of the argon present naturally in the air used to cool the outside surfaces of the reactor vessels and their shields. It is discharged from high stacks to ensure its rapid dispersal in the atmosphere and, being inert, it is not reconcentrated by biological systems.

Caesium-137: radioactive isotope of caesium produced in nuclear reactions, with a half-life of 30 years. It is chemically similar to potassium; when absorbed in the body, it spreads throughout the muscles.

Strontium-90: radioactive isotope of strontium produced in nuclear reactions, with a half-life of 28 years. It is chemically similar to calcium and tends to be concentrated in milk; when absorbed into the body, it is concentrated in the bones.

Tritium: radioactive isotope of hydrogen produced in nuclear reactions, with a half-life of 12.3 years. It has a very low radiotoxicity and is not subject to reconcentration in marine organisms and therefore relatively large quantities may be discharged with relatively little radiological effect.

MEASUREMENTS

The International System (SI) of units for radioactivity, radiation and the effects of radiation are as follows:

Becquerel (Bq): The standard international unit of radioactivity, equal to one radioactive transformation per second. Multiples of the becquerel are frequently used such as the terabecquerel, TBq, which is 1 million million becquerels.

Gray (Gy): The standard unit of absorbed dose.

milli-Sievert (mSv): A unit of effective dose equal to one-thousandth of a Sievert. Natural radiation and natural radioactivity in the environment give an average effective dose to each member of the public of about 2 mSv per year. The internationally recommended limit for prolonged public exposure to artificial radioactivity is 1mSv per year.

Sievert (Sv): The standard unit of biologically-effective dose, taking account of the damage caused by different types of radiation.

Land and nature conservation

Crown density: The amount of light passing through the crown of a tree. Used as an indicator of tree health.

Chapter 1   Air quality and global atmospheric change

This chapter deals with the quality of the air we breathe. Nothing is so all pervading: good air quality is essential for human health and the health of the environment as a whole. Polluted air can seriously affect the quality of life, especially for those with asthma, bronchitis and similar breathing problems. It can damage historic buildings and kill sensitive plant life. In the long term it can even change our soil and water.

Data on pollutants can be presented as exposure concentrations in the atmosphere or deposition loads to the environment. Emission data are very important as they identify the main sources of pollutants and are used in mathematical models to estimate levels of pollutants where they cannot be directly measured.

See page xi for definitions of terms used in this chapter.

For most pollutants the combustion of fuels is the major source of emissions which pollute the atmosphere. Estimates of emissions are prepared for the Department of the Environment (DOE) by Warren Spring Laboratory (WSL) and are available for emission source and type of fuel. For most sources pollutant emissions are estimated by applying emission factors to figures for fuel consumption (see Table 1.1) in the various sectors of activity; for example, industry and power stations. The exception is road transport where UK vehicle driving patterns are also used. It should be noted that emission factors are being updated constantly and that estimates are subject to a degree of uncertainty arising from the uncertainty involved in calculating exact amounts of fuel use and the precise mix of plant in which it is used. The statistics presented here should be regarded as the best estimates currently available.

1.1 Fuel consumption by type of fuel and consumer[1]

United Kingdom

Million tonnes

	1979	1980	1981	1982	1983	1984	1985	1986	1987	1988	1989
Coal:											
Domestic	8.9	7.3	6.9	6.7	6.2	4.8	6.5	7.0	5.7	5.1	4.3
Industry, etc[2]	11.8	10.1	9.3	9.4	9.4	8.0	9.5	10.0	9.6	9.5	8.6
Power stations	88.8	89.6	87.2	80.2	81.6	53.4	73.9	82.6	86.2	82.5	80.6
Gas works[3]	2.9	3.0	2.5	2.3	2.1	1.3	2.2	2.0	2.1	2.0	1.7
Solid smokeless fuel:											
Domestic	4.5	4.4	4.0	4.1	3.9	3.2	4.2	3.5	3.5	3.3	3.0
Industry, etc[4]	3.1	2.0	2.0	1.9	1.9	1.8	2.1	2.0	2.0	2.0	1.9
Petroleum:											
Motor spirit	18.7	19.1	18.7	19.2	19.6	20.2	20.4	21.5	22.2	23.2	23.9
Diesel fuel	6.1	5.9	5.5	5.7	6.2	6.8	7.1	7.9	8.5	9.4	10.1
Burning oil (Kerosene)	2.7	2.1	1.9	1.7	1.7	1.7	1.9	2.0	2.0	2.0	1.9
Gas oil	12.4	10.6	10.0	9.5	9.0	10.0	8.7	9.2	8.6	8.4r	8.3
Fuel oil:											
Power stations	10.7	6.3	4.8	6.3	3.8	19.8	9.5	5.6	4.4	5.1r	5.3
Other uses	16.3	12.7	10.8	9.9	8.7	8.0	6.4	7.0	5.4	6.8	5.8
Refinery fuel	6.5	6.3	5.4	5.5	5.3	5.4	5.2	5.4	5.2	5.5	5.8

Million therms

	1979	1980	1981	1982	1983	1984	1985	1986	1987	1988	1989
Liquified petroleum gas[5]	690	600	564	685	833	912	731	888	905	882r	874
Other petroleum gas[5]	153	139	125	302	379	489	535	680	733	745	648
Coke oven gas[6]	831	619	578	537	544	438	604	600	611	574	565
Blast furnace gas	775	352	503	442	481	486	517	476	573	645	623
Town gas	36	31	27	23	18	17	16	14	11	3	-
Natural gas[7]	17,067	17,278	17,385	17,594	17,954	18,540	19,790	20,019	20,895	20,208r	19,730

[1] Include only those fuels which are sources of air pollution for which estimated emissions are presented in later tables in this chapter.
[2] Final energy users (ie, industry other than fuel conversion industries), and also includes public services, railways, agriculture and miscellaneous.
[3] Includes low temperature carbonisation and patent fuel plants.
[4] Includes public services, railways, agriculture and miscellaneous.
[5] Excludes gas already included under "refinery fuel" which is a mixture of gas and oil fuel.
[6] Unpurified.
[7] Includes substitute natural gas.

Source: *Warren Spring Laboratory, Department of Trade and Industry using the* Digest of United Kingdom Energy Statistics *published by the Department of Energy*

Note:
1 million therms is approximately equivalent to 4,000 tonnes of coal or 2,400 tonnes of petroleum.

Figure 1.1 UK automated air quality monitoring sites 1989/90

Site Locations

1 Strath Vaich
2 Glasgow
3 Bush
4 Eskdalemuir
5 Great Dun Fell
6 Wharley Croft
7 Billingham
8 High Muffles
9 Featherstone
10 Glazebury
11 Manchester
12 Ladybower Res.
13 Bircotes
14 Bottesford
15 Aston Hill
16 Walsall
17 Sibton
18 Stevenage
19 Harwell
20 West London

21 Cromwell Road
22 Central London
23 Lullington Heath
24 Yarner Wood
25 Mace Head[1]
26 Lough Navar
27 Belfast

Pollutants

● Ozone
● Nitrogen dioxide
● Sulphur dioxide
● Carbon monoxide

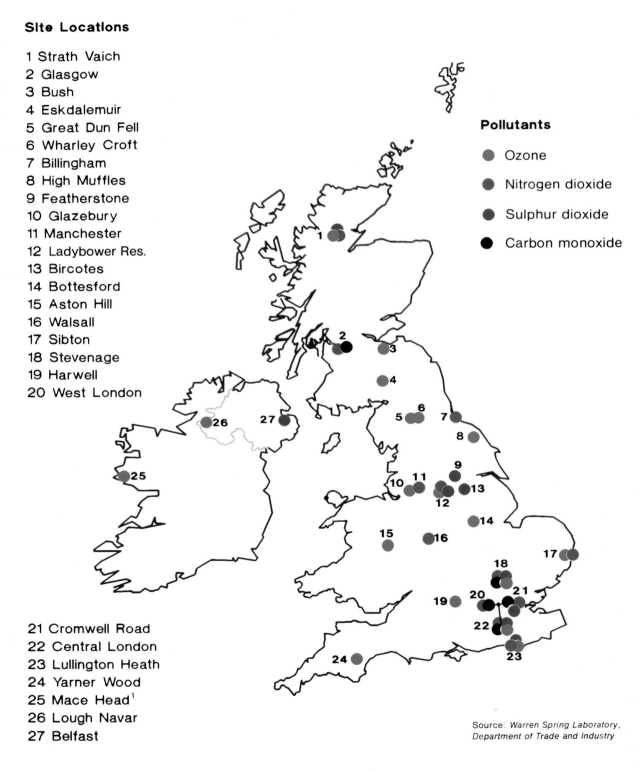

Source: *Warren Spring Laboratory,
Department of Trade and Industry*

1 Established with the co-operation of the Department of the Environment of the Republic of Ireland

Monitoring networks, which measure atmospheric concentrations of pollutants directly, have been developed on the basis of advice from expert Review Groups sponsored by DOE. The number and location of monitoring sites are reviewed periodically to ensure that they provide a representative and cost effective coverage of the UK and networks are adapted where necessary to comply with EC directives. The UK also recognises the value of World Health Organisation (WHO) pollutant concentration guidelines.[1] Table 1.2 shows the number of sites used in the UK to measure concentrations of major air pollutants. The location of sites providing automatic monitoring of air pollution is shown in Figure 1.1. In October 1990, the DOE announced a new scheme[2] to include UK air quality information in weather bulletins from the Meteorological Office for use by national television and the press and via recorded telephone messages for members of the public. Under the new scheme, air quality will be designated "very good", "good", "poor" or "very poor" on a daily basis in relation to airborne concentrations of sulphur dioxide, nitrogen dioxide and ozone.

Concentration data from monitoring sites are used to monitor compliance with air quality standards set in EC directives for sulphur dioxide, particulates, lead and nitrogen dioxide. Concentrations of pollutants are highly dependent on weather conditions and much of the year-to-year variability can be attributed to the variability of the weather. For example, sulphur dioxide concentrations tend to be higher in years with cold winters because fuel consumption increases and because associated weather conditions prevent dispersion. Peak ground-level ozone concentrations become elevated during extended periods of warm sunny summertime weather and year-to-year variability exerts a significant influence on ground-level exposure levels.

The order in which the major pollutants are dealt with in this chapter reflects the geographical scale at which impacts are felt and the level at which decisions about reducing them have to be made: firstly, pollutants with local effects; secondly, pollutants which cross international boundaries and which are subject to international agreement between neighbouring countries, including those contributing to acid rain; and, finally, pollutants that contribute to stratospheric ozone depletion and to global warming and that require worldwide international agreement.

LOCAL ISSUES

Sulphur dioxide (SO₂) and smoke

Sulphur dioxide is a gas released by the combustion of sulphur-containing fuels such as coal and oil. Smoke consists of fine suspended particulate air pollutants arising from incomplete fuel combustion. The potential

1.2 Air quality monitoring sites:[1] December 1990

United Kingdom

Pollutant	Number of sites[2]
Ozone[3]	17
Carbon monoxide[3]	5
Nitrogen oxides[3]	12
Acid deposition, nitrogen dioxide, sulphur dioxide and ammonia	32
Atmospheric hydrocarbon	2
Trace gases	1
PAN, hydrogen peroxide, hydrocarbons and aerosols	2
Smoke and sulphur dioxide sites	261
Other sulphur dioxide sites[3]	9
Lead	18
Multi-element sites including lead	5

Source: *Warren Spring Laboratory, Department of Trade and Industry*

[1] Monitored on behalf of the Department of the Environment by Warren Spring Laboratory, Department of Trade and Industry; Harwell Laboratory; University of Manchester Institute of Science and Technology and the Institute of Terrestrial Ecology.
[2] Monitoring sites for different air pollutants may be located in the same place.
[3] Automated monitoring sites.

Figure 1.2 Sulphur dioxide (SO₂): estimated emissions source

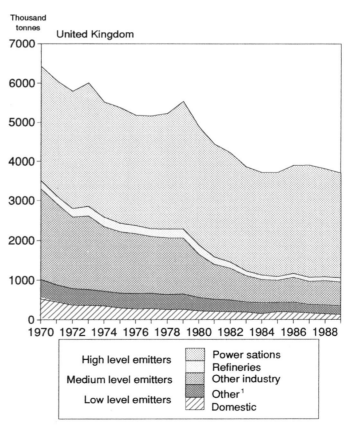

1. Commercial / public service; agriculture; railways; road transport; civil aircraft; shipping.

Source: *Warren Spring Laboratory, Department of Trade and Industry*

health effects of sulphur dioxide include temporary respiratory problems in sensitive groups exposed to high levels for short periods and an increased prevalence of respiratory problems from long term exposure. Smoke has similar effects. In addition, sulphur dioxide affects vegetation by inducing lesions and reducing growth and is a major contributor to acid rain (see below).

Total emissions of sulphur dioxide were relatively stable in the 1960s at around 6 million tonnes per annum but, as Figure 1.2 shows, declined during the 1970s and early 1980s to under 4 million tonnes in 1983 (the temporary increase in 1979 was due to an exceptionally cold winter). The causes of this decline

included increasing use of sulphur-free fuels such as natural gas in place of coal and oil, lower industrial energy demand and energy conservation. Table 1.3 shows recent trends in sulphur dioxide emissions for each emission source and by type of fuel. Total emissions fell to 3.7 million tonnes in 1984 and 1985 during the miners' strike because power stations and industry switched from coal to oil but returned in 1986, 1987 and 1988 to the 1983 pre-strike level of over 3.8 million tonnes. In 1989 emissions fell by 3 per cent to 3.7 million tonnes, mainly because of a decline in emissions from power stations. Emissions per unit of gross domestic product (GDP) indicate an almost 50 per cent reduction between 1979 and 1989.

1.3 Sulphur dioxide (SO$_2$): estimated emissions by emission source and type of fuel

United Kingdom   Thousand tonnes

	1979	1980	1981	1982	1983	1984	1985	1986	1987	1988	1989	Percentage of total in 1989
a) By emission source												
Domestic	264	226	210	202	195	158	202	197	171	155	135	4
Commercial/public service[1]	221	197	178	170	143	148	128	135	107	101r	88	2
Power stations	3,242	3,007	2,847	2,748	2,631	2,589	2,627	2,722	2,830	2,730r	2,644	71
Refineries	228	237	185	165	117	115	96	108	102	97	109	3
Agriculture	30	21	17	15	12	10	8	9	8	7	7	-
Other industry[2]	1,409	1,089	879	792	662	593	556	621	583r	617r	595	16
Railways	14	11	9	8	5	6	5	5	4	4	3	-
Road transport	55	42	53	49	42	43	45	50	46	54	60	2
Civil aircraft	2r	2r	2r	2r	2r	2r	2r	-	2r	1r	1	-
Shipping	67r	62r	53r	57r	52r	55r	50r	48r	45r	46r	57	2
Total	5,531r	4,894r	4,431r	4,208r	3,861r	3,719r	3,718r	3,895r	3,898r	3,813r	3,699	100
b) By type of fuel												
Coal	3,333	3,225	3,113	2,945	2,986	2,103	2,707	3,006	3,119	2,959r	2,832	77
Solid smokeless fuel	64	64	58	60	58	44	61	51	50	47	42	1
Petroleum:												
Motor spirit	19	11	26	23	16	16	16	17	9	19	22	1
Derv	36	30	27	26	26	27	28	33	37	36	38	1
Gas	171r	121r	96r	98r	76r	75r	70r	69r	67r	60r	58	2
Fuel oil	1,847r	1,378r	1,054r	1,010r	652r	1,404r	787r	672r	568r	646r	660	18
Burning oil	2	2	2	1	1	1	1	2	2	1	2	-
Other petroleum	22r	27r	25r	18r	20r	22r	21r	21	22r	23r	23	1
Other emissions	36	35	30	26	27	27	26	24	22r	23r	22	1
Total	5,531r	4,894r	4,431r	4,208r	3,861r	3,719r	3,718r	3,895r	3,898r	3,813r	3,699	100
c) Emissions from large combustion plants												
Large plants[3]	4,273	3,865	3,533	3,364	3,125	3,042	3,040	3,184	3,264r	3,179r	3,092	
Index (1980 = 100)	111	100	91	87	81	79	79	82	84	82r	80	
d) Emissions (tonnes)/GDP (£ million)[4]												
	16.7	15.1	13.9	13.0	11.5	10.8	10.4	10.5	10.1	9.4	8.9	

[1] Includes miscellaneous emission sources.
[2] Excludes power stations, refineries and agriculture.
[3] Power stations, refineries and a proportion (57%) of other industry.
[4] GDP measured at 1985 market prices.

Source: *Warren Spring Laboratory, Department of Trade and Industry; Central Statistical Office*

Figure 1.3 Black smoke: estimated emissions[1] by emission source

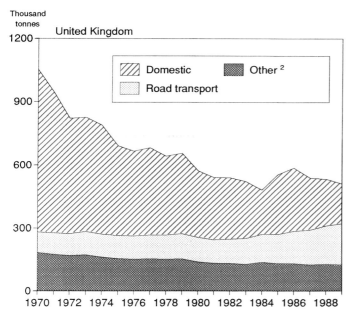

1. Based mainly on constant emission factors.
2. Commercial / public service; power stations; refineries; agriculture; other industry; railways; civil aircraft; shipping.

Source: Warren Spring Laboratory, Department of Trade and Industry

efficiently or switch to an alternative fuel. Table 1.4 shows recent trends in black smoke emissions for each emission source and by type of fuel. Emissions fell continuously from 655,000 tonnes in 1979 to 482,000 tonnes in 1984 during the miners' strike. After a rise to 585,000 tonnes in 1986, emissions fell again to 512,000 tonnes in 1989. The contribution from domestic sources fell from 58 per cent in 1979 to 37 per cent in 1989, whilst that from road transport rose from 18 per cent to 39 per cent over the same period. These changes are reflected in the analysis by fuel type which shows between 1979 and 1989 a substantial reduction in emissions from coal combustion and an almost doubling of emissions from diesel combustion. Total emissions of black smoke per unit of GDP decreased by almost one half over this period.

Ground-level concentrations of sulphur dioxide and smoke are both limited by EC Directive 80/779 which came into force in 1983. The mandatory limit values are intended to act as a protection for human health and are based on WHO guidelines for safe levels of the pollutants. WSL co-ordinates on behalf of DOE a 261-site network to monitor compliance with this directive and for other monitoring purposes. In addition, automatic monitoring data of hourly sulphur dioxide concentrations at nine sites (see Figure 1.1) are made

Table 1.3 shows that 90 per cent of sulphur dioxide is emitted from industrial sources, 71 per cent coming from power stations which burn fossil fuel. The combustion of coal and fuel oil account for 95 per cent of sulphur dioxide emissions. Between 1979 and 1989 the contribution from coal combustion rose from 60 to 77 per cent whilst that from fuel oil combustion fell from 33 to 18 per cent.

EC Directive 88/609 on emissions from large combustion plants sets emission limits for sulphur dioxide, nitrogen dioxide and dust for new plants and also requires a reduction in total sulphur dioxide emissions from existing combustion installations with a capacity greater than 50 megawatts by 20 per cent by 1993, 40 per cent by 1998 and 60 per cent by 2003, taking 1980 emissions as the baseline. Table 1.3 shows that emissions from large combustion plants in 1989 were 3 per cent lower than in 1988 and were 20 per cent below the 1980 baseline level.

Figure 1.3 shows that emissions of black smoke fell by one-half between 1970 and 1979 due predominantly to reductions from domestic sources. This is largely the successful result of the Clean Air Acts legislated in the 1950s and 1960s to ensure that consumers burn coal

Figure 1.4 Smoke[1] and sulphur dioxide: trends in urban concentrations

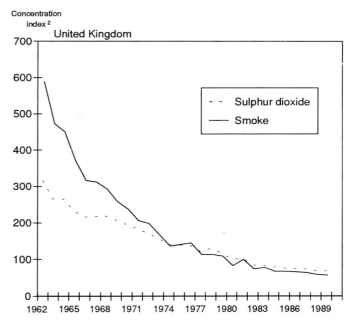

1. Smoke is taken to be suspended matter collected on filter paper in accordance with British Standard (BS) 1747 : Part 2.
2. 1981 / 2 = 100 (for sulphur dioxide = 50Mg/ m³ ;for smoke = 23Mg / m³).

Source: Warren Spring Laboratory, Department of Trade and Industry

1.4 Black smoke: estimated emissions[1] by emission source and by type of fuel

United Kingdom   Thousand tonnes

	1979	1980	1981	1982	1983	1984	1985	1986	1987	1988	1989	Percentage of total in 1989
a) By emission source												
Domestic	382	316	297	292	271	212	285	300	247	223	191	37
Commercial/public service[2]	7	6	6	6	6	6	6	5	5	4	4	1
Power stations	33	29	27	26	24	33	28	26	26	26r	25	5
Refineries	4	4	3	3	3	3	2	2	2	2	2	-
Agriculture	1	1	1	1	1	1	1	1	1	1	1	-
Other industry[3]	102	93	90	91	89	89	89	91	87r	89r	88	17
Railways	2	2	2	2	1	1	1	1	1	1	-	-
Road transport	121	118	112	116	124	135	141	155	167	184	198	39
Civil aircraft	1	1	1	1	1	1	1	1	1	1	1	-
Shipping	3r	3r	2r	3r	3r	3r	3r	2	2r	2	3	1
Total	655r	572r	541r	539r	521r	482r	555	585r	538r	533	512	100
b) By type of fuel												
Coal	413	341	322	315	294	228	306	326	274	251	218	43
Solid smokeless fuel	21	21	19	19	19	15	20	17	17	16	14	3
Petroleum:												
Motor spirit	12	12	12	12	13	13	13	14	14	15	15	3
Derv	109	105	100	103	111	122	128	142	152	169	182	36
Gas	11	10	9	9	8	9r	8	8	7	7	7	1
Fuel oil	32r	24r	20r	20r	16r	31r	19r	15	12	14r	14	3
Other petroleum	1	1	1	1	1	1	1	1	1	1	1	-
Other emissions	56	58	58	60	59	64	60	62	60r	60r	60	12
Total	655r	572r	541r	539r	521r	482r	555	585r	538r	533	512	100
c) Emissions (tonnes)/GDP (£ million)[4]												
	2.0	1.8	1.7	1.7	1.6	1.4	1.6	1.6	1.4	1.3	1.2	

[1] Includes miscellaneous emission sources.
[2] Excludes power stations, refineries and agriculture.
[3] Power stations, refineries and a proportion (57%) of other industry.
[4] GDP measured at 1985 market prices.

Source: *Warren Spring Laboratory, Department of Trade and Industry; Central Statistical Office*

available on a daily basis via the Meteorological Office who also broadcast bulletins when air quality is judged to be "poor" or "very poor" according to criteria set by the Department of Health. Summary indications of site breaches of the directive limit values since 1983/4 are given in Table 1.5. Areas where levels above the limit values were recorded have fallen from 13 in 1983/4 to three in 1989/90. These three exceedences were at sites in Sunderland, Belfast and Newry. Details of the directive limit values themselves and further details of their exceedences are given in Statistical Bulletin (91)1. Sulphur dioxide concentrations at a representative selection of monitoring sites are shown in Table 1.6. The WHO hourly guideline of 122.5 ppb was exceeded at most of these sites in 1989.

Trends in average urban concentrations of both sulphur dioxide and smoke are given in Figure 1.4. Between 1962/3 and 1989/90, urban concentrations of sulphur dioxide fell by nearly 80 per cent reflecting mainly the reduction from low-level sources. The decrease for smoke has been even greater, the 1989/90 concentration being about one-tenth of that in 1962/3. This reduction has come about largely from controls established under the Clean Air Acts of 1956 and 1968. Recent trends in the numbers of smoke control orders in operation, the area and number of premises covered are shown in Table 1.7. Although the majority of smoke control orders were made soon after the enabling legislation, they are still continuing to be issued. The number of orders and premises affected are nearly 20 per cent higher in 1989 than in 1979 with the area covered increased by nearly 30 per cent. Local authorities can also give grant to householders to help them pay for new boilers and fires in newly-declared smoke control zones. Table 1.8 shows the upward trend during the 1980s of sums reimbursed by the Exchequer to local authorities to support such grant incentives.

1.5 Smoke and sulphur dioxide: breaches of limit values - Directive 80/779/EEC

United Kingdom

Local authority	Monitoring site (site no.)	1983/4	1984/5[1]	1985/6	1986/7	1987/8	1988/9	1989/90
Barnsley	Goldthorpe (1)	X						
Barnsley	Grimethorpe (2)	X		X				
Barnsley	Wombwell (2)	X						
Barnsley	Barnsley (9)			X				
Bassetlaw	Langold (1)				X			
Copeland	Whitehaven (2)	X						
Copeland	Crewe (17)					X		
Doncaster	Askern (6)	X						
Doncaster	Askern (8)	X		X				
Doncaster	Doncaster (27)	X						
Doncaster	Doncaster (29)			X				
Doncaster	Doncaster (32)	X		X				
Doncaster	Moorends (1)	X		X				
Doncaster	Mexborough (19)					X		
Easington	Seaham (2)				X	X		
Mansfield	Mansfield (2)	X						
Newark	New Ollerton (2)						X	
Sunderland	Sunderland (8)	X		X		X		
Sunderland	Hetton-le-Hole (3)				X	X	X	X
Sunderland	Houghton-le-Spring (2)					X		
Wakefield	Castleford (9)	X						
Wakefield	Featherstone (1)			X		X		
Wansbeck	Ashington (4)	X				X		
Belfast	Belfast (12)		X	X				
Belfast	Belfast (13)				X			
Belfast	Belfast (17)		X					
Belfast	Belfast (33)		X					
Belfast	Belfast (39)					X	X	
Belfast	Belfast (42)							X
Derry	Londonderry (8)		X					
Newry and Mourne	Newry (3)		X	X				X
Newry and Mourne	Newry (4)		X		X			
		13	6	10	5	9	3	3

[1] No pollution levels above the Directive limits were recorded in England in 1984/5 due to reduced coal burning during the miners' strike.

Source: *Warren Spring Laboratory, Department of Trade and Industry*

7

1.6 Sulphur dioxide (SO$_2$): concentrations[1] at selected sites

United Kingdom

Site	Year	Annual average (ppb)	98th percentile of hourly average for year (ppb)	Number of hours exceeding WHO hourly guideline of 122.5 ppb	Data capture for year[2] %
EC Directive 80/779 sites					
Belfast	1989	45	285	243	31
Bircotes	1989	21	109	40	29
Featherstone	1989	27	97	22	27
Kerbside					
Cromwell Road	1987	..	..	..	..
	1988	..	..	..	..
	1989	20	62	15	72
Urban site					
Central London	1985	11	47	11	56
	1986	16	71	45	86
	1987	11	52	14	68
	1988	10	47	1	89
	1989	12	56	18	87
Suburban site					
Stevenage	1985	15	81	37	83
	1986	20	89	48	68
	1987	10	55	16	79
	1988	7	38	3	89
	1989	8	31	-	90
Rural sites					
Sibton	1988	7	20	-	47
	1989	4	17	-	41
Lullington Heath	1988	3	18	-	56
	1989	4	17	-	37
Ladybower Reservoir	1988	7	41	2	51
	1989	8	44	7	75

[1] Measurements are made with continuous pulsed UV-fluorescent analysers; "-" refers to nil exceedences (rather than nil or negligible exceedences).

[2] Percentage of possible values available throughout the year.

Source: *Warren Spring Laboratory, Department of Trade and Industry*

1.7 Smoke control orders: number in operation, area and premises covered

United Kingdom

	1979	1980	1981	1982	1983	1984	1985	1986	1987	1988	1989
Total number of orders	5,375	5,581	5,667	5,763	5,840	5,933	6,025	6,102	6,168	6,237	6,293
Total area covered (thousand hectares)	729	759	774	794	812	847	869	887	899	924	943
Total number of premises[1] affected (thousands)	7,862	8,080	8,256	8,436	8,595	8,767	8,899	9,001	9,109	9,245	9,380

[1] Domestic and industrial premises.

Source: *Department of the Environment; Welsh Office; Scottish Development Department; Department of the Environment (Northern Ireland)*

1.8 Clean air grants:[1] expenditure by central government: by country

United Kingdom

£ thousands

Area	1979/80	1980/1	1981/2	1982/3	1983/4	1984/5	1985/6	1986/7	1987/8	1988/9	1989/90
England	1,380	1,946	1,399	1,115	1,055	951	1,757	1,164	1,243	1,304	1,927
Wales	-	-	-	-	-	-	6	9	5	5	4
Scotland	65	66	84	94	54	70	165	131	178	53	190
Northern Ireland	222	165	237	180	192	230	254	172	142	379	548
United Kingdom	1,667	2,177	1,720	1,389	1,302	1,251	2,182	1,476	1,568	1,741	2,669

[1] Local authority grants are available for the cost of conversion work required as a result of smoke control orders. These are at the rate of 70 per cent for private sector householders and 100 per cent for public sector tenants and hardship cases. Local authority grants are reimbursed by the exchequer at the rate of 40 per cent for the first two categories and 56 per cent for hardship cases. The figures relate only to the sums reimbursed by the exchequer.

Source: *Department of the Environment; Welsh Office; Scottish Development Department; Department of the Environment (Northern Ireland)*

Nitrogen dioxide (NO_2) and nitrogen oxides (NO_x)

A number of nitrogen compounds including nitrogen dioxide, nitric oxide and nitrous oxide are formed in combustion processes as nitrogen in the air and the fuel combines with oxygen. Almost all oxidised nitrogen pollution is emitted as nitric oxide (NO) which at ambient temperatures, is oxidised to the more toxic secondary pollutant, nitrogen dioxide (NO_2). This process is accelerated in the presence of reactive hydrocarbons and ozone. The effects of oxides of nitrogen on human health are varied. Nitrogen dioxide is of particular concern - acute exposure can cause transient respiratory problems and reduce lung function. Oxides of nitrogen can also have adverse effects on plants, reducing growth and inducing lesions in sensitive crops; contribute a large part to acid deposition; and are important in the formation of tropospheric ozone. Nitrous oxide contributes to global warming (see below).

Trends in emissions of nitrogen oxides are shown in Figure 1.5 and Table 1.9. Total emissions declined during the early 1980s from a peak of 2.6 million tonnes in 1979 to 2.3 million tonnes in 1984, reflecting a reduction in emissions from power stations - particularly during the miners' strike in 1984 - which more than offset the steady increase in emissions from road transport. From 1985 increases in emissions from power stations (up to 1987) and road transport resulted in total emissions reaching 2.7 million tonnes in 1989. The main sources of nitrogen oxides are road transport (48 per cent in 1989) and power stations (29 per cent). Almost all emissions are produced by fuel combustion, the main contributors in 1989 being coal (32 per cent), motor spirit (26 per cent) and diesel fuel (22 per cent). Emissions per unit of GDP have decreased by nearly 20 per cent since 1979 although the rate of decline has slowed down in recent years.

EC Directive 88/609 on large combustion plants sets limits on emissions of nitrogen oxides. There are standards for new plants and the UK is committed to reducing total NO_x emissions from existing combustion installations with a capacity greater than 50 megawatts (thermal) by 15 per cent by 1993 and by 30 per cent by 1998 taking 1980 emissions as the baseline. Table 1.9 shows that emissions from large combustion plants in 1989 were 2 per cent lower than in 1988 and were 12 per cent below the 1980 baseline level. To meet the directive targets, all 12 of the major coal-fired power stations (73 per cent of coal fired capacity) will be fitted with low-NO_x burners.

Figure 1.5 Nitrogen oxides (NO_x):[1] estimated emissions[2] by emission source

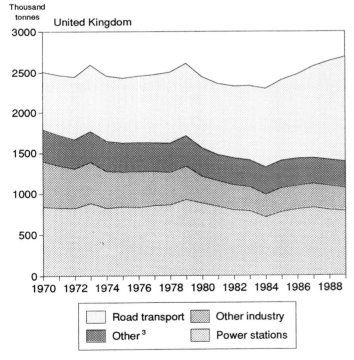

Thousand tonnes
United Kingdom

Road transport
Other[3]
Other industry
Power stations

1. Expressed as nitrogen dioxide equivalent.
2. Based mainly on constant emission factors.
3. Domestic; commercial / public service; refineries; agriculture; railways; civil aircraft; shipping.

Source: Warren Spring Laboratory, Department of Trade and Industry

1.9 Nitrogen oxides (NO_x):[1] estimated emissions[2] by emission source and by type of fuel

United Kingdom — Thousand tonnes

	1979	1980	1981	1982	1983	1984	1985	1986	1987	1988	1989	Percentage of total in 1989
a) By emission source												
Domestic	71	68	68	67	67	64	72	75	74	72	68	3
Commercial/public service[3]	65	62	61	61	62	63	64	65	61	60r	55	2
Power stations	926	880	839	799	787	711	775	807	826	800r	785	29
Refineries	42	43	38	37	36	36	34	35	34	34	36	1
Agriculture	6	5	5	5	5	5	5	5	4	4	4	-
Other industry[4]	412	328	314	303	294	273	292	289	290	294r	282	10
Railways	42	41	39	35	37	35	37	37	35	35	32	1
Road transport	908	884r	881r	886r	920r	973r	997r	1,042r	1,142r	1,228r	1,298	48
Civil aircraft	9r	10r	9r	10r	10r	11r	11r	11r	12r	13r	14	1
Shipping	131r	121r	104r	119r	111r	123r	116r	108r	101r	102r	126	5
Total	2,613r	2,442r	2,359r	2,322r	2,330r	2,293r	2,402r	2,475r	2,578r	2,642r	2,690	100
b) By type of fuel												
Coal	1,008	957	937	869	882	610	822	900	931	900	866	32
Solid smokeless fuel	7	7	6	6	6	4	6	5	5	5	4	-
Petroleum:												
Motor spirit	466	449r	461r	474r	487r	520r	535r	568r	616r	664r	702	26
Derv	442	435r	420	412r	433r	453r	462r	474r	526r	564r	596	22
Gas	192r	174r	158r	168r	160r	170r	168r	157r	147r	147r	161	6
Fuel oil	296r	220r	180r	188r	148r	315r	186r	149r	122r	139r	139	5
Burning oil	6	5	4	4	4	4	4	4	4	4	4	-
Other petroleum	32r	32r	30r	35r	41r	41r	33r	35r	36r	37r	39	1
Other gas	141	140	139	141	143	150	160	157	166	160	156	6
Other emissions	24	24	24	25	25	25	25	25	25	22r	21	1
Total	2,613r	2,442r	2,359r	2,322r	2,330r	2,293r	2,402r	2,475r	2,578r	2,642r	2,690	100
c) Emissions from large combustion plants												
Large plants[5]	1,203	1,110	1,056	1,009	991	903	975	1,007	1,025	1,002r	982	
Index (1980 = 100)	108	100	95	91	89	81	88	91	92	90	88	
d) Emissions (tonnes)/GDP (£ million)[6]												
	7.9	7.5	7.4	7.2	6.9	6.7	6.7	6.7	6.7	6.5	6.5	

[1] Expressed as nitrogen dioxide equivalent.
[2] Most of the figures in this table are based on constant emission factors.
[3] Includes miscellaneous emission sources.
[4] Excludes power stations, refineries and agriculture.
[5] Based on the latest information available on fuel used in power stations, large industrial boilers and boiler complexes above 50 megawatts and on the latest emission factors; emission factors are published annually by Warren Spring Laboratory.
[6] GDP measured at 1985 market prices.

Source: *Warren Spring Laboratory, Department of Trade and Industry; Central Statistical Office*

In 1989, the EC agreed Directive 89/458 on emission standards for small cars. A consolidated directive imposing similar standards for all new passenger vehicles will require that from the end of 1992 emissions of NO_x from each new car will be reduced by 75 per cent. In addition to the above action by the EC, the UN/ECE NO_x Protocol requires the UK to reduce total NO_x emissions to 1987 levels by 1994-5, with further reductions thereafter. The protocol is based on the "critical load" concept which provides a scientific rationale for deriving emission reductions (see also introduction to the national issues section).

Ground-level concentrations of nitrogen dioxide are limited by EC Directive 85/203 as a protection for human health. Since 1987, nitrogen dioxide has been monitored continuously at 12 sites in urban and suburban locations (see Figure 1.1) where the risk of exposure to high levels of nitrogen dioxide pollution was expected to be greatest. Nitrogen dioxide concentrations at a selected number of these sites are given in Table 1.10. The only sites at which the directive limit value of 104.6 ppb for the 98th percentile of average hourly readings for the year have been exceeded are the kerbside site in Cromwell Road and the west London site. Both sites are heavily influenced by road traffic.

DOE formed the Photochemical Oxidant Review Group (UKPORG) to study and report on the extent of existing knowledge and to make recommendations for future research and monitoring. The second UKPORG report[3] provides more detailed information on concentrations of nitrogen oxides with respect to both EC limit values

1.10 Nitrogen dioxide (NO$_2$): concentrations[1] at selected automated monitoring sites

United Kingdom

Site	Year	Annual average (ppb)	98th percentile of hourly average for year (ppb)	Number of hours exceeding EC limit value of 104.6 ppb	Data capture for year[2] %
Directive sites[3]					
Central London	1985	32	63	5	63
	1986	35	65	13	84
	1987	39	85	69	87
	1988	35	74	42	98
	1989	37	79	33	98
West London	1987	35	84	48	70
	1988	37	92	81	100
	1989	42	112	202	94
Glasgow	1987	31	69	40	91
	1988	30	57	6	85
	1989	27	61	34	99
Manchester	1987	29	65	38	84
	1988	28	67	60	89
	1989	25	62	27	100
Walsall	1987	30	62	-	61
	1988	26	54	5	90
	1989	29	59	9	94
Billingham	1987	23	63	3	87
	1988	21	58	12	93
	1989	22	60	4	96
Kerbside					
Cromwell Road	1985	48	128	202	49
	1986	40	109	113	54
	1987	..	..	..	..
	1988	..	..	..	..
	1989	45	105	142	80
Suburban site					
Stevenage	1985	25	57	-	49
	1986	21	52	1	70
	1987	27	72	9	55
	1988	24	53	7	89
	1989	25	56	13	92

[1] Measurements are made with continuous chemiluminescent gas analysers; "-" refers to nil exceedences (rather than nil or negligible exceedences).
[2] Percentage of possible value available throughout the year.
[3] The six-site nitrogen dioxide monitoring network was established in 1987.

Source: *Warren Spring Laboratory; Department of Trade and Industry*

and WHO guidelines. The report collects together all the continuous monitoring data for nitrogen oxides carried out in the UK since 1972 at over 50 sites. Increasing trends in nitrogen dioxide have been documented at a range of urban, suburban and rural sites. The report also drew attention to the importance of passive diffusion tubes in allowing detailed spatial coverage of nitrogen dioxide concentrations to be mapped. In this way nitrogen dioxide levels in Wales, Manchester, Birmingham, Glasgow, west London and central London and across the entire UK have been described.

Volatile organic compounds (VOCs)

Volatile organic compounds consist of a large number of compounds including hydrocarbons and oxygenated and halogenated organics which are released from oil refining, petrol distribution and garage forecourts, motor vehicle activity, various industrial processes and from solvents such as those used in paint. They are usually liquid, in the form of an aerosol or solid. Some hydrocarbons can cause unpleasant effects such as drowsiness, eye irritation and coughing and others, for example, benzene, are carcinogenic. VOCs are directly

11

1.11 Volatile organic compounds (VOCs):[1] estimated emissions[2] by emission source and by type of fuel

United Kingdom   Thousand tonnes

	1979	1980	1981	1982	1983	1984	1985	1986	1987	1988	1989	Percentage of total in 1989
a) By emission source												
Domestic	97	80	76	75	69	55	73	77	64	58	50	2
Commercial/public service[3]	1	1	1	1	1	1	1	1	1	1	1	-
Power stations	14	14	13	12	12	10	12	13	13	13	12	1
Other industry[4]	43	42	42	42	42	41	42	42	42	42	42	2
Processes and solvents[5]	1,031	1,033	1,031	1,034	1,035	1,039	1,040	1,046	1,050	1,056	1,059	51
Gas leakage[6]	31	31	31	30	31	32	32	34	36	34	34	2
Forests[7]	80	80	80	80	80	80	80	80	80	80	80	4
Railways	11	10	10	9	10	9	9	9	9	9	8	-
Road transport[8]	490r	580r	595r	614r	607r	623r	621r	640r	674r	705r	762	37
Civil aircraft	3r	3r	3r	3r	3r	3r	3r	3r	3r	4r	4	-
Shipping	14r	13r	11r	13r	12r	13r	13r	12r	11r	11r	14	1
Total	1,813r	1,887r	1,893r	1,912r	1,903r	1,907r	1,926r	1,957r	1,984r	2,013r	2,066	100
b) By type of fuel												
Coal	105	88	83	81	76	58	78	84	72	65	57	3
Solid smokeless fuel	5	5	4	4	4	3	4	4	4	3	3	-
Petroleum:												
Motor spirit	356r	448r	470r	491r	480r	492r	488r	503r	524r	544r	590	29
Derv	134r	131r	125r	123r	127r	131r	133r	137r	150r	161r	173	8
Gas	22r	21r	19r	20r	20r	20r	21r	20r	19r	19r	20	1
Fuel oil	5r	4r	3r	4r	3r	5r	3r	3r	3r	3r	3	-
Other petroleum	3r	3r	3r	3r	3r	3r	3r	4r	4r	4r	4	-
Other gas	4	4	4	4	4	4	5	5	5	5	5	-
Other emissions	1,180	1,182	1,179	1,182	1,184	1,189	1,190	1,198	1,204	1,208	1,211	59
Total	1,813r	1,887r	1,893r	1,912r	1,903r	1,907r	1,926r	1,957r	1,984r	2,013r	2,066	100
c) Emissions (tonnes)/GDP (£ million)[9]												
	5.4	5.8	5.9	5.9	5.7	5.5	5.4	5.3	5.1	5.0	5.0	

[1] Excluding methane.
[2] Most of the figures in this table are based on constant emission factors.
[3] Includes miscellaneous emission sources.
[4] Excludes power stations.
[5] Including evaporation of motor spirit during production, storage and distribution.
[6] Gas leakage is an estimate of losses during transmission along the distribution system.

Source: *Warren Spring Laboratory, Department of Trade and Industry; Central Statistical Office*

[7] An order of magnitude estimate of natural emissions from forests.
[8] Includes evaporative emissions from the petrol tank and carburettor of petrol-engined vehicles.
[9] GDP measured at 1985 market prices.

involved in the formation of tropospheric ozone (see below). Methane is not classed as a VOC but is considered separately in the section on global warming.

Figure 1.6 Volatile organic compounds (VOCs):[1] estimated emissions[2] by emission source

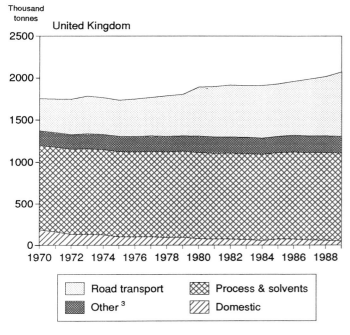

1. Excluding methane.
2. Based mainly on constant emission factors.
3. Commercial / public service; power stations; other industry; gas leakage; forests; railways; civil aircraft; shipping.

Source: Warren Spring Laboratory, Department of Trade and Industry

Figure 1.6 shows that total emissions of volatile organic compounds have increased gradually since 1970 to reach 2.1 million tonnes in 1989 largely due to increased emissions from road transport. Table 1.11 shows recent trends in VOCs emissions for each emission source and by type of fuel. The main sources of emissions are processes and solvents (51 per cent in 1989) and road transport (37 per cent). Emissions from road transport increased by over 50 per cent since 1979. In 1989, only 41 per cent of emissions came from fuel combustion, the main fuel being motor spirit (29 per cent). The EC directive measures on vehicle emissions described in the previous section will reduce VOC emissions from new cars from the end of 1992. Discussion is underway within the Convention on Long-range Transboundary Air Pollution on possible measures to control VOC emissions.

Carbon monoxide (CO)

Carbon monoxide is derived from the incomplete combustion of fuel, mainly from road transport. It is one of the most directly toxic of substances, interfering with respiratory biochemistry. It can impair physical co-ordination, vision and judgement and affect the central nervous and cardiovascular systems. Other pollutants can exacerbate the effects. Carbon monoxide can also indirectly contribute to global warming (see later section).

Trends in emissions of carbon monoxide are shown in Figure 1.7 and Table 1.12. Emissions fluctuated around 5 million tonnes between 1970 and the early 1980s but rose since then to 6.5 million tonnes in 1989. Emissions from road transport increased by over 40 per cent between 1979 and 1989 and their share of total emissions rose from 78 to 88 per cent. Emissions from the combustion of motor spirit accounted for 87 per cent of total emissions in 1989. Emissions per unit of GDP have declined slightly between 1979 and the mid-1980s but have increased in 1989. Future emissions of carbon monoxide from road transport will be reduced by the EC vehicle directives.

The WHO air quality guideline is that, to minimise health risks, concentrations of carbon monoxide should not exceed 10 ppm over an eight-hour period. Carbon monoxide monitoring is under development and data from five automated monitoring sites (see Figure 1.1) are available for the first time in 1990. Table 1.13 shows concentrations at each of these sites and indicates that the one-hour guideline has not been exceeded over recent years, whilst the eight-hour WHO guideline has been exceeded relatively infrequently.

Figure 1.7 Carbon monoxide: estimated emissions[1] by emission source

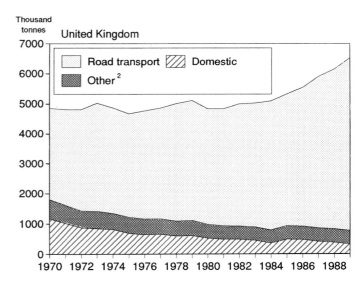

1. Based mainly on constant emission factors.
2. Commercial / public service; power stations; refineries; agriculture; other industry; railways; civil aircraft; shipping.

Source: Warren Spring Laboratory, Department of Trade and Industry

1.12 Carbon monoxide (CO): estimated emissions[1] by emission source and by type of fuel

United Kingdom   Thousand tonnes

Emission source	1979	1980	1981	1982	1983	1984	1985	1986	1987	1988	1989	*Percentage of total in 1989*
a) By emission source												
Domestic	611	532	496	493	464	370	490	482	423	388	339	*5*
Commercial/public service[2]	13	12	11	12	12	11	12	11	10	9	8	-
Power stations	58	53	50	48	46	52	49	48	49	48r	47	*1*
Refineries	2	2	2	2	2	2	1	1	1	1	1	-
Agriculture	1	1	1	1	1	1	1	1	1	1	1	-
Other industry[3]	376	333	333	328	329	314	334	334	334	338	334	*5*
Railways	16	15	15	14	14	13	14	14	13	13	12	-
Road transport	3,992	3,855r	3,900r	4,071r	4,119r	4,296r	4,391r	4,618r	5,036r	5,316r	5,751	*88*
Civil aircraft	7r	8r	7r	8r	8r	8r	9r	9r	9r	10r	11	-
Shipping	20r	18r	16r	18r	17r	18r	17r	16r	15r	15r	19	-
Total	5,096r	4,829r	4,831r	4,993r	5,010r	5,085r	5,318r	5,535r	5,892r	6,140r	6,522	*100*
b) By type of fuel												
Coal	635	514	493	479	456	366	477	497	439	413	396	*6*
Solid smokeless fuel	169	169	154	157	152	120	160	135	136	128	116	*2*
Petroleum:												
Motor spirit	3,911	3,776r	3,824r	3,996r	4,043r	4,217r	4,312r	4,537r	4,947r	5,211r	5,649	*87*
Derv	81	79r	76r	75r	76r	79r	79r	81r	89r	105r	102	*2*
Gas	33r	31r	28r	29r	29r	29r	30r	29r	27r	27r	28	-
Fuel oil	29r	22r	18r	19r	15r	35r	20r	15r	13r	14r	15	-
Other petroleum	8r	8r	8r	8r	9r	9r	9r	9r	10r	11r	11	-
Other gas	9	9	10	10	10	10	11	11	12	11	11	-
Other emissions	220	220	220	220	220	220	220	220	220	220	220	*3*
Total	5,096r	4,829r	4,831r	4,993r	5,010r	5,085r	5,318r	5,535r	5,892r	6,140r	6,522	*100*
c) Emissions (tonnes)/GDP (£ million)[6]												
	15.4	14.9	15.1	15.4	14.9	14.8	14.9	15.0	15.2	15.2	15.8	

[1] Most of the figures in this table are based on constant emission factors.
[2] Includes miscellaneous emission sources.
[3] Excludes power stations, refineries and agriculture.
[4] GDP measured at 1985 market prices.

Source: *Warren Spring Laboratory, Department of Trade and Industry; Central Statistical Office*

1.13 Carbon monoxide (CO): concentrations[1] at automated monitoring sites

United Kingdom

Site	Year	Annual average (ppm)	98th percentile of hourly average for year (ppm)	Number of hours exceeding		Data capture for year[2] %
				WHO hourly guideline of 25 ppm	WHO 8-hour guideline of 10 ppm	
Kerbside						
Cromwell Road	1987	..	..	..	..	..
	1988	..	..	..	..	..
	1989	4	10	-	7	66
Urban sites						
Central London	1985	1	3	-	-	68
	1986	1	2	-	-	49
	1987[3]	-	-	-	-	19
	1988	1	4	-	1	72
	1989	1	6	-	1	77
West London	1989	2	10	-	2	16
Glasgow	1989	2	8	-	3	43
Suburban site						
Stevenage	1987	..	..	..	..	..
	1988	..	..	..	..	..
	1989	1	3	-	-	49

[1] Measurements are made with continuous infrared absorption analysers; "-" refers to nil exceedences (rather than nil or negligible exceedences).
[2] Percentage of possible values available throughout the year.
[3] Data capture too low to warrant calculation of statistics.

Source: *Warren Spring Laboratory, Department of Trade and Industry*

Lead and other elements

Lead is of concern because of its effects on health, particularly that of children. Lead enters the body primarily by absorption of ingested lead and from inhaled lead. The main sources of lead in air are from lead in petrol, coal combustion and metal works.

In 1981 the maximum amount of lead permitted in petrol was reduced from 0.45 grams per litre (g/l) to 0.40 g/l to comply with EC Directive 78/611. The permitted level was reduced further in December 1985 to 0.15 g/l. A further step to reduce lead emissions from petrol was taken in 1986 when unleaded petrol was first sold in the UK. This followed the adoption of EC Directive 85/210 which required unleaded petrol to be made available throughout the Community from 1 October 1989, or earlier if member states wished. The tax differential between leaded and unleaded petrol was raised to 14p a gallon in March 1989 and to 16p in March 1990 and during 1989 and 1990 there was a very effective campaign by the Government, the oil and motor industries and others to encourage drivers to use unleaded petrol. The number of petrol stations selling unleaded petrol rose rapidly in 1989 and 1990 from 11 per cent in October 1988, to 80 per cent in September 1989 and to 98 per cent in September 1990. Figure 1.8 shows that unleaded petrol deliveries rose from under 3 per cent in November 1988 to 38 per cent in November 1990. From October 1989 new car models had to be capable of running on unleaded petrol as have all cars coming off the production line from October 1990.

Table 1.14 shows that emissions of lead from petrol-engined road vehicles fell after the reductions in lead content in 1981 and 1985 described above. The increase in petrol consumption over the period tended to offset these steep falls to a small extent. The slight increases in 1987 and 1988 reflect similar increases in the consumption of petrol. The large increase in consumption of unleaded petrol during 1989 resulted in total lead emissions for 1989 falling by about 15 per cent to about 2,600 tonnes and this has been reflected in decreased airborne lead concentrations.

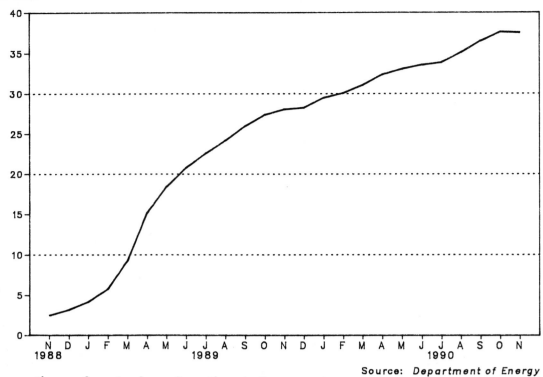

Figure 1.8 Unleaded petrol: percentage of total deliveries of motor spirit

Source: *Department of Energy*

1.14 Consumption of petrol and estimated emissions of lead from petrol-engined road vehicles

United Kingdom

	Consumption of petrol		Estimated emissions of lead from petrol-engined road vehicles[1,2]	
	Million tonnes	Index 1975 = 100	Thousand tonnes	Index 1975 = 100
1975	16.12	100	8.0r	100
1976	16.88	105	8.4r	105r
1977	17.34	108	7.9r	98r
1978	18.35	114	7.2r	90r
1979	18.68	116	7.3	92r
1980	19.15	119	7.5	94r
1981	18.72	116	6.7	83r
1982	19.25	119	6.8	85r
1983	19.57	121	6.9	86r
1984	20.22	125	7.2	90r
1985	20.40	127	6.5	81r
1986	21.47	133	2.9	36r
1987	22.18	138	3.0	37r
1988	23.25	144	3.1	39r
1989	23.93	148	2.6	33

Source: *Department of Energy; Warren Spring Laboratory, Department of Trade and Industry*

[1] These figures are based on lead contents for petrol published by the Institute of Petroleum. It has been assumed that only 70 per cent of this lead in petrol is emitted from vehicle exhausts, the remainder being retained in lubricating oil and exhaust systems.

[2] Estimated lead emissions for 1975-8 have been revised to reflect higher lead content figures closer to the maximum permissible levels. As a result the Index based on 1975 values has also been revised.

EC Directive 82/884 limits airborne lead concentrations to 2.0 µg per cubic metre of air expressed as an annual average. DOE operates a monitoring network to measure compliance with this directive. Currently (1990), three works and 11 sampling locations are being monitored. Since 1985, only one works (in Walsall) has exceeded the limit value. This site was in a derogation area, requiring compliance with the directive by the end of 1989. Compliance was achieved in 1990.

In addition to the directive network, a lead in petrol monitoring survey is operated at selected rural and urban sites. Average airborne lead concentrations at these sites for 1985, 1987 and 1989 are shown in Figure 1.9 and further information on airborne lead monitoring surveys in Statistical Bulletin (91)1. These show that there was an average fall of 55 per cent between 1985 and 1986, following the reduction of lead in petrol at the end of 1985. The decrease in airborne lead concentrations between 1987 and 1989 shown in Figure 1.9 reflects largely the recent uptake in unleaded petrol. The results of surveys carried out by DOE to investigate the effect on blood lead concentrations of the reduction in lead content of petrol were reported in Digest no 11.

Figure 1.9 Average monthly airborne lead concentrations: 1985, 1987 and 1989

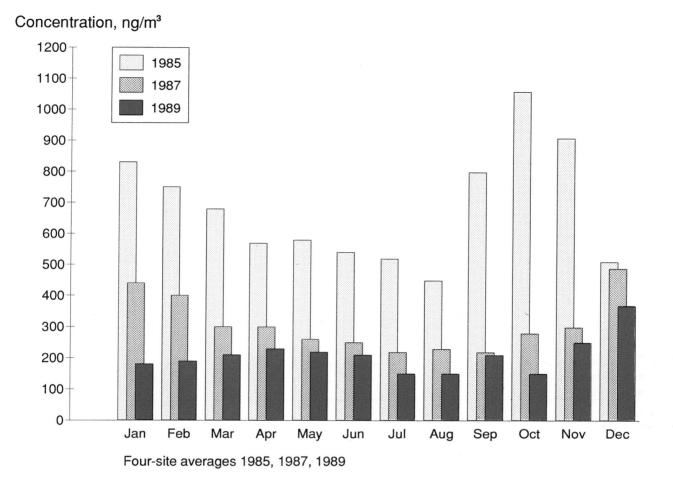

Concentration, ng/m³

Legend:
- 1985
- 1987
- 1989

Four-site averages 1985, 1987, 1989

Source: *Warren Spring Laboratory, Department of Trade and Industry*

Data on urban concentrations of lead and other trace elements are collected as part of Multi-element and Sulphate Surveys that have been in operation since 1976. Initially the survey involved monitoring 16 elements at 20 urban sites but in 1978 the number of sites was reduced to the five shown in Table 1.15(a). Trends in the concentrations of zinc, iron, vanadium and lead (the elements found in the most significant amounts) were generally downwards. The United Kingdom Atomic Energy Authority (UKAEA) also monitors about 30 trace and major elements in air at non-urban sites. The main objectives are to provide data to compare with urban measurements, to study the longer term trends in atmospheric concentrations and to record the deposition inventory to the ground. Trends in the concentrations of the four elements shown in Table 1.15(b), zinc, arsenic, selenium and lead which come primarily from industrial processes are generally downwards.

1.15 Trace elements: annual average concentrations by site

(a) Urban concentrations
Great Britain

nanograms/m³ air[1]

	1979/80	1980/81	1981/82	1982/3	1983/4	1984/5	1985/6	1986/7	1987/8	1988/9
Central London										
Zinc	160	120	130	110	92	100	945	93	94	95
Iron	1,260	1,150	1,040	970	800	980r	840	940	1,000	710
Vanadium	22	20	24	23	19r	32r	14r	14	14	10
Lead	730	610	600	570	410	570r	380r	280	270	200
LB Brent										
Zinc	91	96	88	71	82	86r	72	64	160	130
Iron	700	590	670	810	520	490r	530	530	610	510
Vanadium	..	..	19	15	..	..	..	..	..	..
Lead	970	680	850	710	640	640r	620	310	290	320
Leeds										
Zinc	150	..	140	91	100	88r	110	90	79	89
Iron	830	..	820	680	680	550r	640	640	690	520
Vanadium	..	..	18	19	..	..	..	..	..	..
Lead	620	..	450	350	340	280	2,705	180	180	120
Glasgow										
Zinc	790	520	450	120	120	120	110	130	160	140
Iron	660	700	660	500	640	550r	530	420	510	480
Vanadium	13	12	20	13	..	..	..	..	..	..
Lead	470	360	340	210	240	210	210r	140	160	110
Motherwell										
Zinc	140	..	200	190	130	120	240	220	220	400
Iron	1,510	..	2,000	2,130	2,180	1,400r	2,100r	1,600	1,500	2,400
Vanadium	..	..	17	14	..	..	..	..	..	..
Lead	300	..	260	280	260	170r	250r	180	120	..

(b) Non-urban concentrations
England and Wales

nanograms/kg air[1]

	1979	1980	1981	1982	1983	1984	1985	1986	1987	1988	1989
Chiltern (Oxon)[2]											
Zinc	44	57	56	22	21	26	41	30	43	32	43
Arsenic	2.3	2.8	1.5	2.4	0.9	0.69	1.4	1.8	1.8	1.2	1.1
Selenium	0.81	1.4	1.5	0.6	1.0	0.71	0.93	1.0	1.2	0.75	0.79
Lead	67	90	46	54	53	71	73	27	49	42	39
Styrrup (Notts)[3]											
Zinc	125	100	96	145	120	112	135	92	88	78	130
Arsenic	12	6.2	4.6	5.5	2.4	3.4	4.0	4.6	3.8	3.2	3.2
Selenium	2.7	3.4	3.7	4.0	4.1	3.5	1.9	2.8	3.5	2.8	3.6
Lead	130	145	110	140	94	140	105	53	57	77	70
Wraymires (Cumbria)[4]											
Zinc	21	19	26	23	19	14	13	12	15	11	12
Arsenic	2.2	2.4	1.6	1.4	0.7	0.47	<0.4	<0.8	1.0	0.71	0.62
Selenium	0.62	0.81	1.5	1.1	0.94	0.63	0.46	0.60	0.69	0.65	0.76
Lead	33	38	32	38	37	39	29	12	16	19	18
Trebanos (W Glam)[5]											
Zinc	33	39	38	45	27	75	47	31	32	57	36
Arsenic	4.5	4.2	4.5	3	1.3	2.3	3.5	3.5	2.4	3.5	2.4
Selenium	0.79	1.4	1.6	1.1	0.99	1.4	0.87	0.98	0.92	1.3	0.73
Lead	68	67	65	64	75	80	66	32	39	45	53

[1] A nanogram is a thousand millionth (10⁻⁹) of a gram. The following conversion formula may be used to convert from nanograms/kg of air to nanograms/m³ of air - the more common measurement of pollutant concentrations in the atmosphere. 1 m³ air at 15°C, 760 mm Mercury (Standard Cubic Metre) = 1.226 kg.

[2] The site at Chilton is located in central southern England, about 90 km from the English Channel. The sampling apparatus is situated on the westerly perimeter of UKAEA Harwell and the surroundings are predominantly rural.

[3] This site is in a rural area but industrial influences are very strong. It lies only 25 km east of the Sheffield industrial complex with steel works and coal mining.

Source: *Multi-element surveys, Warren Spring Laboratory, Department of Trade and Industry; United Kingdom Atomic Energy Authority*

[4] A rural site near Lake Windermere, about 25 km from the Irish Sea, and 32 km to the north-east of Barrow-in-Furness.

[5] This site is in the River Tawe Valley, 11 km inland from Swansea Bay, and is on the outer limit of the industrial zone (oil refineries, steel works and nickel smelting).

NATIONAL ISSUES

Individual air pollutants can be transported great distances, and some interact chemically to produce secondary pollutants. The following sections consider the direct and indirect effects of pollutants on a national and transboundary scale. The main forum for co-operation between the governments of east and west Europe and north America is the 1979 UN/ECE Convention on Long Range Transboundary Air Pollution which is aimed at assessing and limiting transboundary air pollution. Part of its programme includes monitoring nitrogen dioxide and sulphur dioxide emissions, and modelling their transport and deposition within Europe.

In 1988 the UK signed the Sofia NO_x Protocol arising from the convention which is based on the concept of "critical loads". This is a scientifically based pollution control policy that allows the effective targeting of resources directed at abatement by assessing the maximum pollutant load permissible before environmental damage is observed.

The UK and fellow EC Member States will review the Large Combustion Plants directive in 1994. In doing so, the Government will assess the progress made in reducing sulphur dioxide emissions and measure this against the latest scientific understanding of the effects of acid rain, including the critical loads approach, and the need to reduce emissions of greenhouse gases. The UK will also take part in the revision to the existing UN/ECE Protocol on sulphur dioxide emissions. The new agreement should be based on the critical loads approach. The Government will be working with other countries in both East and West Europe to agree on achievable longer-term targets.

Acid deposition and acid rain

Acid deposition causes concern in many parts of Europe and North America because of the long term effects on freshwater, groundwater and soils and, possibly, on forests, crops and buildings. Acid deposition can occur in three ways: dry deposition, occult deposition and acidified rain. Dry deposition of gases and particles from the atmosphere is particularly important in low-lying areas of the UK. The majority of sulphur, particularly in low-lying areas and close to emission sources, is deposited by dry deposition of sulphur dioxide gas. The deposition of sulphur due to the impact of cloud droplets onto vegetation, known as occult deposition, is significant for land above 500 metres. Rain is naturally slightly acidic because carbon dioxide dissolves in rainwater to form carbonic acid. The additional acidification of rain is due to oxides of sulphur and nitrogen which dissolve to form dilute sulphuric and nitric acids. Hydrochloric acid may also make a contribution to acidity of rainfall in the vicinity of power stations burning coal with a high chloride

content. Acid rain may occur hundreds of kilometres away from the source of acidic pollutants.

DOE has established two networks to monitor acid deposition. The number and location of sites was determined on the advice of the Review Group on Acid Rain (RGAR) who reported in 1983[4] that the available data from 40 rural sites were inadequate for mapping annual average concentrations and deposition of relevant ions in all regions of the UK. New networks were established in 1986 to determine the spatial distribution of acidity and relevant ions; to assess the impact of acid deposition on sensitive areas; to permit trend analysis as information accumulated; and to assist understanding processes leading to acid deposition and allow validation of models. The networks consisted of about 60 sites altogether and provided a considerable increase in the understanding of acid deposition. RGAR recommended that from 1989 the networks be reduced in size by about half to maintain long-term monitoring of acid rain. The current networks consist of 32 sites, of which five are primary sites utilising "wet only" rainfall collectors and providing daily information for a wide range of ions in precipitation as well as concentrations of sulphur dioxide, nitrogen dioxide and aerosol sulphate. The remainder are secondary sites using bulk rain collectors but measuring the same range of ions and are designed to give more spatial detail to the network as a whole. A map of the acid rain networks is given in Figure 1.10.

Figure 1.10 Acid rain monitoring networks, 1990

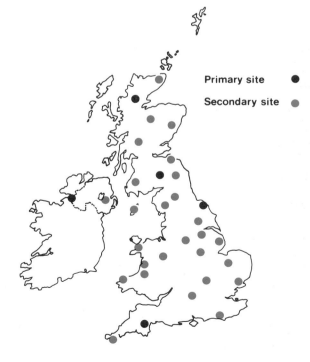

Primary site ●

Secondary site ●

Source: *Warren Spring Laboratory, Department of Trade and Industry*

Figure 1.11 Acidity[1] of rain 1989

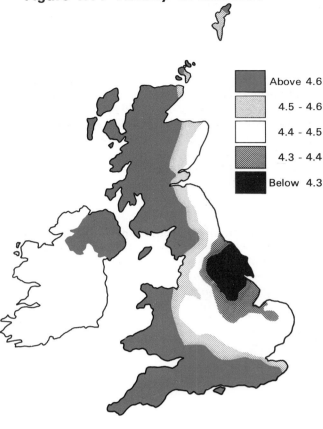

▨	Above 4.6
▨	4.5 - 4.6
□	4.4 - 4.5
▨	4.3 - 4.4
■	Below 4.3

1. Average acidity of precipitation.

Figure 1.12 Wet deposited acidity 1989

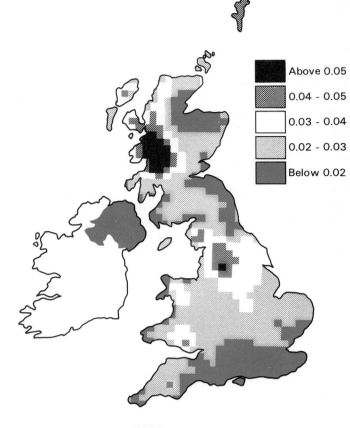

■	Above 0.05
▨	0.04 - 0.05
□	0.03 - 0.04
▨	0.02 - 0.03
▨	Below 0.02

*Source: Warren Spring Laboratory,
Department of Trade and Industry*

Results from the networks for 1989 are shown in Figures 1.11 and 1.12. In Figure 1.11 the data from the secondary network are expressed as rainfall acidity. Acidity and alkalinity are measured using a scale of pH units from 1, which is highly acid, through 7 (neutral) to 14 which is alkaline. The scale is constructed so that a drop of one pH unit represents a ten-fold increase in acidity. It is widely believed that without man-made influence rainfall pH may fall as low as pH 5. Figure 1.11 shows that in 1989 rainfall acidity was highest in the region of Yorkshire and Humberside and lowest in north-west Scotland, Northern Ireland, west Wales and south-west England.

It is however the total acidic load which often determines the potential stress on the environment at any particular place and this is a function of the amount of rain falling on an area as well as the acidity of the rain. Figure 1.12 combines these two factors producing a map of wet deposited acidity expressed in grams of hydrogen ion per square metre. In contrast with Figure 1.11, deposition is highest in parts of Scotland, north Wales, Cumbria and the Pennines. This pattern has remained essentially the same for the last four years. Levels are comparable to the acid rain

damaged regions of southern Norway. Maps of wet deposition of sulphate and nitrate ions show a similar pattern to that of hydrogen, reflecting the influence of the amount of rainfall upon acid deposition and the broadly similar emission patterns of sulphur and nitrogen oxides.

The third RGAR report[5] published in 1990 summarises the understanding of acid deposition over the UK for the years 1986-8. The spatial patterns of non-marine sulphate, ammonium and acidity in rainwater are similar and since 1986 have been consistent from year-to-year.

Many of the processes involved in acid deposition and its effects are poorly understood. DOE has established three review groups to study the effects of acid rain. The second report of the UK Acid Waters Review Group (UKAWRG), published in 1988,[6] concluded that parts of Scotland, Wales and England, especially northern England, possess moderately severe acid waters leading, in some cases, to depletion of fish stocks. Acid deposition appears to be the major causal factor. In some regions of the UK, afforestation has exacerbated freshwater acidity.

The UK Terrestrial Effects Review Group (UKTERG) acknowledged in its first report,[7] published in 1988, that acid deposition was accelerating acidification of some soils and changes in soil biology might result. Such changes were likely to alter plant nutrition and change the chemistry and biology of freshwaters. Major agricultural crops were unlikely to be damaged directly by current rural concentrations of sulphur dioxide and nitrogen oxides but few data existed on the impact of air pollution on natural vegetation. There was no direct proof of pollution-related forest decline in the UK, although some forests were subjected to pollution climates which might be expected to cause stress. A report on forest health surveys carried out by the Forestry Commission is included in Chapter 6.

The main conclusions of the first report of the UK Buildings Effects Review Group (UKBERG), published in 1989,[8] were that: current rates of weathering of stone on historic buildings appeared to be higher than natural rates and weathering on all buildings was greater in urban areas; there is no unequivocal evidence that current rates of weathering of stone and most metals in the structure of historic buildings is significantly different from those in the recent past; and, natural stone buildings face a greater risk than modern buildings. The review groups have made a number of recommendations for further research.

The DOE has established the Critical Loads Advisory Group to prepare maps of the critical loads and levels of pollutant-target combinations across the UK. A critical load map displays the spatial variations in the maximum pollutant load that sensitive ecosystems can accept without damage occurring. These maps will become available during 1991.

Tropospheric ozone

Ozone is a naturally occurring gas and is found throughout the atmosphere reaching maximum concentrations in the stratosphere (15 to 50 km

Figure 1.13   Number of exceedences of 60 ppb hourly average tropospheric ozone concentrations during summer (April–September) 1989

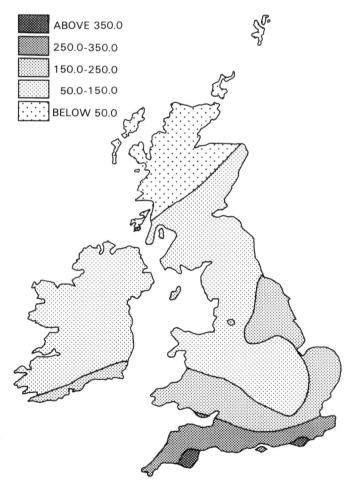

ABOVE 350.0
250.0-350.0
150.0-250.0
50.0-150.0
BELOW 50.0

Source: Warren Spring Laboratory
Department of Trade and Industry

1.16 Ozone: concentrations[1] at automated monitoring sites[2]
United Kingdom

Site	Year	Annual average (ppb)	98th percentile of hourly averages for year (ppb)	Number of hours exceeding			Data capture for year[3] %
				60 ppb	80 ppb	100 ppb	
Urban site							
Central London	1985	16	59	137	49	17	87
	1986	10	47	68	19	1	76
	1987	5	28	9	-	-	71
	1988	7	29	3	-	-	98
	1989	10	46	74	13	1	96
Suburban site							
Stevenage	1985	15	50	75	17	4	89
	1986	13	58	85	22	1	61
	1987	10	42	36	1	-	78
	1988	12	41	10	-	-	92
	1989	13	48	85	18	1	90
Rural sites[4]							
Sibton	1985	18	50	54	5	-	70
	1986	..	..	..	..	..	..
	1987	22	51	46	4	-	59
	1988	24	54	76	7	2	93
	1989	25	65	216	62	13	90
Aston Hill	1987	24	50	45	-	-	69
	1988	30	56	83	18	2	88
	1989	31	58	143	33	6	92
Lullington Heath	1987	23	61	106	21	2	58
	1988	27	56	112	10	2	93
	1989	31	76	422	128	26	95
Strath Vaich	1987	31	50	32	7	-	47
	1988	34	52	53	-	-	96
	1989	32	48	28	-	-	77
High Muffles	1987	18	35	-	-	-	46
	1988	24	53	49	1	-	98
	1989	26	63	184	56	-	89
Lough Navar	1987	22	46	34	3	-	66
	1988	25	48	49	-	-	90
	1989	25	48	74	11	3	99
Yarner Wood	1987	25	43	22	2	-	67
	1988	29	49	51	9	3	95
	1989	32	76	367	136	17	95
Ladybower Reservoir	1987	..	..	..	..	..	..
	1988	24	41	20	5	-	69
	1989	26	60	173	64	22	96
Harwell	1989	21	68	170	57	6	87
Bottesford	1989	17	47	82	4	-	92
Bush	1989	27	50	63	13	3	97
Eskdalemuir	1989	28	52	99	21	-	90
Great Dun Fell	1989	31	65	204	33	2	93
Wharley Croft	1989	26	57	129	18	3	87
Glazebury	1989	17	45	39	2	-	77
Mace Head[5]	1989	34	53	65	7	-	91

[1] Measurements made with continuous UV-absorption instruments; "-" refers to nil exceedences (rather than nil or negligible exceedences).

[2] Monitored on behalf of the Department of the Environment by Warren Spring Laboratory, AEA Technology, Power Gen plc, London Scientific Services, University of Manchester Institute of Science and Technology, Institute of Terrestrial Ecology Bush Estate.

[3] Percentage of possible values available throughout the year.

Source: *Warren Spring Laboratory, Department of Trade and Industry*

[4] The rural zone networks was established after 1986.

[5] Established with the co-operation of the Department of the Environment of the Republic of Ireland and part of the Global Atmospheric Gases Experiment (GAGE).

approximately) where it acts as a shield to harmful ultra-violet radiation (see below). In the lower part of the atmosphere, known as the troposphere, ozone occurs naturally but can be enhanced by other pollutants. It is therefore referred to as a secondary pollutant and is formed by a complex series of reactions between nitrogen oxides, oxygen and volatile organic compounds in the presence of sunlight. High levels of ozone increase susceptibility to infections and respiratory disease and irritate the eyes, nose, throat and respiratory system. Ozone is also involved in the processes that lead to acid deposition and can reduce the yield of some sensitive crops and damage natural vegetation.

There is evidence that the pre-industrial near ground-level concentrations of ozone were typically 10 to 15 ppb. Such concentrations result from natural in situ photochemical production of ozone and a small downward flux of ozone from the stratosphere. Since then, it appears that atmospheric pollution has increased the background concentrations by a factor of about two over the past 100 years and current concentrations are approximately 30 ppb over the UK. Ozone episodes in which concentrations rise substantially above background levels occur in summer heat waves when there are long hours of bright sunlight, temperatures above 20°C, and light winds. Once formed, ozone can persist for several days and can be transported long distances.

The first UKPORG report[9] concluded that summer ozone episodes were the result of photochemical reactions involving nitrogen oxides and volatile organic compounds; that long range transport of ozone from the continent of Europe can initiate high ozone episodes in the UK under particular meteorological conditions; and that there are instances when ozone levels have exceeded guidelines established elsewhere.

There are no UK or EC controls on concentrations of ozone, but the UK gives regard to WHO guidelines which recommend a maximum hourly average concentration of 75-100 ppb in ambient air. EC directives which aim to reduce emissions of nitrogen oxides and volatile organic compounds will also help to reduce ozone episodes.

In 1985 the DOE substantially expanded the national ozone monitoring network (see Figure 1.1) in response to recommendations from the Royal Commission on Environmental Pollution and the Commons Select Committee on the Environment. Figure 1.13 shows distribution over the country of episodes that exceeded the WHO health guideline of 60 ppb hourly average concentrations during the summer of 1989. The contours indicate the number of high ozone episodes and show a marked gradient increasing in a north-west/south-east direction, a trend that was also observed in 1987 and 1988. From this distribution it would seem likely that pollution transported with

European air masses plays a significant role in UK ozone episodes. Details of the ozone concentrations at each of the automated monitoring sites and the number of hours exceeding the WHO guideline as well as more stringent concentration limits are given in Table 1.16.

GLOBAL ISSUES

Stratospheric ozone depletion

The so-called *ozone layer* is a region of relatively high ozone concentrations which occur in a stable part of the atmosphere known as the stratosphere (15 to 50 km). Ozone concentrations reach a maximum in the stratosphere at a height of between 25-35 km but even there never exceed 10 ppm.

The ozone layer is important for two reasons: it shields the earth from ultraviolet-C radiation which is lethal to man and living things, and substantially reduces the amount of harmful ultraviolet-B reaching the earth's surface. An increase in ultraviolet-B would be detrimental to human health, for example increasing the incidence of skin cancer, and have serious effects on plants, including agricultural crops and marine organisms. It also plays a role in regulating the earth's temperature.

Ozone in the stratosphere is created photochemically and destroyed in chain reactions with trace species which naturally generates a state of equilibrium in which the average amount of ozone varies little from year-to-year. There are, in the natural state, substantial variations in ozone levels between seasons and at different latitudes because of natural variations in the intensity of solar radiation. However, since 1984 there has been evidence of increasing ozone depletion, particularly in the stratosphere over the Antarctic. Each Antarctic spring severe reduction in ozone has occurred over the region and has been popularly referred to as the "ozone hole". There is also evidence of a more general but less severe decline in ozone concentrations elsewhere, with reductions of up to 3 per cent being observed in mid-latitudes of the northern hemisphere over the past decade.[10] There is now unequivocal evidence that serious stratospheric ozone depletion is being caused by chlorofluorocarbons (CFCs) and halons emitted as a result of their use as aerosol propellents, refrigerants, foam blowing agents, degreasers for electronic components, and fire extinguishers. These substances release chlorine and bromine into the stratosphere which are particularly effective in destroying ozone even though they are present in very small amounts. Other substances implicated in the destruction of the ozone layer are carbon tetrachloride and methylchloroform.

The Montreal Protocol of 1987, following on from the Vienna Convention of 1985, set a goal of 50 per cent reduction in the production and consumption of CFCs by 1999 compared with the 1986 level. The UK fulfilled

1.17 Chlorofluorocarbons and halons: EC production and consumption[1]

European Community   Tonnes

| Year | CFCs 11 and 12 | | CFCs 113, 114 and 115[2] | | Halons[3] | |
	Production	Consumption[4]	Production	Consumption[4]	Production	Consumption
1976	326,433	244,019	23,524	17,567	..	..
1977	319,107	232,986	23,879	19,307	..	..
1978	307,033	231,437	..	..	..	..
1979	304,238	219,561	..	..	..	..
1980	295,718	216,828	..	..	..	..
1981	300,144	209,765	..	..	..	..
1982	288,979	206,762	..	..	..	..
1983	310,193	216,420	..	..	..	..
1984	322,209	217,729	53,568	38,629	..	..
1985	336,276	228,450	64,334	43,665	..	..
1986[5]	371,914	259,369	57,465	44,444	70,203	44,040
1987	376,065	271,395	59,056	46,040	73,662	54,571

[1] Member States: 1976-80: 9; 1981-5: 10; 1986-7: 12.

[2] From 1986. Previously no EC data was available for CFC 115 but production is believed to have been small.

[3] Halon 1211, 1301 and 2402.

[4] 1976-85: total EC sales by EC producers. As imports of CFCs into the EC are negligible these figures approximate to consumption; from 1986: consumption.

Source: *European Council of Chemical Manufacturers' Federations (CEFIC)*

[5] From 1986 figures are not straight tonnes produced or consumed. Instead, the quantity of each CFC and halon is multiplied by a factor reflecting its potential to damage the ozone layer.

its obligations for consumption under the protocol by 1989, ten years ahead of schedule. The parties to the Montreal Protocol at their second meeting held in London in June 1990 agreed that CFCs be phased out by the year 2000 with intermediate cuts of 50 per cent by 1995 and 85 per cent by 1997. Data on the production and sales of CFCs for the EC are given in Table 1.17. In the UK, consumption of CFCs was halved between 1986 and 1989. In December 1990, EC countries agreed unanimously to phase out the production of CFCs by mid-1997, with exemptions for essential uses such as medical aerosols should they still be necessary.

Global climate change

The earth's atmosphere is largely transparent to incoming radiation from the sun (light). This radiation heats the earth's surface which in turn emits infra-red radiation (heat). Certain gases normally found within the atmosphere absorb and subsequently re-emit this radiation back to the surface. As a result the atmosphere acts like a blanket reducing the losses of infra-red radiation to space and the surface of the earth is some 33°C warmer than if these gases were not present. This is known as the "greenhouse effect" by analogy with the warming effect of glass in greenhouses, and without it life would not be possible on earth.

The abundance of these "greenhouse" gases helps to determine the average global temperature. Significant changes in their concentrations have occurred in the history of the earth and, coupled with other changes, for example in the earth's orbit, have contributed to changes in the global climate.

Water vapour is by far the most important natural greenhouse gas in our atmosphere but its amount is largely determined by atmospheric temperature and the amount of heating of the earth's surface. The remaining natural greenhouse gases have fairly long lifetimes in the atmosphere (from 10 to 200 years) and vary relatively slowly in response to other changes. Their amounts had changed little since the last glacial period over 10,000 years ago. However, the concentrations of other greenhouse gases in the atmosphere has been altered in the recent past by man's activities. For example, average carbon dioxide concentrations in the atmosphere are estimated to have risen from about 280 ppm before the industrial revolution to 353 ppm in 1990. The main cause has been the burning of fossil fuels. Of man-made greenhouse gases, the most important are carbon dioxide (CO_2), methane (CH_4), nitrous oxide (N_2O), and the halocarbons, of which the chlorofluorocarbons (CFCs) are the most significant. Ozone (O_3) in the lower atmosphere, whose concentration is affected by man's activities, is also an important greenhouse gas. Apart from the CFCs these gases also occur naturally. Different gases absorb and trap infra-red radiation from the earth at different levels of efficiency.

Table 1.18 shows the average atmospheric concentrations of greenhouse gases and how they are changing and their relative importance for global climate change[11]. The global warming potential (GWP) of a greenhouse gas is the likely total warming contribution of an emission of that gas over a selected time period (in this case 100 years) relative to the emission of an equal weight of carbon dioxide. All other

1.18 Aspects of key man-made greenhouse gases

	Current (1990) average atmospheric concentration (ppmv)	Current rate of change (per cent per annum)	Lifetime[1] (years)	Global Warming Potential (GWP)[2]	Relative effect of 1990 emissions (per cent)
Carbon dioxide	353	0.5	120 [a]	1	61
Methane	1.72	0.9	10	21	15
Nitrous Oxide	0.31	0.25	150	290	4
CFC[3] 11	0.00028	4	60	3500	11
CFC[3] 12	0.000484	4	130	7300	
Ozone (lower atmosphere)	0.06	1.5	0.2	18 [b]	9 [c]

[1] The period over which almost one-third of each greenhouse gas will remain is the atmosphere.
[2] The likely total warming contribution of an emission of each greenhouse gas (in this case 100 years) relative to the emission of an equal weight of carbon dioxide.
[3] CFC = Chlorofluorocarbon.
[a] An approximate estimate.
[b] Ozone is generated indirectly; this figure represents an approximate estimate based on an infinite timescale.
[c] Includes some other minor trace gases.

Source: *Climate Change, the IPCC Scientific Assessment*

1.19 Carbon dioxide (CO_2): estimated emissions[1] by emission source and by type of fuel

United Kingdom — Million tonnes

Emission source	1979	1980	1981	1982	1983	1984	1985	1986	1987	1988	1989	Percentage of total in 1989
a) By emission source												
Domestic	25	24	24r	23	23	22r	25	26r	25	24	23	14
Commercial/public service[2]	10	9	9	9	9	9	10	10	9	9	8	5
Power stations	62	58	56	53	52	49	52	54	55	53r	52	33
Refineries	5	6	5	5	5	5	5	5	5	5	5	3
Agriculture	1	1	1	1	1	1	1	1	1	1	1	-
Other industry[3]	53	42	40	39	38	36	37	36	36	38r	36	23
Railways	1	1	1	1	1	1	1	1	1	1	1	-
Road transport	21	21	21	21	22	23	24	25	26	28	29	19
Civil aircraft	-	-	-	-	1r	1	1	1	1	1	1	-
Shipping	2r	2r	1	2r	1	2r	2r	1	1	1	2	1
Total	181r	164	158r	154	152	148r	155r	158r	159	159r	157	100
b) By type of fuel												
Coal	77	71	70	65	66	47	62	68	69	67	65	41
Solid smokeless fuel	3	3	3	3	3	2	3	2	2	2	2	1
Petroleum:												
Motor spirit	16	16	16	16	17	17	17	18	19	20	20	13
Derv	5	5	5	5	5	6	6	7	7	8	9	6
Gas	12	10	10r	9	9	9	9r	8	8r	7	7	5
Fuel oil	27r	20r	16	17r	13	26	16r	13	10	12r	12	7
Burning oil	2	2	2	2	1	2	2	2	2	2	2	1
Other petroleum	4	4	4	4	5	5	4	5	5	5	5	3
Other gas	26	27	27	27	28	28	30	31	32	31	30	19
Other emissions	8	6	6	6	6	6r	5	5	5	6r	6	4
Total	181r	164	158r	154r	152	148r	155r	158r	159	159r	157	100
c) Emissions (tonnes)/GDP (£ million)[4]												
	546	508	494	475	452	430	434	427	412	394	380	

[1] Expressed in terms of weight of carbon emitted. In terms of weight of carbon dioxide emitted the figures should be multiplied by 44/12. Most of the figures in this table are based on constant emission factors.
[2] Includes miscellaneous emission sources.
[3] Excludes power stations, refineries and agriculture.
[4] GDP measured at 1985 market prices.

Source: *Warren Spring Laboratory, Department of Trade and Industry; Central Statistical Office*

Figure 1.14 Carbon dioxide (CO_2): estimated emissions[1] by emission source

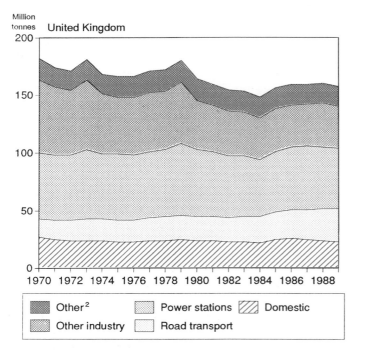

Other[2] Power stations Domestic

Other industry Road transport

1. Based mainly on constant emission factors.
2. Commercial / public service; refineries; agriculture; railways; civil aircraft; shipping

Source: Warren Spring Laboratory, Department of Trade and Industry

greenhouse gases are more potent than carbon dioxide, particularly the man-made CFCs. This is partly due to their physical characteristics and their atmospheric lifetimes. The lifetime of a greenhouse gas is an important factor in determining its likely contribution to global warming. The lifetime is defined as the time taken for 63 per cent of the original emission to be removed from the atmosphere. This also gives a measure of the response time for any measures which are taken to reduce atmospheric concentrations of greenhouse gases. The final column in Table 1.18 shows the relative importance of one year's (1990) global emissions of greenhouse gases to global warming over the next 100 years. It is clear that although carbon dioxide is the least potent greenhouse gas on an equal mass basis, the volume of emissions is so large that it remains the main contributor to global warming. The increase in greenhouse gases from man's activities may contribute to an increase in global mean surface air temperatures (see below).

The most important greenhouse gas is carbon dioxide. The UK contributes 2.3 per cent to global man-made emissions of carbon dioxide which are currently about 7,000 million tonnes per annum (expressed as carbon). Figure 1.14 and Table 1.19 show that total UK emissions of carbon dioxide (expressed as carbon) rose in the late 1970s to 181 million tonnes in 1979 and then declined steadily in the early 1980s to 148 million tonnes in 1984. Emissions then rose again to reach 157 million tonnes in 1989. The main sources of carbon dioxide emissions in 1989 were power stations (33 per cent), other industry (23 per cent), road transport

1.20 Methane (CH_4): estimated emissions[1] by emission source

United Kingdom

Thousand tonnes

	1979	1980	1981	1982	1983	1984	1985	1986	1987	1988	1989	Percentage of total in 1989
a) By emission source												
Domestic	1	1	1	1	1	1	1	1	1	1	1	-
Deep mined coal	1,272	1,326	1,304	1,253	1,200	416	888	1,066	1,014r	988r	940	27
Open cast coal	5	6	6	6	6	5	6	5	6	7	7	-
Oil and gas venting	154	158	176	201	222	203	229	261	273	219	175	5
Road transport	6r	7r	8r	8r	8r	8r	8r	8r	9r	9r	10	-
Gas leakage[2]	313	309	310	303	311	321	326	348	365	345	340	10
Landfill	575	587	599	611	626	643	663	682	700	716	728	21
Sewage disposal	86	86	86	86	86	86	87	87	87	87	87	3
Cattle	927	914	897	903	895	887	867	846	818	801r	804	23
Sheep	240	252	257	265	273	278	285	296	310	328r	344	10
Other animals[3]	15r	15r	15r	15r	16r	15r	15r	15r	15r	15r	15	-
Other emissions[4]	1	1	1	1	1	1	1	1	1	1	1	-
Total	3,595r	3,662r	3,658r	3,653r	3,644r	2,865r	3,376r	3,617r	3,599r	3,517r	3,452	100
b) Emissions (tonnes)/GDP (£ million)[5]												
	10.9	11.3	11.5	11.2	10.8	8.3	9.5	9.8	9.3	8.7	8.3	

[1] Most of the figures in this table are based on constant emission factors. It should be noted that these figures are approximate and represent best current estimates; they will be revised as more accurate information becomes available. The number of significant figures quoted in this table should not be taken as an indication of the accuracy of the estimate.
[2] Gas leakage is an estimate of losses during transmission along the distribution system.

Source: Warren Spring Laboratory, Department of Trade and Industry; Central Statistical Office

[3] Pigs, poultry, horses, humans.
[4] Includes emissions from commercial/public service, power stations, refineries, processes and solvents, forests, railways, aircraft or shipping.
[5] GDP measured at 1985 market prices.

(19 per cent) and domestic (14 per cent). Most carbon dioxide emissions are from fuel combustion: coal (41 per cent), gas (19 per cent) and motor spirit (13 per cent). Total emissions per unit of GDP decreased by 30 per cent between 1979 and 1989.

Methane emissions have been rising at a rate of 1 per cent per annum in the last few decades. Agricultural production, waste disposal and mining are thought to be the main man-made sources. The annual global release of methane to the atmosphere is about 540 million tonnes of which the UK contributes 0.6 per cent. Figure 1.15 and Table 1.20 show that total methane emissions increased gradually in the 1970s and early 1980s to 3.6 million tonnes in 1983, followed by a sharp fall to 2.9 million tonnes in 1984 due to the miners' strike. Emissions rose again to the pre-strike levels thereafter but fell slightly to 3.4 million tonnes in 1989. The main sources of methane emissions in the UK are animals (33 per cent), coal mines (27 per cent) and landfill (21 per cent) with only 1 per cent coming from fuel combustion. It should be noted that these figures are approximate and represent best current estimates; they will be revised as more accurate

information becomes available. The number of significant figures quoted in the table should not be taken as indicative of the accuracy of the estimate.

In order to improve assessment of the science of climate change and of its possible impacts and to consider possible responses, the United Nations Environment Programme and the World Meteorological Organisation in 1988 established the Intergovernmental Panel on Climate Change (IPCC). The IPCC[11] confirmed the reality of the greenhouse effect and the proposition that increasing concentrations of greenhouse gases would lead to a general warming of the earth's surface. They reported that, without controls of greenhouse gas emissions, global mean temperatures will increase by about 0.3°C per decade during the next century leading to a temperature increase of 1°C by 2025 on today's levels and 3°C before the end of the next century. Sea levels are likely to increase by 20 cm and 65 cm respectively on the same timescale. They also drew attention to the observations that over the past century global average temperatures have increased by between 0.3°C and 0.6°C and sea levels by between 10 and 20 cm. It appears that 1990 was the warmest year on record and five of the next warmest years have all occurred during the 1980s. Although it is too early to attribute unequivocally these changes to an enhancement of the greenhouse effect, they are consistent with the predictions which have been made.

The IPCC reported in 1990 and its conclusions were considered at the second World Climate Conference in November 1990. The 137 countries present called for negotiations to begin on a framework convention on climate change, welcomed the commitments made to control greenhouse gas emissions, and agreed that developed countries should co-operate with developing countries to enable them to play their full part in the international response to climate change. The UN General Assembly passed a resolution in December 1990 which established an Inter-Governmental Negotiating Committee to carry forward the negotiations for a framework convention and related instruments. These negotiations are due to begin in February 1991 with the aim of completing the convention by the time of the UN Conference on Environment and Development in Brazil in June 1991.

The UK stated in its 1990 environment white paper[12] that provided other countries take similar action, it is prepared to set itself the demanding target of returning emissions of CO_2 to 1990 levels by the year 2005. At the meeting of Environment and Energy States in October 1990, the European Community and its Member States,

Figure 1.15   Methane (CH_4): estimated emissions[1] by emission source

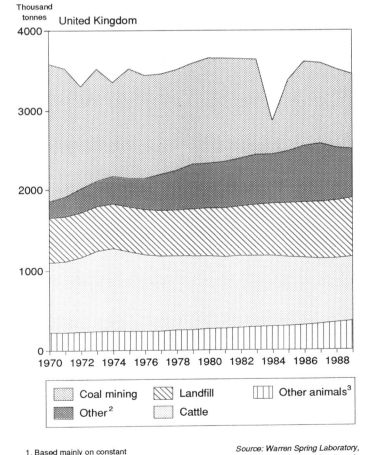

1. Based mainly on constant emission factors.
2. Domestic; oil and gas venting; road transport; gas leakage; sewage disposal; other emissions.
3. Sheep; pigs; poultry; horses; humans.

Source: Warren Spring Laboratory, Department of Trade and Industry

assuming that other leading countries undertake similar commitments, agreed to take actions aimed at reaching stabilisation of the total of CO_2 emissions by 2000 at 1990 levels in the Community as a whole.

[1] *An Assessment of the UK Position with Respect to the 1987 WHO Air Quality Guidelines*, LR650, Warren Spring Laboratory.

[2] *New Air Quality Bulletins System*, Department of the Environment News Release, no 586, 24 October 1990.

[3] *Oxides of Nitrogen in the United Kingdom: the Second Report of the UK Photo-chemical Oxidants Review Group*, Harwell Laboratory,1990.

[4] *Acid Deposition in the United Kingdom: UK Review Group on Acid Rain*,Warren Spring Laboratory,1983.

[5] *Acid Deposition in the United Kingdom, 1986-8: UK Review Group on Acid Rain*, Warren Spring Laboratory,1990.

[6] *Acidity in United Kingdom Fresh Waters: Second Report UK Acid Waters Review Group*, HMSO,1988.

[7] *The Effects of Acid Deposition on the Terrestrial Environment in the United Kingdom: UK Terrestrial Effects Review Group*, HMSO,1988.

[8] *The Effects of Acid Deposition on Buildings and Building Materials: UK Building Effects Review Group Report*, HMSO,1989.

[9] *Ozone in the United Kingdom: the First Report of the UK Photo-chemical Oxidants Review Group*, Harwell Laboratory,1987.

[10] *Stratospheric Ozone, 1990*, United Kingdom Stratospheric Ozone Review Group, HMSO, 1990.

[11] *Climate Change, the IPCC Scientific Assessment*, F T Houghton, G J Jenkins, and J J Ephraums (eds), Cambridge University Press, 1990.

[12] *This Common Inheritance: Britain's Environmental Strategy*, Environment White Paper,1990.

Chapter 2   Water quality

This chapter covers pollution of water by sewage, water quality of rivers and canals, causes of freshwater pollution incidents, bathing waters quality, quality of the North Sea, the dumping of wastes at sea and oil spills at sea.

On 1 September 1989, a major reorganisation of the water industry in England and Wales took place. Before this reorganisation, industrial and other private effluents discharged into sewers or directly into rivers, estuaries and coastal waters were regulated through consents granted by the water authorities, whilst discharges made by water authorities (eg, from sewage treatment works) were regulated through consents granted by Her Majesty's Inspectorate of Pollution (HMIP) on behalf of the Secretary of State for the Environment.

New water service companies established under the Water Act 1989 took over responsibility in England and Wales from the water authorities for sewage collection, treatment and disposal, and for water supply and treatment, on 1 September 1989. At the same time the National Rivers Authority (NRA) was established as an independent regulatory body with responsibility for the management of water resources, and the control and monitoring of water pollution. The NRA also has certain responsibilities for flood defence and land drainage, fisheries, navigation in some areas, and nature conservation and recreation in inland waters and associated land.

Water may become polluted by discharges (eg, from industry, agriculture or sewage treatment works), run-off (eg, from roads, industrial sites or land), or incidents (eg, spillages). Consents for discharges to watercourses are granted by the NRA and consents for discharges into sewers by the water service companies. Consent applications for discharges to sewers containing substances prescribed in the Trade Effluent (Prescribed Processes and Substances) Regulations 1989 as amended are dealt with by HMIP.

Consents to discharge into watercourses generally have conditions imposed which take into account both the present and future uses of the waters into which the discharge is to be made. Public registers are required to be maintained by the NRA under the 1989 Water Act, containing details of consents to discharge, together with the results of samples taken both of the effluents discharged and of the waters protected by the legislation. These registers are open to inspection by

---

See page xi for definitions of terms used in this chapter.

Figure 2.1   Water Service Companies' expenditure on sewage collection, treatment and disposal[1]

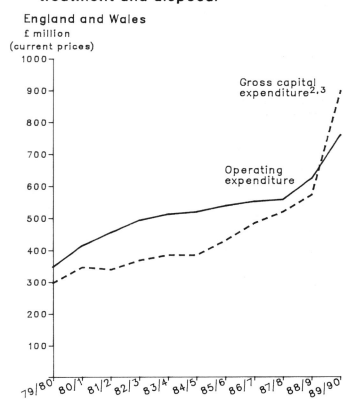

England and Wales
£ million
(current prices)

1. In addition a small amount is spent on water quality regulation, pollution alleviation and specific environmental improvement.

2. Gross capital expenditure is expenditure on the construction, provision or purchase of fixed assets or on their replacement, improvement or major renewal, and is shown as the cost before deducting any capital grants or contributions receivable. These figures are presented on the basis of accounting used by the Water Service Companies

3. Infrastructure renewals expenditure is treated as gross capital expenditure rather than operating expenditure

Source: *former water authorities; annual accounts of Water Service Companies*

the public, free of charge, at the regional offices of the NRA.

From 1 April 1991 onwards, discharges to water from "scheduled processes" will progressively come under the control of HMIP under the system of Integrated Pollution Control introduced by the Environmental Protection Act 1990. Authorisations issued by HMIP will incorporate conditions over such discharges at least as stringent as those required by the NRA in order to meet water quality objectives.

The 1989 Water Act provides a strong basis for preventing and controlling pollution. Previously, individual water authorities set water quality objectives on a non-statutory basis, which were not necessarily consistent from area to area. Under the new arrangements, statutory water quality objectives will in due course be set by the Secretary of State for the Environment, on the advice of the NRA, and following the results of the 1990 River Quality Survey, to provide a clear and consistent framework for ensuring that different waters are of a high enough standard for all their uses.

The 1990 River Quality Survey is one of a number of reviews, studies and measures the NRA has embarked on since its establishment. A major review of the way in which discharge consents are set and how compliance with their terms is assessed was published in July 1990, and the NRA is considering responses it received from interested parties.

The NRA has been actively reviewing the water quality monitoring and data gathering procedures it inherited from the water authorities, in order to ensure that these are adequate to fulfil the statutory duties placed on it. As a result, a number of tables in this chapter have not been updated from those published last year in Digest no 12; these relate to sewage treatment compliance (Table 2.2), quality of rivers and canals (Table 2.4) and water pollution incidents and prosecutions (Table 2.5). Limited information on some of these subjects were published in Autumn 1990 by the NRA in its first Corporate Plan and in its first Annual Report but this information is not necessarily on a basis which enables direct comparisons to be made with information published in previous Digests. The NRA intends to publish detailed data on a range of water quality and pollution matters in Spring 1991 once the necessary data validation exercise has been completed.

The NRA has, since its establishment, had considerable success in carrying out its pollution control functions, and is taking action against polluters. Action following a major oil pollution incident in the estuary of the River Mersey resulted in a £1 million fine against Shell UK.

2.1 Water Service Companies' expenditure on sewage collection, treatment and disposal[1]

England and Wales
Operating expenditure

£ million (current prices)

Water region	1979/80	1980/1	1981/2	1982/3	1983/4	1984/5	1985/6	1986/7	1987/8	1988/9	1989/90
Anglian	36.6	43.6	47.7	50.6	52.7	51.9	54.3	57.9	58.1	71.8	85.9
Northumbria	12.6	15.8	18.2	19.4	20.7	18.1	18.8	19.8	20.6	24.7	29.1
North West	43.3	53.2	58.7	63.8	66.9	71.1	73.1	78.8	77.6	85.1	100.7
Severn Trent	64.0	74.2	75.7	80.7	85.2	85.0	91.3	92.7	91.6	101.0	124.4
Southern	24.4	28.9	32.8	34.9	36.4	37.5	38.6	40.4	39.1	44.2	62.6
South West	9.3	11.9	13.2	14.5	14.3	14.9	15.2	15.9	15.3	17.6	22.0
Thames	83.2	98.4	110.1	122.7	127.8	131.3	134.7	132.5	146.7	158.1	183.0
Welsh	24.5	30.3	34.1	35.9	38.3	37.9	38.1	38.7	37.9	38.8	48.0
Wessex	17.6	20.4	22.6	24.2	25.0	25.8	26.6	25.8	26.5	29.4	41.5
Yorkshire	34.0	39.1	43.9	48.2	47.1	48.3	50.3	52.1	47.6	55.9	65.3
England and Wales	349.5	415.8	457.0	494.9	514.4	521.8	541.0	554.6	561.0	626.6	762.5

Gross capital expenditure[2,3]

	1979/80	1980/1	1981/2	1982/3	1983/4	1984/5	1985/6	1986/7	1987/8	1988/9	1989/90
Anglian	41.0	52.2	62.9	62.5	66.2	56.6	55.6	62.2	70.3	67.4	111.2
Northumbria	24.0	19.7	18.6	23.9	19.0	17.7	25.1	23.9	19.9	21.4	50.5
North West	45.3	56.6	54.8	66.2	83.1	92.8	101.9	106.5	105.0	113.7	150.5
Severn Trent	45.4	58.1	44.2	47.0	46.1	45.8	46.9	62.8	69.9	86.3	151.8
Southern	30.7	28.5	28.5	29.3	33.9	33.3	42.9	42.5	43.3	50.2	73.5
South West	7.3	9.4	7.2	8.6	9.9	10.9	13.6	15.3	23.2	23.8	30.8
Thames	46.3	51.4	49.2	56.4	67.5	58.2	63.1	66.2	69.1	74.8	123.8
Welsh	15.2	14.5	17.7	22.8	12.6	12.5	16.5	23.1	26.2	28.0	47.2
Wessex	14.9	16.6	20.0	19.9	23.8	22.9	31.7	36.5	40.1	46.0	61.1
Yorkshire	28.2	40.7	36.9	33.3	29.7	35.7	35.3	47.6	55.1	63.4	101.1
England and Wales	298.3	347.6	340.0	369.8	386.8	386.3	432.6	486.5	522.1	575.0	901.5

[1] In addition a small amount was spent on water quality regulation, pollution alleviation and specific environmental improvement.

[2] Gross capital expenditure is expenditure on the construction, provision or purchase of fixed assets or on their replacement, improvement or major renewal, and is shown as the cost before deducting any capital grants or contributions receivable. These figures are presented on the basis of accounting used by the Water Service Companies.

Source: *former water authorities; annual accounts of Water Service Companies*

[3] Infrastructure renewals expenditure is treated as gross capital expenditure rather than operating expenditure.

Sewage

Ninety-three per cent of the population of England and Wales are served by sewers, which have often been managed by local authorities acting on an agency basis for water authorities (and, for 1989/90, the water service companies) who reimbursed their costs. Figure 2.1 and Table 2.1 show the water industry's operating and capital expenditure on sewage collection, treatment and disposal between 1979/80 and 1989/90, including payments to local authorities. Both operating and capital expenditure have increased each year throughout the 1980s with particularly large increases between 1988/89 and 1989/90. Over the last decade, while retail prices almost doubled, operating expenditure more than doubled and capital expenditure trebled.

Over 80 per cent of sewage produced in England and Wales receives secondary (biological) treatment. About 95 per cent of the polluting load of sewage is removed by treatment before being discharged into inland rivers; for discharge into tidal waters, over 50 per cent is removed. In March 1990 the Secretary of State for the Environment announced that in future all significant discharges of sewage should be treated at sewage treatment works before discharge to estuarial or coastal waters. Under this new policy, priority is being given to schemes intended to improve the quality of bathing waters so that virtually all will comply with the EC bathing water directive by the mid-1990s.

The 1985 River Quality Survey identified deteriorating sewage works effluents, sometimes due to increased loads, as one of the main causes of local deteriorations in water quality. From 1986 to 1988, water authorities were required to make returns to the Department of the Environment (DOE) and the Welsh Office on those works failing to meet the annual performance measure specified in the consent. Table 2.2 summarises returns on non-compliance for the period 1986 to 1988 for those works with numerical consent conditions. (Some smaller works have descriptive consents.) The number of non-compliant works fell from 1,002 in 1986 to 742 in 1988, a fall of 26 per cent. Failure to comply was often because plant was inadequate to deal with the increased load placed upon it due to increased population. Since 1 September 1989, the monitoring of sewage works' compliance has been the responsibility of the NRA.

The water industry is now committed to a large capital investment programme, £28 billion at 1989 prices between 1990 and 2000, including £14 billion on sewage works, pipe networks and sea and estuarial outfalls. In particular, £1 billion has been planned to be spent on enabling poorly performing sewage works to comply with their discharge consents by March 1992 wherever possible, whilst some £3.5 billion is being spent to improve the quality of coastal waters.

About one million tonnes, dry weight, of sewage sludge is produced annually in England and Wales and nearly all is disposed of on land or at sea; a small amount (about 6 per cent) is incinerated. In 1980, 72 per cent of all sewage sludge was disposed of to land, two-thirds of this as a nutrient on farm land and horticultural areas, and the remainder as landfill. The disposal of sewage sludge at sea is controlled under the Food and Environment Protection Act 1985 which prohibits

2.2 Sewage treatment works:[1] non-compliance: 1986, 1987 and 1988

Water region	Number[2]			Number tested			Works in breach of consent					
							Number			Percentage of works tested		
	1986	1987	1988	1986	1987	1988	1986	1987	1988	1986	1987	1988
Anglian	782	760	775	774	754	748	309	260	208	40	34	28
Northumbria	196	182	178	196	182	178	37	27	26	19	15	15
North West	458	448	441	458	448	441	62	55	43	14	12	10
Severn Trent	773	753	808	762	742	751	179	160	112[3]	23	22	15
Southern	282	274	273	282	274	271	54	39	41	19	14	15
South West	226	226	232	188	219	228	55	65	67	29	30	29
Thames	374	382	378	374	379	378	67	70	60	18	18	16
Welsh[4]	803	764	710	668	611	650	112	108	107	17	18	17
Wessex	272	272	272	272	270	272	39	29	17	14	11	6
Yorkshire	380	360	360	380	351	354	88	74	61	23	21	17
England and Wales	4,546	4,421	4,427	4,354	4,230	4,271	1,002	887	742	23	21	17

[1] Works with numerical consents and tested for compliance.
[2] Because a number of works were abandoned, and the consents for a number of small works changed to descriptive consents, there were 125 fewer works with numerical consents in 1987 than 1986.
[3] In addition, three works were reported as non-compliant because they had one failure out of respectively 3, 2 and 2 samples taken during the year.

Source: *former water authorities*

[4] The majority of works with numerical consents which were not tested for compliance are understood to be small works, for which the authority asked for descriptive consents.

dumping without a licence issued by the Minister of Agriculture, Fisheries and Food (MAFF). The Secretary of State for the Environment announced in March 1990 that the UK would cease the dumping of sewage sludge in the North Sea by 1998, and (as indicated above) that large scale discharges of sewage to coastal and estuarial waters would at least receive primary treatment in future (details on the dumping of sewage sludge at sea are given later in the marine section of this chapter). There will therefore be a substantial increase in the amount of sewage sludge to be disposed of on land.

Freshwater quality

River water quality has been monitored in a series of national surveys beginning in 1958. The results, which are summarised in Table 2.3 and Figure 2.2, show very little change in river quality since 1970. Results from the 1985 river quality survey published in 1986[1]

showed that the waters of England and Wales continued to be of a high quality with around 90 per cent of river and canal length and the length of estuaries assessed as of good or fair quality. Similar surveys in Scotland, using the classification system in operation in England and Wales up to 1980, showed that around 95 per cent of the lengths of non-tidal rivers and canals and around 65 per cent of the length of tidal rivers were unpolluted.[2]

Data on the quality of rivers and canals were collected by the water authorities up to 1988 in England and Wales. Table 2.4 and Figure 2.3 show the lengths of rivers and canals in different quality classes for the period 1985-8 in each water region. During the period 1985-8 the results show a slight improvement in river quality with a decline in the length of poor and bad quality rivers of 326 km for England and Wales overall. These results are not comparable with the results of the 1985 river quality survey as differing stretches of river

2.3 Water quality: 1958-85[1]

England and Wales

Class	Former classification 1958-80 surveys									Class	New classification 1980-5 surveys				
	Non-tidal rivers and canals										Freshwater rivers and canals				
	1958		1970		1975		1980				1980		1985		
	km	%	km	%	km	%	km	%			km	%	km	%
Unpolluted	24,950	72	28,500	74	28,810	75	28,810	75		Good 1A	13,830	34	13,470	33
										Good 1B	14,220	35	13,990	34
Doubtful	5,220	15	6,270	17	6,730	17	7,110	18		Fair 2	8,670	21	9,730	24
Poor	2,270	7	1,940	5	1,770	5	2,000	5		Poor 3	3,260	8	3,560	9
Grossly polluted	2,250	6	1,700	4	1,270	3	810	2		Bad 4	640	2	650	2
All classes	34,690	100	38,400	100	38,590	100	38,740	100		All classes	40,630	100	41,390	100

Class	Tidal rivers									Class	Estuaries				
	1958		1970		1975		1980				1980		1985		
	km	%	km	%	km	%	km	%			km	%	km	%
Unpolluted	1,160	41	1,380	48	1,360	48	1,410	50		Good A	1,870	68	1,860	68
Doubtful	940	32	680	23	780	27	950	34		Fair B	620	23	650	24
Poor	400	14	490	17	420	15	220	8		Poor C	140	5	130	5
Grossly polluted	360	13	340	12	280	10	220	8		Bad D	110	4	90	3
All classes	2,850	100	2,880	100	2,850	100	2,800	100		All classes	2,730	100	2,730	100

Scotland

Class	Non-tidal rivers and canals						Tidal rivers					
	1974		1980		1985		1974		1980		1985	
	km	%	km	%	km	%	km	%	km	%	km	%
Unpolluted	45,190	95	45,080	95	45,400	96	310	66	280	60	310	66
Doubtful	1,760	4	2,000	4	1,710	4	100	21	130	28	110	23
Poor	390	1	260	1	270	1	30	6	40	9	20	4
Grossly polluted	170	-	170	-	140	-	40	9	30	6	30	6
All classes	47,510	100	47,510	100	47,510	100	470	100	470	100	470	100

[1] Lengths are rounded to the nearest 10 km and may not sum to totals.

Sources: *River Quality in England and Wales, 1985: a Report of the 1985 Survey. Department of the Environment and Welsh Office, 1986; Scottish Development Department*

Figure 2.2 River water quality: 1958-85

England and Wales

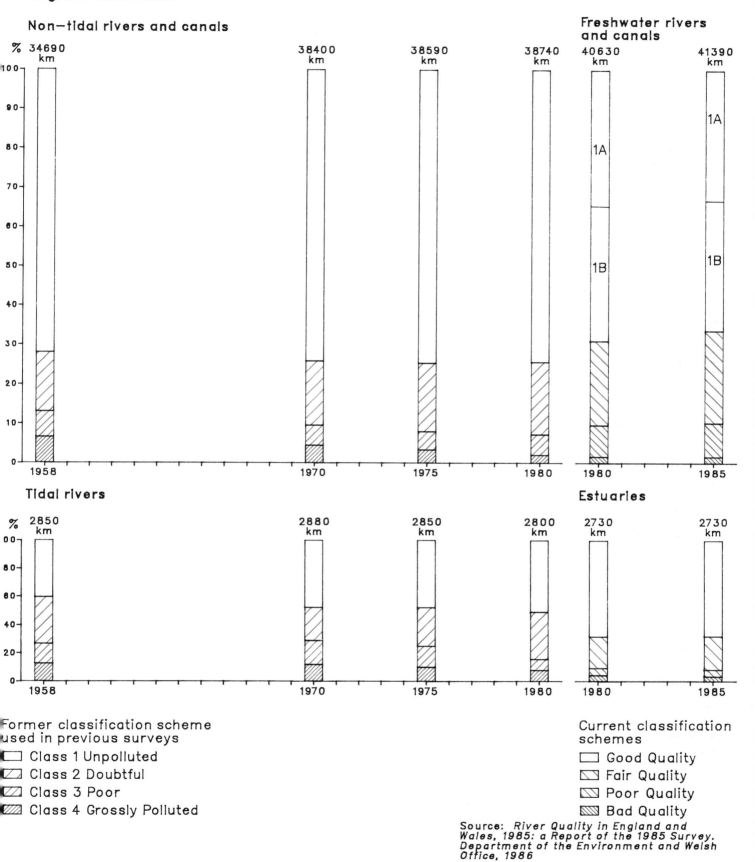

Former classification scheme
used in previous surveys

☐ Class 1 Unpolluted
▨ Class 2 Doubtful
▨ Class 3 Poor
▨ Class 4 Grossly Polluted

Current classification
schemes

☐ Good Quality
▨ Fair Quality
▨ Poor Quality
▨ Bad Quality

Source: *River Quality in England and Wales, 1985: a Report of the 1985 Survey. Department of the Environment and Welsh Office, 1986*

and canal were classified by the water authorities for their own purposes. As mentioned previously, since 1 September 1989, the NRA has been responsible for monitoring water quality in England and Wales. As one of its first major tasks, the NRA carried out during 1990 a further comprehensive river and estuary quality survey and is now compiling and validating the results for publication.

2.4 Quality of rivers and canals: 1985-8[1]

England and Wales

Length in km

Water region	Year	1A Good quality	1B Good quality	2 Fair quality	3 Poor quality	4 Bad quality	Total
Anglian	1985	443	2,144	1,467	392	7	4,453
	1986	414	2,068	1,524	400	48	4,453
	1987	379	2,100	1,578	378	18	4,453
	1988	360	2,197	1,526	352	18	4,453
Northumbrian	1985	1,729	708	264	62	22	2,785
	1986	1,729	717	257	62	20	2,785
	1987	1,730	716	273	61	5	2,785
	1988	1,730	722	284	44	5	2,785
North West	1985	2,710	762	1,239	921	268	5,900
	1986	2,669	764	1,238	963	266	5,900
	1987	2,590	821	1,265	964	260	5,900
	1988	2,601	785	1,334	915	265	5,900
Severn-Trent	1985	802	2,444	2,346	504	71	6,167
	1986	827	2,411	2,299	549	71	6,156
	1987	827	2,407	2,285	557	80	6,156
	1988	834	2,402	2,278	564	78	6,156
Southern	1985	378	1,029	584	152	18	2,161
	1986	373	949	690	128	21	2,161
	1987	628	773	596	164	0	2,161
	1988	565	1,052	413	124	7	2,161
South West	1985[2]	594	749	757	485	16	2,601
	1986	609	791	814	358	29	2,601
	1987	650	769	827	328	27	2,601
	1988	513	897	872	286	33	2,601
Thames	1985	389	1,129	648	249	3	2,418
	1986	358	1,035	791	228	6	2,418
	1987	702	951	643	117	5	2,418
	1988	540	1,057	704	117	0	2,418
Welsh	1985	2,573	1,343	566	275	24	4,781
	1986	2,495	1,299	677	298	33	4,802
	1987	2,469	1,297	728	274	34	4,802
	1988	2,739	1,105	606	311	41	4,802
Wessex	1985	650	864	781	156	15	2,466
	1986	627	880	816	126	17	2,466
	1987	640	853	839	115	19	2,466
	1988	632	852	857	106	19	2,466
Yorkshire	1985	2,304	2,192	773	571	194	6,034
	1986	2,275	2,193	781	614	170	6,034
	1987	2,264	2,198	779	629	165	6,034
	1988	2,261	2,140	839	646	148	6,034
England and Wales	1985[2]	12,572	13,364	9,425	3,767	638	39,766
	1986	12,376	13,107	9,887	3,726	681	39,777
	1987	12,879	12,885	9,813	3,587	613	39,777
	1988	12,775	13,209	9,713	3,465	614	39,776

[1] In some cases estimates of river quality have been based upon financial years and/or more than one year's data.

[2] Adequate data are not available to classify 97 km of river length in 1985. For these 97 km the 1986 assessment of river class has been used.

Source: *former water authorities*

Figure 2.3 Quality of rivers and canals : 1985-88 : percentage in each class

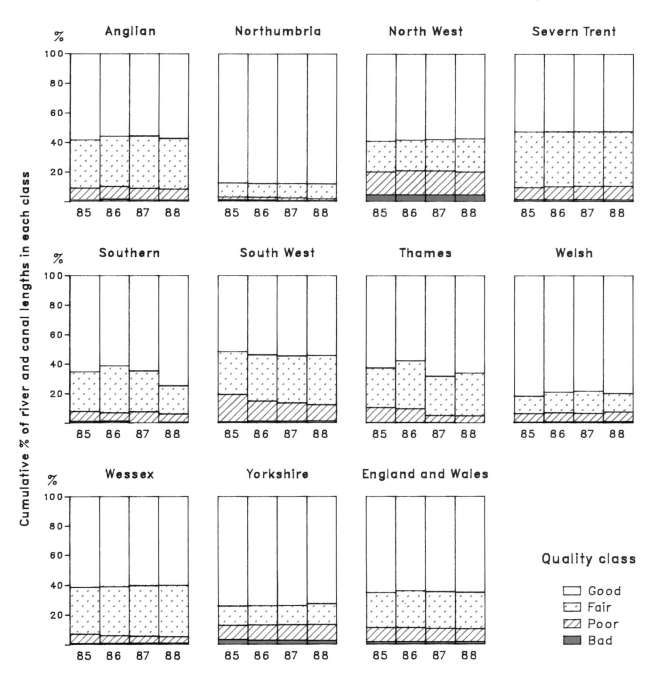

Source: *former water authorities*

Pollution incidents

Table 2.5 shows the number of water pollution incidents, their cause and prosecutions by cause. Table 2.5a shows that the total number of pollution incidents reported in England and Wales more than doubled between 1981 and 1988. The causes of pollution incidents reported in 1988 are shown in Table 2.5b. Thirty-eight per cent were identified as being attributable to industry, 17 per cent to farm pollution and 19 per cent to problems of sewage and sewerage. The remaining 26 per cent fell into the "other"

2.5 Water pollution incidents and prosecutions

England and Wales

a) **Water pollution incidents[1]**

Water region	1981	1982	1983	1984	1985	1986	1987	1988
Anglian	1,095	1,077	1,288	1,544	1,707	1,468	1,605	1,446
Northumbria	509	544	613	654	722	729	671	795
North West	1,350	1,288	1,385	2,241	2,202	2,480	2,965	3,365
Severn Trent	2,401	2,681	3,354	4,372	4,524	4,497	4,435	5,292
Southern	1,300	1,327	1,400	1,574	1,668	1,725	1,795	1,742
South West	1,143	1,227	1,639	1,685	1,796	2,220	2,251	2,760
Thames	1,810	2,120	2,345	2,486	2,695	2,890	2,969	3,925
Welsh	..	..	..	1,418	1,681	1,619	2,489	2,707
Wessex	844	790	966	1,125	993	1,332	1,339	1,920
Yorkshire	1,136	1,020	1,165	1,536	2,006	2,444	2,738	2,974
England and Wales	12,600[2]	13,100[2]	15,400[2]	18,635	19,994	21,404	23,257	26,926

b) **Water pollution incidents[1] reported in 1988: by cause**

Water region	Industrial			Farm[3]	Sewage		Sewerage	Other	Total[4]	Nothing found[5]
	Oil	Chemical	Other		Own	Other				
Anglian	478	98	71	203	← 373 →			223	1,446	-
Northumbrian	135	← 66 →		80	← 273 →			141	695	100
North West	508	← 338 →		612	100	115	399	495	2,567	798
Severn Trent	1,300	567	541	582	73	73	626	1,530	5,292	-
Southern	459	← 182 →		120	98	114	133	409	1,515	227
South West	254	← 341 →		840	← 488 →			463	2,386	374
Thames	1,256	← 323 →		188	← 610 →			997	3,374	551
Welsh	197	79	274	582	122	105	249	577	2,185	522
Wessex	435	← 160 →		392	← 168 →			506	1,661	259
Yorkshire	403	← 620 →		353	← 459 →			698	2,533	441
England and Wales	5,425	← 3,660 →		3,952	← 4,578 →			6,039	23,654	3,272

c) **Water pollution prosecutions in 1988:[6] by cause**

Water region	Industrial			Farm[3]	Sewage		Sewerage	Other	Total
	Oil	Chemical	Other		Own	Other			
Anglian	3	1	3	21	-	-	-	-	28
Northumbrian	-	-	-	1	-	-	-	-	1
North West	3	14	1	22	-	3	-	-	43
Severn Trent	3	3	13	21	-	-	-	-	40
Southern	1	-	-	11	-	-	-	-	12
South West	← 10 →			46	-	-	-	-	56
Thames	1	← 1 →		18	-	3	-	-	23
Welsh	← 40 →			32	-	-	-	-	72
Wessex	← 4 →			10	-	-	-	-	14
Yorkshire	6	19	7	6	-	-	-	-	38
England and Wales	← 133 →			188	-	6	-	-	327

[1] In some cases the figures given are for financial rather than calendar years.

[2] Assumes that the number of incidents in the Welsh water region in the years 1980-3 accounts for the same percentage of national pollution incidents as in the years 1984-6.

[3] Data may differ from that published in *Water Pollution from Farm Waste 1988 England and Wales* (1989) because of differences in definition.

Source: *former water authorities*

[4] Incidents reported where pollution was found.

[5] Incidents reported for which upon investigation no evidence of pollution was found. The pollution may have dispersed. These are not included in the total.

[6] May relate to incidents which took place in a previous year.

category, including dumping/fly-tipping, fires and vandalism. Oil pollution represented 60 per cent of the total number of industrial incidents.

Table 2.5c gives the number of prosecutions for pollution offences in 1988. Farm pollution incidents were the subject of 188 prosecutions followed by industrial incidents which led to 133 prosecutions. There were also six prosecutions for sewage-related incidents. There were no prosecutions for incidents in the sewerage and other categories. Comparison of Tables 2.5c and 2.5b shows that for incidents for which evidence of pollution was found, 4.8 per cent of farm-related pollution incidents resulted in prosecution compared with 1.5 per cent for industrial-related incidents. The higher proportion of farm pollution incidents which resulted in prosecution reflects the higher proportion of serious farm incidents which can involve the discharge of large amounts of organic matter which can cause great damage. Silage effluent is up to 200 times as polluting as untreated sewage whilst cattle slurry is 100 times as strong. In some instances water authorities were unable to provide a full breakdown of the information in Tables 2.5b and 2.5c. The collection of information concerning pollution incidents has, since 1 September 1989, been the responsibility of the NRA.

Nitrate concentrations

The Water Supply (Water Quality) Regulations 1989, which incorporate the requirements of the EC Directive on the Quality of Water intended for Human Consumption, set a maximum concentration of 50 mg/l for nitrate in drinking water supplies. Water companies have given undertakings under section 20(5)(b) of the Water Act 1989 to comply with this standard by 1995. In most cases this will involve blending with low nitrate supplies or treatment using a denitrification process.

The main source of nitrate in water is leaching from the soil, although some nitrate goes directly into waterways through run-off from agricultural land and from sewage works. Groundwater provides about 30 per cent of the public water supplies in Britain though the percentage varies a great deal from region to region, being highest in the southern and eastern areas of England.

Water companies provide regular information to the DOE about sources (eg, boreholes) and supplies of water (eg, leaving water treatment works) in England and Wales where the nitrate concentration had exceeded 50 mg/l as nitrate at any time in the year. Reports were made quarterly from 1983 to 1987, and annually since 1988. A summary of the information for 1983-9 is given in Table 2.6. The number of water supplies which exceeded 50 mg/l as nitrate ranged from 74 to 90 and shows no clear trend. The high number of supplies in 1989 is probably due to the exceptionally dry weather which resulted in abnormally high peaks of nitrate in some rivers.

The areas worst affected by nitrates are in the Anglian and Severn Trent water regions but problems were also experienced in some parts of the Southern, Thames and Yorkshire regions. Powers were taken in the 1989 Water Act to designate Nitrate Sensitive Areas (NSAs) in which certain agricultural operations, such as cropping and fertiliser use, can be regulated. In April 1990, the Government designated 10 pilot NSAs in England covering around 15,000 hectares. In these areas farmers will be advised on ways to reduce the risk of nitrate leaching and will qualify for grants to help them change their farming operations, such as switching from arable to low intensity grassland cultivation. In an additional nine areas, not designated as NSAs, farmers will get similar advice on reducing nitrate leaching.

2.6 Number of water supplies exceeding 50 mg/l nitrate limit[1] at any time

England

Former water authority[2]	1983	1984	1985	1986	1987	1988	1989
Anglian	30	35	30	33	31	34	33
Northumbrian	-	-	-	-	-	-	-
North West	-	-	-	-	-	-	1
Severn Trent	32	34	35	38	36	26	30
Southern	3	-	1	-	-	4	7
South West	1	-	-	-	-	-	1
Thames	8	6	7	7	4	4	7
Wessex	1	-	1	1	-	1	5
Yorkshire	7	6	4	3	3	7	6
England	82	81	79	82	74	76	90

[1] EC Directive limit which was incorporated into the Water Supply (Water Quality) Regulations 1989.
[2] Includes statutory water companies.

Source: *Department of the Environment*

Bathing waters and beaches

EC Directive 76/160/EEC set mandatory values for specified parameters of bathing water quality and member states were required to conform with these limits for all bathing waters by December 1985 unless a derogation had been granted. The directive requires samples of bathing water to be taken at regular intervals during the bathing season, which is regarded as being from mid-May to October in Britain but shorter in Northern Ireland. In the UK a minimum of 20 samples are taken at each site during the bathing season. The DOE has made the NRA the competent authority for bathing water sampling in England and Wales and the data presented here have been provided by the NRA. Data for Scotland and Northern Ireland have been provided by the river purification boards and the Department of the Environment (Northern Ireland) respectively.

To comply with the directive in respect of each coliform parameter, at least 95 per cent of samples must have counts not exceeding the mandatory limit value (2,000/100 ml for faecal coliforms and 10,000/100 ml for total coliforms). The directive also set a series of stricter values which member states should endeavour to observe as guidelines. Failure to meet the mandatory values does not necessarily imply a danger to health.

Twenty-seven bathing waters were identified in 1979 for the purpose of the Directive and sampling began in 1980. Following a survey in 1985-6 of popular coastal bathing waters in the UK the number of identified bathing waters formally brought within the scope of the Directive was increased in 1986 to 391. Subsequently the number of identified bathing waters was further increased to 397 in 1987, 403 in 1988, 440 in 1989 and 446 in 1990. The increase in the number of identified bathing waters between 1988 and 1989 resulted from the sub-division of a number of bathing waters in the Northumbrian and South West regions, and the identification of an additional bathing water at Shoebury near Southend-on-Sea. Six additional bathing waters were identified in 1990, four in England and two in Wales.

The 1988, 1989 and 1990 results for the United Kingdom are summarised in Table 2.7. This shows that 345 of the 446 identified bathing waters complied with the Directive in 1990, a compliance rate of 77 per cent and similar to the previous year. The compliance rate in 1990 ranged from 30 per cent in the North West to 100 per cent in the Thames and Wessex regions. The 1988 and later results are based on a more extensive sampling programme than before and are not comparable with the results for previous years. Table 2.8 shows the number of bathing waters complying or failing to comply in both 1989 and 1990 and also the number of bathing waters where compliance changed between the two years. Figure 2.4 shows the location of each bathing water in the UK in 1990 and which ones that passed or failed the directive criteria. Details of individual bathing waters in 1989 and 1990 are given in Statistical Bulletin (91)1. Details for earlier years are given in previous statistical bulletins.

The European Blue Flag Campaign was launched in 1987 by the Foundation for Environmental Education in Europe to improve the standard of bathing beaches and marinas used by large numbers of holidaymakers. Sponsored by the European Commission the campaign

2.7 Bathing water surveys: 1988-90

United Kingdom

| Region | Compliance with EC Bathing Water Directive[1] coliform standards[2] | | | | | | | | |
| | Identified bathing waters[3] | | | Number complying | | | Percentage complying | | |
	1988	1989	1990	1988	1989	1990	1988	1989	1990
Northumbria	19	32	32	9	20	21	47	63	66
Yorkshire	22	22	22	21	18	17	95	82	77
Anglian	28	28	29	19	23	27	68	82	93
Thames	2	3	3	-	3	3	-	100	100
Southern	65	65	66	27	45	48	42	69	73
Wessex (south coast)	27	27	28	26	25	28	96	93	100
South West	109	132	133	92	113	118	84	86	89
Wessex (north coast)	11	11	11	4	6	11	36	55	100
Welsh	48	48	50	37	40	35	77	83	70
North West	33	33	33	6	11	10	18	33	30
England and Wales	364	401	407	241	304	318	66	76	78
Scotland	23	23	23	12	16	12	52	70	52
Northern Ireland	16	16	16	14	16	15	88	100	94
United Kingdom	403	440	446	267	336	345	66	76	77

[1] 76/160/EEC.

[2] At least 95 per cent of samples must have counts not exceeding the mandatory limit values for total and faecal coliforms (see text).

[3] The increase in 1989 is due to subdivision of some bathing waters.

Source: *former water authorities; National Rivers Authority; Scottish Development Department; Department of the Environment (NI)*

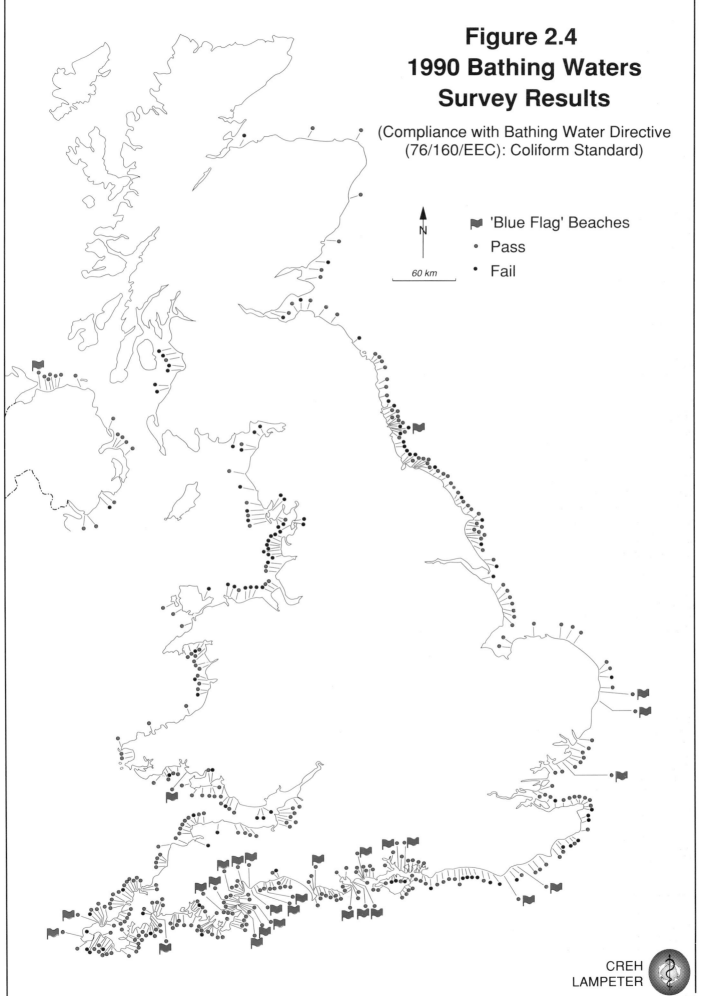

Figure 2.4
1990 Bathing Waters
Survey Results

(Compliance with Bathing Water Directive
(76/160/EEC): Coliform Standard)

N

60 km

'Blue Flag' Beaches

• Pass

• Fail

CREH
LAMPETER

2.8 Bathing water surveys: compliance with EC Bathing Water Directive[1] in both 1989 and 1990

United Kingdom

Region	Number complying in both 1989 and 1990	Number not complying in 1989, complying in 1990	Number complying in 1989, not complying in 1990	Number not complying in both 1989 and 1990	New bathing waters identified in 1990	
					Number complying	Number not complying
Northumbria	15	6	5	6	-	-
Yorkshire	15	2	3	2	-	-
Anglian	23	3	-	2	1	-
Thames	3	-	-	-	-	-
Southern	39	8	6	12	1	-
Wessex (south coast)	25	2	-	-	1	-
South West	106	11	7	8	1	-
Wessex (north coast)	6	5	-	-	-	-
Welsh	31	3	9	5	1	1
North West	7	3	4	19	-	-
England and Wales	270	43	34	54	5	1
Scotland	11	1	5	6	-	-
Northern Ireland	15	-	1	-	-	-
United Kingdom	296	44	40	60	5	1

[1] 76/160/EEC

Source: *National Rivers Authority; Scottish Development Department; Department of the Environment (NI)*

also has a number of public and private sponsors throughout the community. To be eligible for the blue flag award bathing beaches have to meet the guideline micro-biological parameters on bathing water quality specified in the EC bathing water directive and satisfy a broad range of other criteria including safe bathing water, good beach area management and safety, provision of basic facilities and environmental information to users. Blue flags are awarded annually by a jury and can be withdrawn in the course of the season if a bathing beach ceases to meet the required standards. In 1990, 29 beaches were awarded the blue flag out of 63 applications. This compares with the 22 blue flags awarded in 1989. The locations of the blue flag beaches in the UK in 1990 are also shown in Figure 2.4.

Marine

Waste products and effluents containing contaminants reach the marine environment principally from rivers and direct pipeline discharges into coastal and estuarial waters. Other inputs of contaminants reach the sea via the atmosphere and the disposal of harbour dredgings which, together with a diminishing quantity of industrial waste and sewage sludge, are dumped at sea from licensed disposal vessels. Oil and other operational wastes may be discharged from ships and oil rigs.

In 1987 the UK hosted the Second International Conference on the Protection of the North Sea. The key

2.9 Inputs[1] to the North Sea:[2] 1985-6

United Kingdom[3]

Tonnes per annum

Substance	River inputs[4]		Direct discharges	Dredgings	Sewage sludge	Industrial waste		Incineration at sea	Total input to the North Sea from all countries[1]
	Min	Max				Liquid	Solid		
Cadmium	8	14	16	5	3	<1	<1	<1	90
Mercury	4	5	3	5	1	<1	<1	<1	40
Copper	240	283	215	262	103	1	160	<1	2,700
Lead	245	303	133	338	99	1	206	<1	3,500
Zinc	1,440	1,451	986	970	219	5	396	<1	17,000
Chromium	98	141	439	453	39	<1	17	<1	4,000
Nickel	233	265	88	117	14	<1	51	<1	1,150
Arsenic	28	65	220	-	<1	38	4	<1	800

[1] Excluding atmospheric inputs.
[2] Excluding English Channel.
[3] Figures for other North Sea countries are available from the source.
[4] River flow was 90 million cubic metres per day.

Source: *Quality Status of the North Sea, Second International Conference on the Protection of the North Sea, 1987*

scientific background document for the conference was a report on the *Quality Status of the North Sea*[3] which described the physical oceanography of the North Sea, the major inputs of pollutants and contaminants and their theoretical dispersion patterns. It also reviewed what was known about the effects of these inputs and other human activities in the various sectors of the North Sea. The report confirmed that the state of the North Sea was generally good and that environmental damage was largely confined to localised areas such as coastal regions.

Table 2.9 gives data for the UK from the report showing inputs of selected contaminants into the North Sea in 1985-6 from all main sources except the atmosphere. The main sources of most contaminants from the UK into the North Sea were rivers, direct discharges and dredged spoil. It should be noted, however, that data on atmospheric inputs are insufficient to allow inputs from each country to be reliably quantified. For the most important source of contaminants, rivers and estuaries, the UK accounted generally for about 20 per cent of inputs to the North Sea and 15-30 per cent of the total input via dredged spoil. The main sources of waste incinerated at sea were Belgium and West Germany. The UK was the main source of contaminant inputs by direct discharge and was the only country disposing of sewage sludge to the North Sea.

At the Second North Sea Conference a wide range of issues were addressed and a number of measures

agreed. These included an end to the dumping of harmful industrial wastes in the North Sea by 1989, an end to marine incineration by 1994, and, the reduction of inputs of dangerous substances into rivers by the order of 50 per cent by 1995. A North Sea Task Force was subsequently established to ensure better co-ordination of North Sea scientific research and monitoring, and is currently preparing a new quality assessment of the North Sea or publication in 1993.

The Third North Sea Conference held in the Hague in March 1990 agreed further measures to improve the North Sea, including reductions in inputs of a wider range of dangerous substances both by river and atmosphere, in some cases by 70 per cent or more. The conference also agreed the phase out and the destruction of polychlorinated biphenyls (PCBs), oily substances used mainly in transformers and other electrical equipment, which are highly persistent and harmful if released into the environment. The UK manufacture of PCBs ended in 1977 and new applications were restricted to sealed equipment in 1976. The UK, along with other North Sea countries, has agreed to ensure that the use of all identifiable PCBs is phased out by the end of 1999 and that they are destroyed in an environmentally sensitive way. Other initiatives agreed at the conference included new controls on operational discharges from ships and offshore oil platforms and new international measures on research, survey and protection of marine wildlife, and specifically small cetaceans (dolphins and

2.10 Dumping of sewage sludge, industrial waste and dredgings at sea: amounts dumped and content of certain metals

United Kingdom[1]   Tonnes, unless otherwise stated

	1980	1981	1982	1983	1984	1985	1986	1987	1988
Sewage sludge:									
Mercury	3.6	2.4	1.4	1.1	0.9	1.2	1.1	1.2	0.9
Cadmium	9.3	6.5	5.1	4.0	4.0	3.6	3.4	3.4	2.4
Copper	220.7	199.8	203.9	158.6	156.8	150.6	147.0	142.3	130.0
Lead	182.3	159.8	164.8	160.8	158.0	166.3	166.0	164.9	142.7
Zinc	684.8	640.8	442.0	439.2	500.3	326.8	485.4	462.0	347.7
Total amount dumped (million tonnes)	8.9	8.5	8.1	7.3	7.5	7.5	8.0	7.3	7.2
Industrial waste:[2]									
Mercury	<0.4	<0.4	0.4	0.3	-	0.2	0.2	0.2	0.3
Cadmium	<0.2	<0.4	0.4	0.3	-	0.3	0.2	0.3	0.3
Copper	188.3	203.7	194.0	224.3	44.1	161.7	197.8	197.2	199.9
Lead	237.3	251.1	244.8	283.2	48.0	207.1	250.4	251.5	252.4
Zinc	452.8	470.8	472.1	546.6	112.0	401.0	491.1	486.3	485.5
Total amount dumped (million tonnes)	2.5	2.5	2.2	2.5	0.7	2.0	2.2	2.2	2.3
Dredgings:[1]									
Mercury	18.2	11.3	11.2	12.2	10.6	8.8	6.9	5.9	4.0
Cadmium	10.7	7.1	7.0	7.9	6.9	7.8	11.2	9.3	3.0
Copper	744.0	451.7	474.3	508.6	585.0	409.2	466.6	387.5	286.6
Lead	1,335.0	723.4	789.1	795.3	928.3	574.9	679.4	540.0	387.3
Zinc	2,814.0	1,923.0	1,920.3	2,188.9	2,287.6	1,649.8	1,981.0	1,461.7	940.6
Total amount dumped (million tonnes)	16.0	12.8	12.9	12.7	20.2	12.5	15.2	13.0	9.1

[1] Figures on the metal content of dredgings for 1980-3 cover England and Wales only.
[2] Includes colliery wastes and flyash.

Source: *Ministry of Agriculture, Fisheries and Food. Figures as supplied to the Oslo Commission*

porpoises). Details of the steps the UK will take to implement the agreements reached at the third North Sea Conference were published in an *Implementation Guidance Note*[4] in July 1990.

The dumping of wastes at sea, except under licence, is prohibited by the Food and Environment Protection Act 1985. Conditions in the licence may specify the site, the volume and the method of disposal. Details of all dumping operations in external waters are sent to the Oslo Commission, of which the UK is one of the several European signatories. "External waters" are defined as those beyond the baselines described in the Territorial Waters Order in Council 1984 (baselines generally follow the low water line along the coast but cross bays and inlets). Table 2.10 shows that in 1988 7.2 million tonnes of sewage sludge (wet weight), 2.3 million tonnes of industrial waste and 9.1 million tonnes of dredgings were dumped in the external waters around the UK. The main dumping areas were Liverpool Bay, the Thames Estuary, off north east England and the Clyde Estuary. The amount of dumped sewage sludge rose to a peak of 8.9 million tonnes in 1980, but has since fallen by 19 per cent. The amounts of dumped industrial waste and dredgings have shown no clear trend but the amount of dredgings in 1988 was much lower than in recent years. The relatively large tonnage for dredgings in 1980 and in 1984 were the result of a number of "one-off" projects. The amounts of various metals in dumped industrial waste and dredgings has fluctuated in recent years with no underlying trend. However, the trend in the volume of these metals in sewage sludge has been downwards and this trend was maintained in 1988 with falls in some cases of 20-30 per cent. These reductions have been achieved by the close control of the sewage treatment authorities and the licensing authorities, allied to improvements in processes, and industrial effluent control by industry and the water authorities.

Oil pollution, as a result of discharges from tankers, oil rigs and other sources, can cause great damage to the marine environment and result in the death of birds, fish and plants. The Advisory Committee on Pollution of the Sea (ACOPS) is an independent organisation which carries out annual surveys of oil pollution and its effects around the UK coast.

Table 2.11 gives various data relating to oil spills. Table 2.11a shows that for the fourth successive year there was an increase in the number of oil spills with 764 separate incidents reported in 1989. This is 205 more than in 1988 and the most in the past 10 years. The Department of Energy was notified by offshore operators of 307 spills in the North Sea in 1989, compared to 269 in 1988, 254 in 1987 and 91 in 1985. This markedly upward trend has resulted from the more accurate reporting of spillages, irrespective of size, by offshore operators, which began in 1986 with the help of improved surveillance and overflights by the Department of Energy. The evidence available suggests that the size of spills has not changed significantly in recent years. Despite recent improvements in reporting and surveillance it is probable that current operational and accidental oil discharges from installations in the North Sea are still much greater than those reported.

Because most spillages are small and no clean-up action is necessary (the oil being removed by natural processes), the number of spills reported is not necessarily the best indication of the overall effect on the environment. Decisions to clean up small spills are also influenced by likely damage from clean-up operations, type of oil, problems of access to beaches and the cost of clean-up operations. Table 2.11b shows that in 1989 there were 132 oil spills of 100 gallons or more.

Table 2.11c shows that in 1989 clean-up action was undertaken on 160 occasions, 21 per cent of the total oil spills reported. This is the highest figure in recent years. Clean-up data are not available for the large number of spills in the North Sea but it is likely that the oil was left to degrade naturally without treatment. Clean-up action was taken for 39 spills in the Bristol Channel and south Wales coastal region, 24 per cent of all clean-ups, followed by east Scotland where there were 33 clean-ups, and Orkneys and Shetlands. Table 2.11d shows that the costs of clean-up operations incurred by reporting organisations in 1989 were £234,000, the highest figure in the past 10 years, and the fifth succesive year that costs have risen.

A total of 19 spills over two tonnes were reported during 1989. Spillages of 50 tonnes or more are given below:

> 17 September: 900 tonnes crude oil following a collision between two tankers, the *Phillips Oklahoma* and *Fiona* at the Humber anchorage;
>
> 19 August: 150 tonnes crude oil accidentally discharged into the River Mersey following a collision with a tug;
>
> 22 November: 84 tonnes intermediate fuel oil from the tanker *Texaco Westminster* in Milford Haven following a collision with a tug.

Table 2.12 shows prosecutions by port authorities and convictions for offences relating to the illegal discharge of oil or of mixtures containing oil. It covers offences committed in harbours and coastal waters and includes deliberate discharges of oil from ships and discharges of ballast water in harbours. There is a rising trend of convictions and in 1989 there were 29 convictions, double that in 1988, and fines of £48,400 imposed. Foreign ships accounted for over a half of the convictions. For offences committed outside UK territorial limits the Department of Transport is the prosecuting authority. Only one prosecution has been undertaken since 1983 leading, in 1989, to a conviction and a fine of £15,000.

2.11 Oil spills: incidents reported, size, effect and costs incurred

United Kingdom

	1979	1980	1981	1982	1983	1984	1985	1986	1987	1988	1989
a) Number of incidents reported											
North east England	23	17	23	31	20	11	22	23	23	25	22
East England	26	32	61	37	30	15	18	9	12	10	37
Essex and Kent[1]	109	110	130	131	89	85	53	47	27	41	83
Southern England	56	77	79	48	36	36	24	36	36	33	57
South west England[2]	55	25	21	27	15	13	21	14	15	19	49
Bristol Channel and south Wales	58	36	47	37	27	29	20	30	28	37	65
Lancashire and Irish Sea	35	14	33	31	16	19	30	30	23	26	31
West Scotland	10	18	21	22	18	16	11	13	18	19	15
East Scotland	123	88	46	66	49	42	50	46	21	50	77
Orkneys and Shetlands[3]	35	23	15	35	24	35	26	23	43	30	26
Offshore North Sea	38	92	76	52	72	66	91	165	254	269	307
United Kingdom	568	532	552	517	396	367	366	436	500	559	764
b) Number of spills over 100 gallons[3]											
North east England	2	3	3	5	4	3	4	1	2	4	5
East England	-	-	-	-	1	-	-	-	1	2	1
Essex and Kent	1	20	13	9	3	7	4	2	4	4	1
Southern England	6	5	5	1	3	1	1	-	-	2	2
South west England	2	1	-	2	-	1	-	-	-	1	1
Bristol Channel and south Wales	8	3	4	5	3	4	1	7	2	8	3
Irish Sea[4]	2	4	3	2	3	4	2	5	4	1	2
West Scotland	3	5	2	6	3	3	3	1	6	2	6
East Scotland	6	4	4	10	6	8	4	6	2	3	10
Orkneys and Shetlands	6	7	4	9	6	8	12	3	4	8	2
Offshore North Sea	12	32	55	31	41	37	44	78	101	75	99
United Kingdom[4]	48	84	93	80	73	76	75	103	126	110	132
	(119)	(179)	(207)	(186)	(173)	(185)	(200)	(247)	(314)	(362)	(425)
c) Number of spills requiring clean-up[3]											
North east England	6	7	8	10	6	5	11	10	8	10	9
East England	7	9	7	7	4	3	8	4	5	6	5
Essex and Kent	17	49	46	39	23	38	22	15	11	19	12
Southern England	17	31	29	11	15	6	6	12	10	14	14
South west England	13	7	7	4	5	3	14	7	10	7	11
Bristol Channel and south Wales	38	25	24	21	19	23	11	16	18	24	39
Irish Sea[4]	14	6	22	19	7	14	17	17	12	4	9
West Scotland	6	5	7	3	3	4	1	5	1	4	7
East Scotland	17	28	9	33	21	22	21	21	17	15	33
Orkneys and Shetlands	13	7	10	22	14	22	19	19	13	17	21
Offshore North Sea	1	7	2	1	..	..	..	..	..	..	..
United Kingdom[4]	149	181	171	170	117	140	130	126	105	120	160
	(313)	(443)	(505)	(517)	(368)	(345)	(360)	(436)	(500)	(559)	(764)
d) Costs incurred by reporting authority (£ thousand)											
North east England	2	10	3	3	94	5	20	7	15	7	3
East England	2	5	36	2	-	6	6	3	15	7	4
Essex and Kent	2	20	18	11	2	18	11	5	26	34	2
Southern England	24	53	29	16	4	1	1	21	21	15	54
South west England	2	3	5	1	2	5	5	2	4	13	7
Bristol Channel and south Wales	5	3	1	7	6	1	44	2	37	14	6
Irish Sea[4]	-	9	8	-	5	10	1	74	49	6	146
West Scotland	3	2	2	6	3	1	-	7	-	-	1
East Scotland	3	8	-	9	34	9	14	8	-	2	3
Orkneys and Shetlands	25	1	15	10	..	12	7	5	31	-	8
Offshore North Sea	-	-	-	..	..	..	..	..	..	120	..
United Kingdom[4]	69	113	118	66	149	67	107	134	198	217	234

[1] Figures for 1979 include 62 incidents for the Port of London Authority.
[2] Includes the Channel Islands for 1981.
[3] The figures are not strictly comparable with the incidents reported in Table 2.11a since many individual incident reports did not supply complete information. As a guide, the number of incident reports that gave complete information on spill size and clean-up requirements is shown in brackets.
[4] Excluding Northern Ireland in 1979-80.

Source: *Advisory Committee on Oil Pollution of the Sea, Annual Reports 1979-81; Surveys of Oil Pollution around the Coasts of the United Kingdom 1982-9*

2.12 Oil spills: trends in prosecutions and convictions

United Kingdom

	British ships				Foreign ships			
	1986	1987	1988	1989	1986	1987	1988	1989
Procesutions undertaken	3	2	5	8	1	4	7	17
Convictions	3	2	5	7	1	4	6	17
Cases lost/dismissed	-	-	-	1	-	-	-	-
Total fines imposed(£)	10,685	2,200	5,650	2,600	5,150	1,450	11,000	29,700
Awards for clean-up[1] (£)	-	135	150	-	-	412	3,696	223

	Land installations				Total			
	1986	1987	1988	1989	1986	1987	1988	1989
Procesutions undertaken	3	5	3	5	7	11	15	30
Convictions	3	5	3	5	7	11	14	29
Cases lost/dismissed	-	-	-	-	-	-	1	1
Total fines imposed(£)	2,810	9,200	4,000	16,100	18,645	12,850	20,650	48,400
Awards for clean-up[1] (£)	5,301	200	-	-	5,301	767	3,846	223

[1] Additional to fines.

Source: *Advisory Committee on Oil Pollution of the Sea*

2.13 Heavy metals: average concentrations in the muscle of fish: by species: by area

United Kingdom   mg/kg wet weight

			1979	1980	1981	1982	1983	1984	1985	1986	1987	1988	1989
Thames	Cod	Mercury	0.16	0.15	0.11	0.10	0.13	0.12	0.08[1]	..	0.07[1]	0.11	..
		Cadmium	0.1	0.1	0.2	..	..	..	..	..	..	..	..
		Lead	0.2	0.2	0.2	..	..	..	..	..	..	..	..
		Copper	0.4	0.2	0.2	..	..	..	0.2	..	0.3	0.2	..
		Zinc	3.5	4.0	3.3	..	..	..	3.5	..	3.3	4.2	..
	Plaice	Mercury	..	0.09	0.08	0.08	0.06	0.09	0.04	0.04	..	0.06	..
		Cadmium	..	0.1	0.1	..	..	..	..	..	..	..	..
		Lead	..	0.2	0.2	..	..	..	..	..	..	..	..
		Copper	..	0.4	0.3	..	..	..	0.2	0.3	..	0.2	..
		Zinc	..	6.2	7.0	..	..	..	5.5	5.6	..	4.9	..
Liverpool Bay	Cod	Mercury	0.26	..	0.37	0.26	0.30	0.28	0.27	0.15	0.25	0.17	0.15
		Cadmium	0.1	0.1	0.2	..	..	..	..	..	..	..	..
		Lead	0.2	0.6	0.2	..	..	..	..	..	..	..	..
		Copper	0.2	0.3	0.4	..	..	..	0.2	0.2	0.2	0.3	0.1
		Zinc	4.2	3.7	3.6	..	..	..	3.6	3.5	3.2	3.2	3.2
	Plaice	Mercury	0.23	0.26	0.23	0.26	0.29	0.26	0.15	0.20	0.18	0.15	0.13
		Cadmium	0.1	0.1	0.1	..	..	..	..	..	..	..	..
		Lead	0.2	0.2	0.2	..	..	..	..	..	..	..	..
		Copper	0.4	0.2	0.6	..	..	..	0.3	0.3	0.2	0.3	0.3
		Zinc	8.3	6.3	6.0	..	..	..	5.4	5.1	4.4	4.4	4.0
North Sea (Southern Bight)	Cod	Mercury	0.13	0.04	..	0.10	0.10	0.08	0.07	0.08	0.07	0.08	0.10
		Cadmium	0.1	0.1	..	..	..	..	..	..	..	..	..
		Lead	0.2	0.2	..	..	..	..	..	..	..	..	..
		Copper	0.3	0.3	..	..	..	..	0.3	0.2	0.2	0.2	0.2
		Zinc	4.6	3.6	..	..	..	..	3.3	3.1	3.5	3.3	3.3
	Plaice	Mercury	0.05	0.04	..	0.07	0.08	0.06	0.05	0.04	0.05	0.06	0.05
		Cadmium	0.1	0.1	..	..	..	..	..	..	..	..	..
		Lead	0.2	0.2	..	..	..	..	..	..	..	..	..
		Copper	0.2	0.2	..	..	..	..	0.3	0.2	0.2	0.3	0.3
		Zinc	4.7	6.6	..	..	..	..	4.1	4.0	4.4	4.5	3.8

[1] Only small specimens caught.

Source: *Ministry of Agriculture, Fisheries and Food; Fisheries Laboratory*

The concentration of pollutants in the marine environment is monitored by the fisheries laboratories of MAFF, the Department of Agriculture and Fisheries (Scotland), and the NRA. Concentrations of toxic chemicals, such as heavy metals, pesticides and PCBs, are measured in fish and shellfish. Some of the results of this monitoring contribute to the programme of co-operative investigations in the North Sea and North Atlantic which is conducted under the auspices of the International Council for the Exploration of the Sea (ICES). In recent years ICES activity has mainly been confined to "hot spots", ie, areas which are known to receive substantial inputs of contaminants. Major industrial areas are also monitored as part of the joint monitoring programme of the Oslo and Paris commissions.

The major purpose of the programmes has been to check that concentrations do not exceed levels which would be hazardous to either human health or the fish population. Some results of the fish monitoring programme are shown in Table 2.13. The concentrations of chemicals in different species of fish vary, according to environment and diet, but the levels found in all fish sampled in the "hot spots" were not high enough to be a hazard to man or fish.

---

[1] *River Quality in England and Wales, 1985: a Report of the 1985 Survey.*Department of the Environment and Welsh Office,1986.
[2] *The Scottish Environment - Statistics.* Scottish Development Department,1990.
[3] *Quality Status of the North Sea.* Department of the Environment,1987.
[4] *UK Guidance Note on the Ministerial Declaration.* Department of the Environment,1990.

Chapter 3   Radioactivity

SOURCES OF RADIATION

Many sources of radiation are *natural*; these provide about 87 per cent of the total dose of radiation received by the UK population[1] (see Figure 3.1). *Cosmic rays* from the sun and outer space bombard the earth; *gamma rays* are emitted from naturally occurring radioactive materials in the ground (uranium and thorium decay series). Our bodies are slightly radioactive because the food we eat and the air we breathe contain tiny quantities of radioactive material which then can irradiate the body tissues *internally*. *Radon* and *thoron* are decay products of uranium and thorium which enter the atmosphere from the ground and their decay products irradiate the lung when inhaled. Surveys have been carried out in this country to locate areas where radon levels in houses are high so that appropriate action may be taken (see section on radon below). Survey results indicate that radon accounts for 47 per cent of the total dose.

See page xi for definitions of terms used in this chapter.

Artificial, or man-made, sources of radiation account for 13 per cent of the total dose. By far the largest portion of this is attributable to *medical* exposure from diagnostic X-rays. *Fallout* from nuclear weapons tests declined through the 1970s and early 1980s (see Statistical Bulletin (91)1). The Chernobyl reactor accident resulted in some environmental contamination (see Digest no 10) and the combination of this and the remaining weapons fallout contributes 0.4 per cent of the total dose to the population. *Occupational exposure* accounts for 0.2 per cent of the total dose on average. Radioactive waste discharges from the nuclear power industry, and from universities and hospitals, amount to less than 0.1 per cent of the total dose, although levels vary locally. *Miscellaneous* artificial sources include watches luminised with radioactive material, television receivers and air travel: these account for 0.4 per cent of the average dose.

Radioactivity itself is measured in *becquerels* (Bq), and its effect on people is measured in *sieverts* (Sv), the standard international unit of radiation dose which

Figure 3.1   Radiation exposure of the United Kingdom population

Contributions to the average effective dose equivalent [1]

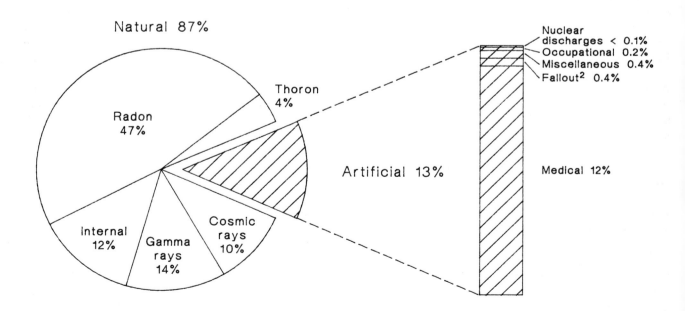

1. Overall effective dose equivalent is about 2.5 mSv a year, on average for people in the UK.

2. About half is due to the Chernobyl reactor accident and half due to nuclear weapons fallout. Both of these components are decreasing with time.

Source: *National Radiological Protection Board*

takes account of the different effects on the body of different types of radiation. The average overall effective dose equivalent from radiation of natural and artificial origin is about 2.5 millisieverts (mSv) for members of the UK population.[1] This is higher than the 2 mSv estimated previously for the early 1980s because of the improved information on radon exposure. The National Radiological Protection Board's (NRPB) publication *Living with Radiation* provides a guide for the general public which describes the nature of ionising radiation, its sources and effects and the means of protection.

NATURAL SOURCES OF RADIATION

Radon

Radon is a natural radioactive gas which causes nearly half of the total radiation received by man in the UK (see Figure 3.1). The gas comes from the radioactive breakdown of uranium which is present in minute quantities in all soils and rocks. It can mix with air in the soil and seep out of the ground. In the open air it is diluted to low levels but higher levels can collect in enclosed spaces such as buildings. Radon levels are higher in some parts of the country than in others because the uranium content of rocks and soils varies from place to place and some rocks and soils allow air to move more freely through them than others. Radon itself breaks down to form radioactive particles called radon daughters or radon decay products. Some of these may be breathed in and deposited in the lungs where radiation from them can damage lung tissue and increase the risk of lung cancer.

The NRPB, which advises the Government on radiation matters, recommended in 1987 that exposure to radon daughters in the home should be limited. The Government accepted these recommendations and started a programme of surveys, research and information.

NRPB has carried out a representative population-weighted national survey[2,3] of radon in dwellings. The survey consisted of a sample of 2,300 dwellings - just over 1 in 10,000 from the UK stock of 21 million dwellings. Measurements of radon gas concentrations were made in these dwellings. The mean weighted radon activity concentration was 20.5 Bq/m³ which corresponds to a mean annual effective dose equivalent from exposure to radon daughters of 1.2 mSv. Selected surveys in regions where high radon concentrations were expected due to particular geological characteristics have also been carried out. The first regional surveys were made in Cornwall, Devon, the central uplands of England and in parts of Scotland. Subsequent surveys have been commissioned by the Government to identify more precisely the extent of household exposure to natural radiation.

Recent assessments indicate that the risk of lung cancer is higher than previously thought. As a consequence, further advice was issued by NRPB in January 1990 and endorsed by the Government that the original Action Level for existing houses be reduced by a half to an annual average indoor radon concentration of 200 Bq/m³. On the basis of the surveys conducted, it is estimated that about 100,000 houses in the UK may have average radon concentrations exceeding the revised Action Level. Figure 3.2 shows that the problem is concentrated in particular areas of the country. In Devon and Cornwall as many as 60,000 houses, equivalent to about 12 per cent of the housing stock, may have radon concentrations above the new Action Level. In Somerset, Northamptonshire and Derbyshire perhaps 10,000 houses, 1 to 2 per cent of houses, may be similarly affected. Although Figure 3.2 is based on a substantial amount of data, there is appreciable uncertainty in the estimation of areas affected by radon and of houses with high levels of radon, and the picture may well change as more data are gathered.

The most appropriate action to reduce radon levels in existing dwellings is to reduce the influx of soil gas carrying radon by diverting it to the open air. The DOE issued a leaflet in August 1988, *The Householder's Guide to Radon*, which advises on appropriate remedial methods. A second edition was published in July 1990 giving fuller advice on how to reduce radon concentrations and reflecting the revised Action Level. The Department of the Environment funds NRPB to provide a free measurement service to householders in areas of potentially high levels. Grants can be available to those on lower incomes to cover the cost of remedial works. The DOE has also issued interim guidance under the building regulations on the construction of new dwellings in radon-prone areas. These give details of construction techniques which may be used in such areas, though other techniques which result in low radon levels are also acceptable. At present all new houses in the parts of Devon and Cornwall which are particularly at risk are built according to this guidance. This guidance is under review and it is likely that the area covered by the guidance will be extended. In all designs, the objective is to construct an airtight barrier across the whole building with provision for natural ventilation under a suspended floor or means of extracting soil gas from under a solid floor. The Building Research Establishment is carrying out further research on remedial and preventive measures.

The Institution of Environmental Health Officers (IEHO) has undertaken radon screening measurements of houses for some local authorities. The IEHO reports that the results point to elevated levels in various locations throughout the country. Confirmatory measurements, funded by DOE, are being offered by NRPB in these cases following its standard procedures. An additional survey based on a 10-kilometre grid is

Figure 3.2 Percentage of homes in the United Kingdom with radon concentrations above 200 Bq/m³

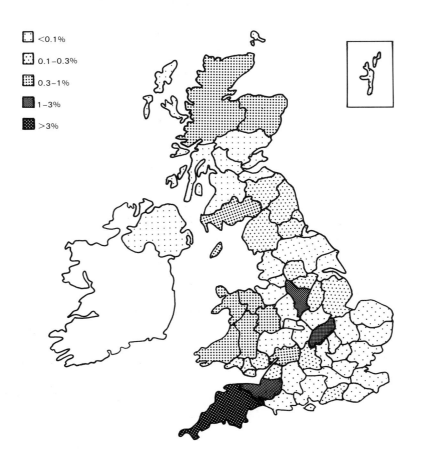

<0.1%

0.1–0.3%

0.3–1%

1–3%

>3%

Source: National Radiological Protection Board

planned by the Government to ensure a consistent coverage of areas of low population density. A study of the relationship between health and indoor pollutants, including radon, is being conducted by the Clinical Trials Unit at Oxford University and the NRPB.

ARTIFICIAL SOURCES OF RADIATION

Control over radioactive discharges

The remainder of this chapter provides information on radioactive discharges from the major sites using radioactive materials, and the resulting exposures of the public. In addition to these major sites there are many smaller users of radioactive material, for example hospitals and universities, which are authorised to dispose of radioactive waste.

UK and European Community objectives for radiological protection are based on the recommendations of the International Commission on Radiological Protection (ICRP). In the UK the NRPB is responsible for advising on the application of ICRP recommendations. The Government's objectives for radioactive waste management in the UK were amended in 1986 to bring them into line with the latest recommendations of the ICRP and NRPB. The current objectives are that:

a) all practices giving rise to radioactive wastes must be justified, ie, the need for the practice must be established in terms of its overall benefit;

b) radiation exposure of individuals and the collective dose to the population arising from radioactive wastes shall be reduced to levels which are as low as reasonably achievable, economic and social factors being taken into account; and,

Figure 3.3 Location of major nuclear establishments

Source: Ministry of Agriculture, Fisheries and Food

● **British Nuclear Fuels plc**
Sellafield: principally concerned with reprocessing nuclear fuel. Also the site of Calder Hall nuclear power station (Magnox type).
Springfields: chemical processing of uranium ore and the manufacture of fuel elements.
Capenhurst: isotopic enrichment of uranium.
Chapelcross: 4 Magnox type reactors.

○ **UKAEA (Research laboratories)**
Harwell: largest UKAEA laboratory. DIDO and PLUTO reactors.
Dounreay: prototype fast reactor.
Winfrith: prototype steam generating heavy water Reactor (SGHWR)(ceased operation in 1990).

△ **Electricity Board Nuclear Power Stations**
All are Nuclear Electric plc except Hunterston A/B and Torness which are Scottish Nuclear Ltd.
Magnox type: *Berkeley (ceased operated in March 1989), Bradwell, Dungeness A, Hinkley Point A, Hunterston A, Oldbury, Sizewell A, Trawsfynydd, Wylfa.*
AGR type: *Dungeness B, Hartlepool, Heysham I and II, Hinkley Point B, Hunterston B, Torness.*

□ **Ministry of Defence**
Aldermaston is the UK nuclear weapons research and development centre.
Devonport and *Rosyth* are Naval Dockyards. *Faslane* is a submarine base.
Chatham Naval Dockyard was closed in 1984.

▲ **Amersham International plc**
Amersham and *Cardiff* manufacture radioactive materials for use in industry, biomedical research, medical diagnosis and treatment.

c) the effective dose equivalent from all sources, excluding natural background radiation and medical procedures, to representative members of a critical group should not exceed 1 mSv in any one year; however effective dose equivalents up to 5 mSv are permissible in some years provided that the total does not exceed 70 mSv over a lifetime.

The ICRP is currently revising its basic recommendations in the light of improved risk estimates. In advance of this review, the NRPB has given interim guidance, which accords with the Government target, suggesting a criterion of 0.5 mSv per year for the effective dose equivalent to the critical group from current discharges of radioactive wastes from a given site.

Discharges in each country of the UK are controlled by the Radioactive Substances Act 1960 which prohibits the disposal of radioactive waste on or from all premises unless authorised by the relevant Secretary of State or Minister. Crown premises are exempt but in practice they conform to the same standards as other premises.

Whenever there is a proposal for the disposal of radioactive waste, whether in liquid, gaseous or solid form, a strict procedure has to be complied with. Applications to dispose are examined to ensure that the need to dispose is justified and any disposals are controlled by the use of best practicable means. Potential exposure pathways for members of the public are examined prior to setting disposal limits. These limits, and other conditions of the authorisation, are designed to achieve the objectives quoted in a) to c) above. Where appropriate, before granting authorisations, the authorising departments consult local and public authorities. In the case of major establishments, the authorisation will include conditions whereby the operator will measure the discharges, sample the waste, monitor the local environment and supply the results to the authorising departments (Environment; Agriculture, Fisheries and Food; Scottish Office; Welsh Office). The major UK nuclear establishments are shown in Figure 3.3.

Atmospheric discharges

Authorisations setting numerical limits to the levels of radioactivity in atmospheric discharges are currently being issued and will eventually cover all major nuclear establishments. Operators will also be required to use the best practicable means to minimise discharges, taking account of local conditions and the current state of technical knowledge as in the past.

The majority of radioactive atmospheric discharges from sites consist of tritium and the chemically inert gases argon-41 and krypton-85. Table 3.1 and

3.1 Radioactive atmospheric discharges: annual emissions: by type of radioactivity and by type of site[1]

TBq

	Inert gases[2]			Tritium		Tritium oxide	
	Sellafield	Power stations[3]	UKAEA[4,7]	Sellafield	Amersham Int.[5]	Chapel-cross	UKAEA[4,6]
1979	35,927	13,373	486	289	85	..	52
1980	32,190	9,280	420	252	94	1,500	38
1981	53,095	10,138	538	459	183	2,100	42
1982	45,347	11,325	483	360	214	1,700	52
1983	43,146	12,697	551	268	253	2,300	161
1984	39,800	11,740	532r	349	251	1,400	114
1985	26,600	16,141	1,109r	268	258	2,200	52
1986	55,890	15,497	1,103r	171	224	1,600	71
1987	36,400	16,956	770r	78	195	1,600	78
1988	42,140r	11,833r	1,226r	186	192	1,900r	101
1989	54,230	11,062	922	679	264	1,400	95

[1] This table contains a selection of the larger discharges (in terms of TBq) made in the UK. The amount of radioactivity is not necessarily the best guide to the significance of a discharge because of differences in half-lives and radiotoxicities between individual radionuclides. Discharges for groups of sites were calculated by adding individual discharges and there may be large site-to-site variations. Fuller details of atmospheric discharges are given in Statistical Bulletin (91)1.
[2] Sellafield: krypton-85 (over 90% of total) and argon-41; power stations: argon-41; UKAEA: argon-41, krypton-85 and other isotopes of krypton and xenon.
[3] All Nuclear Electric plc/Scottish Nuclear Ltd nuclear power stations and Chapelcross. Discharges for Chapelcross prior to 1985

Source: *British Nuclear Fuels plc, United Kingdom Atomic Energy Authority, Nuclear Electric plc, Scottish Development Department, Amersham International plc*

were evaluated differently and are not directly comparable with data for later years.
[4] United Kingdom Atomic Energy Authority (sites at Winfrith, Dounreay and Harwell).
[5] Amersham International plc (sites at Amersham and Cardiff). Discharges mainly from the Cardiff site.
[6] The figures for 1983 and 1984 are estimated upper limits.
[7] The revisions are due mainly to the inclusion of krypton-85 from the Fuel Cycle Area at Dounreay.

Figure 3.4 Radioactive atmospheric discharges: annual emissions

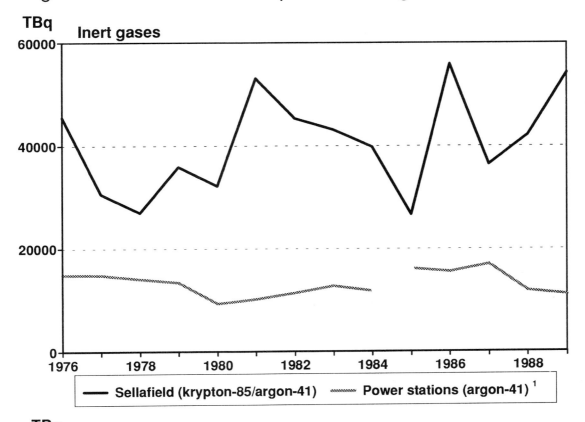

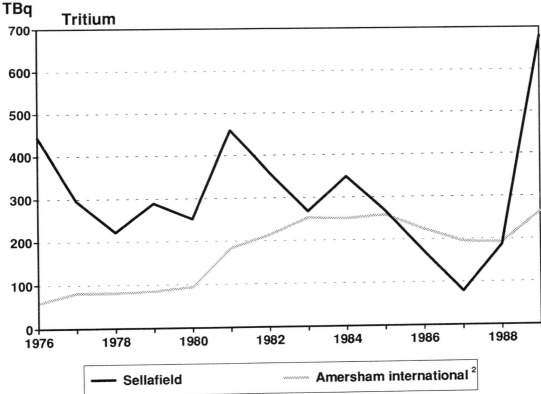

1. All Nuclear Electric plc/Scottish Nuclear Ltd
   sites and Chapelcross. Discharges for
   Chapelcross prior to 1985 were evaluated
   differently and are not directly comparable
   with data for later years.
2. Sites at Amersham and Cardiff.

Source:British Nuclear Fuels plc,
Nuclear Electric plc,
Scottish Development
Department,Amersham
International plc

Figure 3.4 show recent trends in such discharges from particular groups of sites. These trends reflect throughput and reactor operation and should be interpreted with great care since the amount of radioactivity discharged is not necessarily the best guide to its significance. In particular, tritium and krypton-85 make a negligible contribution to the radiation exposure of the local population. The increase in discharges from Sellafield in 1989 reflects that the plant was in continuous operation whereas in 1988 operation was restricted to a nine-month period because of maintenance requirements. Nevertheless, the higher discharges from Sellafield are well within the limits set under the authorisation. Discharges of tritium from sites run by Amersham International more than doubled between 1980 and 1983 but the levels of emissions remain radiologically very low. Further details of atmospheric emissions are given in Statistical Bulletin (91)1.

The dose received by members of the public will be affected by factors such as the nature and activity of the radionuclides released and how they are dispersed and partially reconcentrated in the environment. The principal pathways leading to radiation doses to the public from radioactive atmospheric discharges are direct irradiation, inhalation and ingestion. The latter follows deposition onto soil or vegetation and incorporation into foodstuffs. The radiation dose to the public as a result of radioactive atmospheric discharges is very small. For example, it is estimated that the maximum radiation dose to which a member of the general public may have been exposed during 1989 as a result of airborne emissions to the atmosphere (principally due to argon-41) from steel pressure vessel magnox stations was approximately 0.11 mSv. For stations where reactors are contained in concrete pressure vessels which emit less argon-41, the corresponding maximum radiation dose in 1989 was

3.2 Radioactivity: annual average concentrations of strontium-90 and caesium-137 in milk from farms near Sellafield, Dounreay, Harwell and Winfrith

Bq/l milk[1]

	Sellafield			Dounreay	Harwell	Winfrith
	Farms in zone (km)					
	0-3	3-6	Reference[2]	0-2.5	0-6[3]	0-6
Strontium-90						
1979	0.7	0.3	0.2	..	0.05	0.12
1980	0.4	0.2	0.2	0.4	0.06	0.09
1981	0.4	0.2	0.2	0.4	0.05	0.10
1982	0.4	0.3	0.2	0.3	0.03	0.06
1983	0.4	0.2	0.2	0.4	0.04	0.06
1984	0.5	0.2	<0.2	0.3	0.03	0.06
1985	0.4	<0.3	<0.2	0.3	0.03	0.05
1986	0.5	<0.5	<0.3	0.3	0.03	0.06
1987	<0.4	<0.4	<1.3	0.3	0.03	0.05
1988	<0.4	<0.3	<0.4	0.2r	0.03	0.04
1989	0.4	<0.3	<0.3	..	0.03	0.03
Caesium-137						
1979	7.3	1.6	0.6	<1.1	<1.1	0.2
1980	13.0[4]	3.2[4]	0.9	<1.1	<1.1	0.1
1981	3.8	1.4	0.7	<1.1	<1.1	0.2
1982	3.6	0.7	0.4	<1.1	<1.1	0.2
1983	1.4	0.6	0.4	<1.1	<1.1	0.1
1984	0.9	0.3	0.3	<1.1	<1.1	-
1985	0.6	<0.4	<0.3	<1.1	<1.1	-
1986[5]	13.4	8.9	5.4	8.9r	<1.1[6]	0.8[7]
1987[5]	6.0	13.0	<4.8	7.8	<1.1	0.4
1988	1.1	1.4	1.0	<5.8	<1.0	0.1
1989	0.8	1.2	<0.8	..	<1.0	0.1

[1] Concentrations of strontium-90 were measured in becquerels/gram calcium at Sellafield prior to 1982 and at Dounreay, Harwell and Winfrith prior to 1984. The effect of this change is very small.

[2] About 30 km from the works.

[3] Farms up to 4 km from the site prior to 1981.

[4] Higher levels in 1980 due to temporary increased discharge from a waste silo.

Source: *British Nuclear Fuels plc, United Kingdom Atomic Energy Authority*

[5] Higher levels due to effects of deposition of radionuclides from Chernobyl reactor accident.

[6] Does not include samples obtained in May and June.

[7] 0.03 for first quarter prior to Chernobyl reactor incident.

less than 0.01 mSv. These figures can be compared with the principal dose limit to members of the public of 1 mSv per year and subsidiary dose limit of 5 mSv per year recommended by ICRP.

The most significant pathway back to man is usually through herbage eaten by cows and subsequently transferred to man in milk. For most radionuclides the individual most at risk is assumed to be a one-year old child drinking 0.7 litres of milk each day from a particular source. Table 3.2 shows annual average concentrations of strontium-90 and caesium-137 in milk sampled from farms around Sellafield, Dounreay, Harwell and Winfrith. Concentrations of caesium-137 in milk declined until 1986 when the deposition of radionuclides from the Chernobyl reactor accident that year caused a sharp rise in concentrations. Peak concentrations occurred in May and June 1986 with secondary peaks later on in the year. Levels continued to be high in 1987 but fell considerably in 1988 and 1989. Statistical Bulletin (91)1 gives details of concentrations of radionuclides in milk in the UK as a result of world-wide fall-out from nuclear weapon tests.

Liquid discharges

Authorisations setting numerical limits to the levels of radioactivity in liquid discharges cover all major nuclear establishments. Table 3.3 and Figure 3.5 show trends in liquid radioactive discharges for particular groups of sites. These should be interpreted with great care (see footnotes). In particular the steady increase in tritium discharges from power stations reflects the increased power outputs from advanced gas cooled reactors since commissioning. The large increase in tritium discharges in 1989 is due primarily to Heysham I and II and Hartlepool only comparatively recently achieving full-power operation and the build-up of power generation from Torness which came into operation only at the end of 1987. Statistical Bulletin (91)1 shows liquid discharges for each nuclear site; in 1989 liquid discharges at all sites were well within authorised annual limits.

The liquid discharges from the reprocessing plant operated by British Nuclear Fuels plc at Sellafield have received a considerable amount of attention and a new authorisation was issued in 1986. This set more stringent limits on discharges than previously, and it placed extra controls on the amounts which may be discharged over short periods, and on solvents and particulates. It also included limits on many more individual radioactive isotopes including tritium. As a result of a comprehensive review completed in 1989 lower discharge limits came into force on 1 January 1990. Table 3.3 shows that there have been substantial reductions in the alpha and beta discharges. Reductions in the alpha and beta activity between 1985 and 1986 reflect the successful performance of two new treatment plants in their first full year of operation. This downward trend continued until 1989 when slightly increased alpha and beta discharges were recorded as a

3.3 Radioactive liquid discharges: annual emissions: by type of radioactivity and by type of site[1]

TBq

	Sellafield		Spring-fields	Total alpha and beta[2] (excluding tritium)		Tritium[3]			
	Total alpha	Total beta[4]	Total beta	Power stations[5]	UKAEA[6,8]	Sellafield	Power stations[5]	UKAEA[6]	Amersham Int.[7]
1979	62	4,058	135	24	47	1,176	260	105	8
1980	39	4,306	131	30	71	1,283	296	59	9
1981	30	3,831	97	25	75	1,964	385	54	64
1982	28	3,528	174	26	39	1,745	520	112	63
1983	14	2,490	215	18	93	1,831	600	121	311
1984	14	1,190	152	16	64	1,586	709	103	540
1985	6	587	160	21	33	1,062	820	65	769
1986	4	118	115	12	22r	2,150	782	58	831
1987	2	89	77	9	32	1,375	583	93	826
1988	2	81	110	8	14	1,724	775r	154	662
1989	3	101	114	8	14	2,144	1,071	152	600

[1] This table contains a selection of the larger discharges (in terms of TBq) made in the UK. The amount of radioactivity is not necessarily the best guide to the significance of a discharge because of differences in half-lives and radiotoxicities between individual radionuclides. Discharges for groups of sites were calculated by adding individual discharges and there may be large site-to-site variations. Fuller details of liquid discharges are given in Statistical Bulletin (91)1.
[2] Radionuclides specified in authorisations.
[3] Tritium is the least toxic radionuclide and not subject to reconcentration by marine organisms.
[4] Excluding tritium.
[5] All Nuclear Electric plc/Scottish Nuclear Ltd nuclear power stations and Chapelcross. About one-third of total activity

Source: *British Nuclear Fuels plc, United Kingdom Atomic Energy Authority, Nuclear Electric plc, Scottish Development Department, Amersham International plc*

(excluding tritium) is from sulphur-35. Most tritium discharges come from AGR type power stations.
[6] United Kingdom Atomic Energy Authority (sites at Winfrith, Dounreay and Harwell).
[7] Amersham International plc (sites at Amersham and Cardiff). Discharges mainly from the Cardiff site.
[8] The figure for 1989 is an upper estimate and includes 6.5 TBq of activity, mainly iron-55, with some beta activity.

Figure 3.5 Radioactive liquid discharges: annual emissions

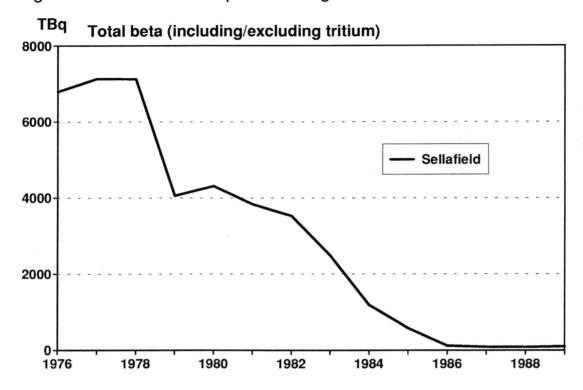

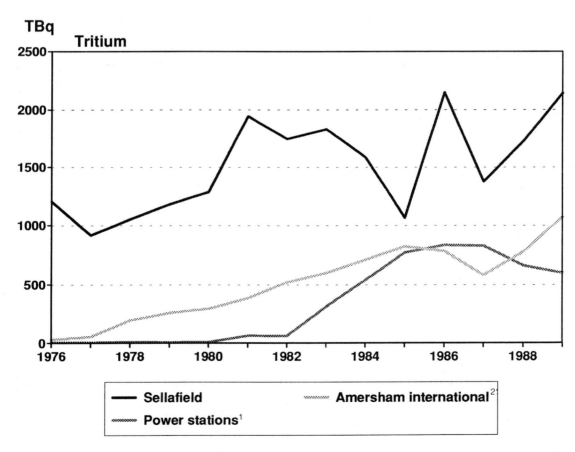

1. All Nuclear Electric plc/Scottish Nuclear Ltd
   sites and Chapelcross.
2. Sites at Amersham and Cardiff.

*Source:British Nuclear Fuels plc,
Nuclear Electric plc,
Scottish Development
Department,Amersham
International plc*

Figure 3.6 Concentration (Bq/kg) of caesium-137 in filtered water from the Irish and North Seas

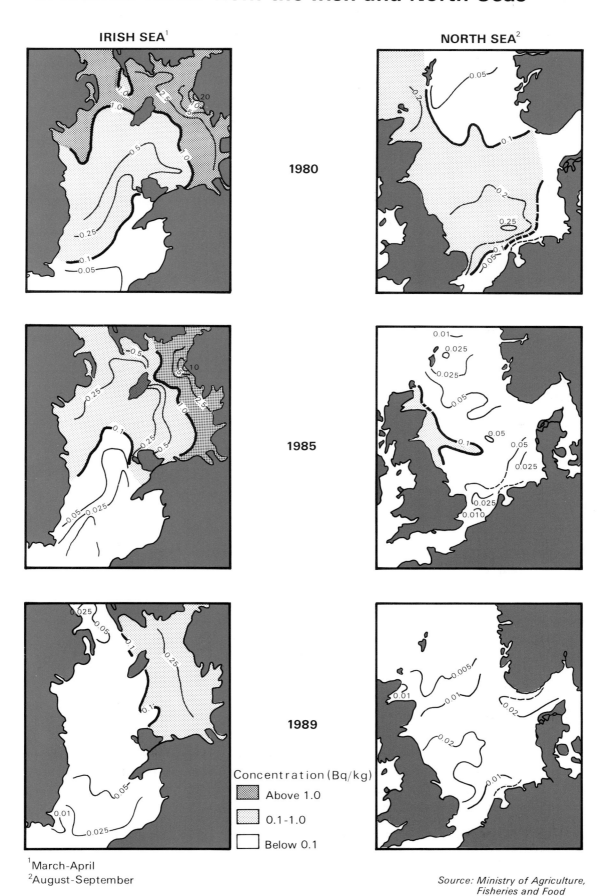

IRISH SEA[1]

NORTH SEA[2]

1980

1985

1989

Concentration (Bq/kg)

Above 1.0

0.1-1.0

Below 0.1

[1]March-April
[2]August-September

Source: Ministry of Agriculture, Fisheries and Food

consequence of the continuous operation of the plant in 1989. A new Thermal Oxide Fuel Reprocessing Plant (THORP) is scheduled for completion in 1992 and the authorisation will be reviewed then to consider any appropriate amendments. The introduction of new effluent treatment plant on the same timescale will ensure that the overall radiation doses to the public will continue to fall.

An important factor in determining public radiation exposure from discharges of liquid radioactive waste from nuclear sites is the distribution of radioactivity in the marine environment. Figure 3.6 shows the distributions of caesium-137 in the Irish and North Seas for 1980, 1985 and 1989. Comparison of the positions of the contour lines shows that concentrations of caesium-137 have decreased over this period. This reflects the reduction in discharges of caesium-137 from Sellafield from 3,000 TBq in 1980 to 29 TBq in 1989. It takes about a year for such discharges to affect concentrations in the Irish Sea and about three years for them to affect concentrations in the North Sea.

The internal radiation *dose* to the public depends on their consumption of fish and shellfish, which take up caesium radioisotopes and other radionuclides from the waste, and on the resulting concentration of radioactivity in this food. Table 3.4 shows estimated public radiation exposure. These figures can be compared with the principal dose limit for members of the public of 1 mSv per year and subsidiary dose limit of 5 mSv per year recommended by ICRP (see section on control over radioactive discharges above). Discharges from Sellafield have given rise to the highest exposures and contribute to exposures near many other nuclear sites. The estimated dose of up to 0.19 mSv for the critical group of seafood consumers near Sellafield in 1989 shows that doses are continuing at a lower level than in years prior to 1986. Doses are expected to decline even further in the next decade as a result of the introduction of new treatment plant. Critical group doses greater than 0.1 mSv in 1989 from the consumption of marine foodstuff were also found at Heysham where exposures are affected by discharges from Sellafield. Figures for earlier years are given as a

3.4 Radioactive liquid waste: trends in estimates of public radiation exposure:[1] by discharge site

mSv

Site[2]	Exposure[3]					
	1984	1985	1986	1987	1988	1989
British Nuclear Fuels plc:						
Sellafield[4]	0.54	0.49	0.12	0.10	0.15	0.19
** Springfields[5]	0.2	0.3	0.34	0.24	0.27	0.17
** Capenhurst[6]	<0.1	<0.1	<0.1	<0.1	<0.1	<0.1
** Chapelcross	<0.2	0.2	0.2	<0.2	<0.14	<0.1
United Kingdom Atomic Energy Authority:						
Winfrith[4]	<0.04	<0.03	0.1	0.11	0.05	0.03
* Dounreay[4]	0.03	<0.05	<0.02	<0.02	<0.02	<0.01
Nuclear Electric plc:						
* Berkeley/Oldbury	<0.001	<0.002	<0.001	<0.01	<0.01	<0.01
* Bradwell	<0.01	<0.01	<0.02	0.01	0.02	<0.02
Dungeness	<0.002	<0.002	<0.002	<0.004	<0.01	0.01
** Hartlepool	<0.02	<0.02	<0.01	<0.01	<0.01	<0.01
** Heysham[4]	<0.43	0.26	0.1	0.06	0.07	0.15
* Hinkley Point	<0.005	<0.01	<0.002	<0.003	<0.01	<0.01
* Sizewell	<0.01	<0.01	<0.01	<0.003	<0.003	<0.003
Trawsfynydd[7]	0.32	0.21	0.17	0.25	0.07	0.09
** Wylfa	0.2	<0.01	<0.1	<0.05	<0.02	0.01
Scottish Nuclear Ltd:						
** Hunterston	0.05	0.03	0.03	0.03	0.02	<0.02
** Torness					<0.005	<0.003
Amersham International plc:						
Cardiff	0.06	0.05	<0.1	<0.1	<0.1	<0.1

** Mainly due to discharges from Sellafield.
* Partly due to discharges from Sellafield.

Source: *Directorate of Fisheries Research, Ministry of Agriculture, Fisheries and Food*

[1] Unless otherwise stated principal exposure pathways are fish and shellfish consumption and external dose. Critical group is usually local fishing community.
[2] See Figure 3.3.
[3] Represents the committed effective dose equivalent, to be compared with the ICRP-recommended principal dose limit of 1 mSv per year or with the subsidiary limit of 5 mSv per year provided the lifetime average does not exceed 1 mSv per year.

[4] From fish and shellfish consumption only.
[5] External dose to houseboat dwellers.
[6] From shellfish consumption only.
[7] From lake fish consumption.

percentage of dose limits and can be found in previous Digests. Care should be taken in interpreting trends because of changes in the habits of local communities over time and changes in ICRP and NRPB advice on calculation of the dose per unit intake.

Another significant pathway back to man is the fine-grained muds and silts prevalent in estuaries and harbours. For discharges from Sellafield this leads to external exposure of the public who frequent the inter-tidal area of the Irish Sea. Since 1986, the critical group for external exposure has consisted of people who live on houseboats moored in muddy creeks of the Ribble estuary who received an effective dose of 0.17 mSv in 1989 compared with 0.27mSv in 1988, 0.24 mSv in 1987 and 0.34 mSv in 1986. The decrease in 1989 was due to reduced equivalent occupancy times, which allow for shielding by the boats themselves and to declining dose rates following the reduced discharges from Sellafield. Details of other discharges and associated environmental impacts are reported in the *Aquatic Environment Monitoring Reports* published by the Ministry of Agriculture Fisheries and Food (MAFF).

Solid waste disposal

Low-level solid wastes, which constitute about 90 per cent by volume of all radioactive waste, are disposed of at authorised landfill sites. Intermediate-level and high-level wastes are currently stored at nuclear establishments. Disposal in drums of low and intermediate-level solid wastes in the Atlantic last took place in 1982. A review by DOE of the best practicable environmental options for low and intermediate-level wastes published in 1986[4] concluded that sea disposal could be the best option for certain low-level wastes.

However, in 1988 the Government announced that it had decided not to resume sea dumping of drummed radioactive wastes. Instead, these will be prepared for eventual disposal in the deep facility for low and intermediate-level wastes which is being investigated by UK Nirex Ltd. The Government has not ruled out sea disposal for large items such as boilers arising from decommissioning operations but will keep under review whether this disposal option needs to be maintained. High-level wastes will be stored for at least 50 years at Sellafield and Dounreay to allow them to cool.

The 300-acre site at Drigg, near Sellafield, is the largest of the authorised land sites and takes the more active of the low-level solid wastes in the form of paper, plastics, scrap metal and protective clothing. This waste is placed in trenches and then buried. The trenches are drained to a stream which flows into the Ravenglass estuary and which is regularly sampled. The principal pathways by which the public could be affected are via the release of radioactive matter into the atmosphere during the tipping process or contamination of the water in the stream draining from the site. The levels of airborne radioactivity at Drigg are regularly measured and are comparable to other levels in the district. The dose incurred from any inadvertent ingestion of the stream water would be negligible. Following a review of waste disposal at Drigg a revised authorisation was brought into effect in February 1988. In addition to placing activity limits on individual consignments, restrictions were also imposed on total activity of specified radionuclides that may be deposited in any year. Engineering work at Drigg, aimed at improving the operation and management of the site, has been completed and waste is now disposed of in containers in a system of concrete-

3.5 Solid radioactive waste: volume disposed of at Drigg by source of waste

m³

	Sellafield	Other BNFL	UKAEA	Power Stations	Amersham Int.	Miscellaneous[1,2]
1979	38,292	1,548	1,783	2,950	1,012	595
1980	89,698	3,611	2,047	3,304	906	1,561
1981	65,064	2,081	1,672	3,937	810	2,413
1982	51,075	3,111	1,961	3,088	2,108	1,883
1983	34,031	2,805	2,038	2,550	1,304	1,315
1984	22,241	3,422	1,931	2,590	1,878	1,094
1985	26,917	5,920	2,071	2,484	1,132	831
1986	26,920	3,917	3,377	2,824	1,290	723
1987	26,622	2,959	3,274	2,194	1,476	3,184
1988[3]	26,711	1,177	1,513	1,644	1,653	2,430
1989[3]	24,843	870	2,520	1,927	1,151	3,210

[1] Ministry of Defence sites and non-nuclear industries.
[2] Disposals from AWE Aldermaston included in Sellafield total prior to 1987.
[3] Figures for 1988 and 1989 from sites other than Sellafield represent gross volumes; this includes additional vault space taken up by the replacement of waste in ISO containers and could be up to 1.9 times the actual volume of waste.

Source: *British Nuclear Fuels plc*

lined vaults. There have also been improvements in the management of water draining from the site which is now discharged through an improved system. In order to reflect these improvements a variation to the authorisation came into force on 1 January 1991, by which the disposal limit for uranium is reduced, discharges of collected contaminated waters are authorised via a new pipeline and the concentration limits on the Drigg stream are consequently reduced.

The Drigg site receives wastes arising mainly from Sellafield operations but also receives wastes from other UK nuclear sites as well as radioactive substances from hospitals, research establishments and industry. The trends in the volume of solid wastes disposed of at Drigg are shown in Table 3.5. All disposals of activity in 1989 were within authorisation limits. Further information on the disposal of solid wastes at Drigg is given in Statistical Bulletin (91)1.

Monitoring and research

The overall responsibility for initiating and co-ordinating *monitoring* in connection with environmental pathways lies with the environment departments in close collaboration with MAFF and NRPB. For this purpose DOE maintains contact with other government departments and the nuclear industry and seeks advice from the Radioactive Waste Management Advisory Committee (RWMAC).

A substantial amount of monitoring is carried out by site operators as a condition of their authorisations. As a check on compliance, representatives of the authorising departments inspect the installations regularly, take independent samples and make measurements in the local environment. Information about these and other regular monitoring programmes is contained in a DOE report *Monitoring of Radioactivity in the UK Environment* (HMSO, 1988).

The objectives of the monitoring programmes are:

a) to assess radiation doses received by members of the public;

b) to provide a suitable check system for compliance with discharge authorisation limits;

c) to measure the distribution and establish the behaviour of radionuclides in the environment; and,

d) to keep the public informed about the behaviour and safety of discharges from nuclear establishments.

In 1987 a *National Response Plan* was announced by the Government to cater for the consequences for the UK of nuclear incidents abroad, such as that which occurred at Chernobyl (see Digest no 10). Under the plan a network, known as the Radioactive Incident Monitoring Network (RIMNET), is being set up so as to be able to detect any abnormal increases in radioactivity of the kind that might arise from an overseas nuclear incident.

The network, which is being installed in two phases, will eventually consist of over 90 continuously operating monitoring stations throughout the UK. An interim Phase 1 system,[5] monitoring gamma-radiation dose rates at 46 sites, has been in operation since the end of 1988. Data collected at the Phase 1 sites have been published regularly in monthly summary form.[6] As an example Figure 3.7 shows the average instrument readings for March 1990 at each of the 46 sites; these readings include cosmic and inherent background components as well as terrestrial gamma-ray dose rates. The size of a site's bar is proportional to the difference between the site's average reading and the lowest of the 46 sites' averages, which is at Marham.

The main factor influencing the observed gamma-radiation dose rate is the geological structure of the site. Higher levels would be found in areas of igneous rocks, which have relatively high uranium and thorium contents, whilst lower levels are typical of clay and chalk areas.[7] The pattern can also be influenced by climatic effects; heavy rain will increase observed levels of gamma-radiation. The level of fluctuation from site to site suggests that background radiation is the main component of the observed levels; it is likely that the pattern of gamma-radiation arising from a nuclear incident would be more regular.

Gamma-radiation dose rate readings from the Phase 1 sites are collected every hour and checked by computer for any indication of abnormal increase. If there is any evidence of a nuclear incident of radiologically significant for the UK, a national alert will be raised. Under the National Response Plan and the RIMNET system[8] there is provision for activating additional Government monitoring programmes in the event of such an alert to establish the incident's effects on the UK and to inform the public what, if any, counter-measures they need to take.

The Phase 1 system will operate until the replacement Phase 2 system becomes available. Phase 2 will double the number of monitoring sites, increase levels of system automation, improve its analytical, interpretive, display and communications facilities and, ultimately, may extend the range of monitoring that is undertaken (eg, to include air and deposition measurements). It is expected that the main part of Phase 2 will become operational during the first quarter of 1992.

DOE is also responsible, with MAFF, for initiating and co-ordinating research on radioactivity in the environment and its pathways to man. Such research

Figure 3.7   Phase 1 RIMNET monitoring sites and bulletin regions: average instrument indications of gamma - radiation for March 1990

Source: RIMNET, Department of the Environment

complements the monitoring programmes and makes possible more accurate predictions of the effects of radioactive discharges. The subjects covered have included transfer mechanisms of radionuclides from one ecosystem to another and atmospheric dispersion and deposition of radionuclides. Relevant DOE-funded research is described in the annual DOE publication *Sponsored Research on Radioactive Waste Management.*

Monitoring of drinking water and food

The environment departments monitor all types of raw drinking water sources with the co-operation of the water authorities who take samples from agreed locations for analysis. Results for 1989-90 for England and Wales are shown in Statistical Bulletin (91)1. Similar measurements are organised in Scotland by the Scottish Development Department. Results at all times were below the World Health Organisation's guideline values.

The Terrestrial Radioactivity Monitoring Programme (TRAMP) carried out by MAFF concentrates on samples of agricultural produce collected from the vicinity of the major nuclear sites in England and Wales and is independent of monitoring undertaken for various purposes by site operators. Milk is of prime importance in this terrestrial monitoring programme. TRAMP also covers a wide range of agricultural and horticultural produce and wild products. Results for 1989 have been published[9] and a summary table showing the maximum committed effective dose equivalents to a one-year old infant from artificial radionuclides measured in milk at all sites is given in Statistical Bulletin (91)1.

The annual Aquatic Environment Monitoring Reports[10] published by MAFF describe results of monitoring aquatic foods and other materials in the vicinity of the major nuclear establishments and further afield. This monitoring is independent of that undertaken by nuclear site operators and was set up to verify the satisfactory control of radioactive waste discharges to the aquatic environment and to ensure that the resulting public radiation exposure is within nationally accepted limits. Results are included in the section on liquid discharges above and in Statistical Bulletin (91)1.

1   *Radiation Exposure of the UK Population - 1988 Review,* NRPB-R227, J S Hughes *et al,* National Radiological Protection Board, 1989.
2   *Exposure to Radon Daughters in Dwellings,* NRPB-GS6, National Radiological Protection Board, 1987.
3   *Natural Radiation Exposure in UK Dwellings,* NRPB-R190, A D Wrixon *et al,* National Radiological Protection Board, 1988.
4   *Assessment of Best Practicable Environmental Options (BPEOs) for Management of Low- and Intermediate-level Solid Radioactive Wastes* (HMSO, 1986).
5   *The National Response Plan and Radioactive Incident and Monitoring Network (RIMNET): Phase 1* (HMSO, 1989).
6   *RIMNET Gamma-radiation Dose Rates at Monitoring Sites throughout the United Kingdom, April 1989-September 1989,* Statistical Bulletin (89)6, Department of the Environment (HMSO, 1989).
    RIMNET Gamma-radiation Dose Rates at Monitoring Sites throughout the United Kingdom, October 1989-March 1990, Statistical Bulletin (90)5, Department of the Environment (HMSO, 1989). (Figures for April 1990-September 1990 will be published in early 1991.)
7   *Gamma-radiation Levels Outdoors in Great Britain,* B M R Green *et al,* National Radiological Protection Board, 1989.
8   *The National Response Plan and Radioactive Incident Monitoring Network (RIMNET): a Statement of Proposals* (HMSO, 1988).
9   *Radioactivity in Food and Agricultural Products in England and Wales: Report for 1989,* Terrestrial Radioactivity Monitoring Programme, Ministry of Agriculture, Fisheries and Food, 1990.
10 *Radioactivity in Surface and Coastal Waters of the British Isles, 1989,* G J Hunt, Aquatic Environment Monitoring Reports, no 23, MAFF, Directorate of Fisheries Research, Lowestoft, 1989.

Chapter 4   Noise

There are many more sources of noise now than there were 20 years ago. In particular, road traffic and aircraft movements have increased substantially. There are large variations in measured noise levels from moment to moment, from place to place, even within relatively short distances, and significantly different levels are experienced at different times of the day or week. These factors make it costly and difficult to set up a continuous and reliable monitoring system throughout the country, although local authorities do undertake a variety of measurements of environmental noise in pursuance of various statutory obligations.

Local authorities have powers to control noise nuisance, to establish noise abatement zones, and to limit construction site noise. The 1990 environment white paper[1] foreshadows the intention to make it easier for authorities to set up noise control zones, to

4.1 Noise: complaints received by Environmental Health Officers: by method of control and source

England and Wales   Number per million persons[1]

	1978	1979	1980	1981	1982	1983/4	1984/5	1985/6	1986/7	1987/8	1988/9
Not controlled by the Act:[2]											
Road Traffic[3]	35	38	31	32	36	36	41	40	41	45	52
Aircraft[4]	14	21	16	16	16	17	15	25	19	23	59
Other	16	10	17	20	17	17	32	27	54	53	43
Total	64	69	63	68	69	70	88	92	114	121	154
Controlled by Section 58 of the Act:[2]											
Industrial premises	220⎫	461	464	478	473	595	636	601	654	741	884
Commercial premises	195⎭										
Road works, construction and demolition	73	68	63	65	84	81	98	103	153	217	289
Domestic premises	420	586	712	764	794	1,016	1,244	1,276	1,269	1,745	2,008
Total	908	1,115	1,239	1,307	1,351	1,692	1,978	1,980	2,076	2,703	3,181
Controlled by Section 62 of the Act:[2]											
Noise in streets[5]	29	32	31	37	46	38	48	45	55	57	85
Total complaints received	1,001	1,216	1,333	1,412	1,466	1,800	2,114	2,117	2,245	2,881	3,420

Scotland   Number per million persons[1]

	1980	1981	1982	1983	1984	1985	1986	1987	1988	1989
Not controlled by the Act:[2]										
Road Traffic[3]	48	101	23	14	26	28	28	32	36	39
Aircraft[4]	9	7	5	5	9	7	4	4	5	7
Other	6	1	2	4	22	9	6	4	6	7
Total	63	109	30	23	57	44	38	40	47	53
Controlled by Section 58 of the Act:[2]										
Industrial premises										
Commercial premises	284	272	326	385	392	427	437	411	436	501
Road works, construction and demolition	35	36	41	39	59	55	90	85	100	129
Domestic premises	65	81	97	112	99	176	169	202	148	161
Total	384	389	464	536	550	658	696	698	684	791
Controlled by Section 62 of the Act:[2]										
Noise in streets[5]	25	18	39	58	47	35	32	27	23	24
Total complaints received	472	516	533	617	654	737	766	765	754	868

[1] For reporting authorities.

[2] Control of Pollution Act 1974.

[3] Most complaints about traffic noise are usually addressed to highway authorities or Department of Transport Regional Directors, and will not necessarily be included in these figures.

[4] Complaints about noise from civil aircraft are generally received by aircraft operators, the airport companies, the Department of Transport or the Civil Aviation Authority. Complaints about military flying are dealt with either by Station Commanding

Source: *Environmental Health Reports; Environmental Health Officers Association (1977-9), Institute of Environmental Health Officers (1980-88/9); Royal Environmental Health Institute of Scotland*

Officers or by Ministry of Defence headquarters. The figures in the table will not necessarily include these complaints.

[5] Primarily includes the chimes of ice-cream vendors and the use of loud speakers other than for strictly defined purposes.

encourage consistent local authority practice on noise, and to carry out further research into sources of noise and the need for further regulations.

The 1990 Batho Report[2] considered aspects of noise control with particular reference to the Control of Pollution Act 1974. The group found that the increase in complaints about noise over the last decade suggests a need to revise parts of the 1974 Act, especially in regard to noise from the highway. The report recommended that the duty of local authorities to investigate complaints be clarified and this was done in the Environmental Protection Act 1990.

Complaints about noise

Evidence of trends in public concern is provided by statistics on complaints about noise, collected by local Environmental Health Officers (EHOs). Table 4.1 shows the trend in the numbers of three types of complaints (per million persons) about noise. The first type is noise from road traffic, aircraft and other sources not subject to control under the Control of Pollution Act 1974. Since most complaints about such noise are usually addressed to various transport bodies and not to EHOs, the coverage of these complaints is far from complete. Also, not all traffic noise complaints are covered. In England and Wales, complaints to EHOs about road traffic noise have increased by nearly 50 per cent over the latest 10-year period. They rose particularly sharply in the last year as did those about aircraft noise which more than doubled. Complaints about noise from "other" sources have also increased substantially in recent years; these cover a wide variety of activities, for example, train movements, roadside car maintenance, sport and refuse collection.

Figure 4.1 Noise: complaints received by Environmental Health Officers about noise sources controlled by Control of Pollution Act 1974[1]

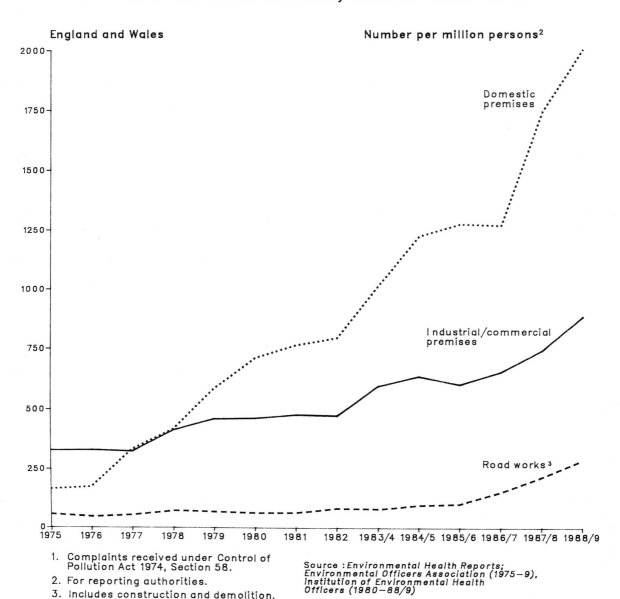

1. Complaints received under Control of Pollution Act 1974, Section 58.
2. For reporting authorities.
3. Includes construction and demolition.

Source : Environmental Health Reports; Environmental Officers Association (1975−9), Institution of Environmental Health Officers (1980−88/9)

Complaints for sources controlled by the Control of Pollution Act 1974 have also increased (see Figure 4.1). Those relating to industrial and commercial premises have more than doubled over the past decade, and the rate for roadworks, construction and demolition quadrupled over the same period. Complaints about noise from domestic premises increased by nearly 15 per cent between 1987/8 and 1988/9 compared with an increase of nearly 40 per cent in the previous year. It is not known whether these increases in complaints were due to declining public toleration of noise or to real increases in noise levels.

Figures for Scotland are included for the first time in this publication. They are presented on the same basis as those for England and Wales except that they relate to calendar years throughout. For sources not controlled by the 1974 Act, the majority of complaints are about road traffic. Total complaints for sources controlled by the 1974 Act have increased steadily, doubling between 1980 and 1989; industrial and commercial premises gave rise to the most complaints.

The number of complaints per million people is much lower than in England and Wales and there are a number of reasons for this. First, the rural area of Scotland, accounting for about a quarter of the total population of Scotland, is much less densely populated than the rural areas of England and Wales. This will have an effect of diluting the complaints per million

4.2 Noise: complaints and prosecutions: by source: 1988/9

England and Wales

	Noise source			All sources[1]	Noise in the street[2]	All complaints[1,2]
	Industrial and commercial premises	Roadworks construction, demolition	Domestic premises			
Complaints received[3]	25,999	8,506	59,061	93,566	2,507	96,073
Sources complained of	12,217	2,561	35,748	50,526	1,077	51,603
Nuisances						
Confirmed[4]	6,791	1,693	13,071	21,555	593	22,148
Remedied informally	8,229	1,977	16,788	26,994	989	27,983
Abatement notices						
Number served	964	1,491	1,865	4,320	-	4,320
Prosecution for contravention[6]	61	185	177	423	23	446
Convictions[6]	53	154	188	395	19	414

Scotland[5]

	Noise source			All sources[1]	Noise in the street[2]	All complaints[1,2]
	Industrial and commercial premises	Roadworks construction, demolition	Domestic premises			
Complaints received[3]	2,486	638	797	3,921	119	4,040
Sources complained of	..	..	..	..	..	..
Nuisances						
Confirmed[4]	927	276	164	1,367	-	1,367
Remedied informally	1,186	446	444	2,076	-	2,076
Abatement notices						
Number served	72	44	12	128	-	128
Prosecution for contravention[6]	7	-	1	8	6	14
Convictions[6]	4	-	1	5	2	7

[1] Complaints received under Control of Pollution Act 1974, Section 58.
[2] Complaints received under Control of Pollution Act 1974, Section 62.
[3] Complaints received by Environmental Health Officers.
[4] Considered to be justified as statutory nuisances.
[5] 1989.
[6] Some prosecutions and convictions may relate to complaints received in previous years.

Source: *Environmental Health Report 1988/9, Institution of Environmental Health Officers; Royal Environmental Health Institute of Scotland*

4.3 Complaints about noise from domestic premises received by Environmental Health Officers

England and Wales   Numbers, rates and *percentages*

Year	1978	1979	1980	1981	1982	1983/4	1984/5	1985/6	1986/7	1987/8	1988/9
Number of complaints[1]	17,980	24,472	31,076	30,289	33,014	41,988	48,645	56,414	46,803	59,132	59,061
Complaints per million	420	586	712	764	794	1,016	1,244	1,276	1,269	1,745	2,008
Number of sources	15,150	18,579	18,047	19,295	23,951	27,285	33,736	35,636	29,223	33,516	35,748
Number of nuisances	7,452	10,344	10,011	11,383	11,690	13,848	15,231	17,780	13,626	14,485	13,071
Abatement notices issued	484	1,100	951	1,215	1,073	1,695	2,156	3,156	1,763	2,636	1,865
Percentage of sources considered a nuisance	*49.2*	*55.7*	*55.5*	*59.0*	*48.8*	*50.8*	*45.1*	*49.9*	*46.6*	*43.2*	*36.6*
Percentage of sources for which an abatement notice was issued	*3.2*	*5.9*	*5.3*	*6.3*	*4.5*	*6.2*	*6.4*	*8.9*	*6.0*	*7.9*	*5.2*

Scotland   Numbers and rates

Year	1980	1981	1982	1983	1984	1985	1986	1987	1988	1989
Number of complaints[1]	269	397	470	554	485	876	844	999	718	797
Complaints per million	65	81	97	112	99	177	169	202	148	161
Number of sources	..	..	..	..	..	..	..	..	..	..
Number of nuisances	..	113	15	165	180	175	245	180	208	164
Abatement notices issued	3	9	11	18	8	9	16	12	5	12

[1] Complaints received by Environmental Health Officers under Control of Pollution Act 1974, Part III, Section 58.

Source: *Environmental Health Reports; Environmental Health Officers Association (1978-9), Institute of Environmental Health Officers (1980-88/9); Royal Environmental Health Institute of Scotland*

people to some extent. Second, the provisions of the Civic Government (Scotland) Act 1982 enables a complainer to seek a court order in cases concerning animals causing noise and disturbance to local residents, and places the onus on the police to deal with noise and disturbance associated with the playing of musical instruments and sound amplification systems, not considered to be a public health nuisance, and may result in many noise complaints of this nature not being directed to the local EHO. Third, the building regulation standards on sound insulation apply to new and refurbished properties, compliance with the regulations being checked by sound insulation tests by EHOs, and may also result in the limiting of complaints in new domestic premises.

A summary of the administrative and legal action taken in England and Wales in 1988/9 and in Scotland in 1989 by the responsible authorities under the Control of Pollution Act 1974, following complaints, is shown in Table 4.2. In England and Wales, over 96,000 separate complaints referred to nearly 52,000 sources. About 22,000 were considered to be justified as statutory nuisances, and about 28,000 nuisances were remedied informally. About 4,300 abatement notices were served, leading to 450 prosecutions and over 400 convictions. In Scotland, over 4,000 complaints were reported, although the number of sources complained of was not identified. Of the complaints, about 1,400 were considered statutory nuisances, over 2,000 nuisances were remedied informally, and nearly 130 abatement notices were served.

Table 4.3 shows complaints about noise from domestic premises reported to EHOs and how they have been dealt with. In England and Wales, although complaints have risen dramatically, the percentage of sources considered to be a nuisance has fallen in recent years. The percentage of sources for which an abatement notice was issued has generally increased over the past 10 years, reflecting the increasing use of a more formal approach to domestic noise abatement. In Scotland, the total number of complaints received nearly quadrupled from 270 in 1980 to a peak of 1,000 in 1987 but fell back in 1988 and 1989 to the lowest levels since 1984.

4.4 Domestic noise complaints by type of source: 1984-6

England and Wales

Type of source	Total mentions	*Percentage of all noises*
Music	895	*34*
Dogs	856	*33*
Domestic activities	243	*9*
Voices	146	*6*
DIY	125	*5*
Car repairs	73	*3*
Other animals	34	*1*
Domestic appliances	27	*1*
Other sources	225	*9*

Source: *Building Research Establishment*

The Building Research Establishment (BRE) organised a survey of domestic noise complaints over a two-year period from mid-1984 to mid-1986. EHOs from 47 local authorities, mostly in areas of high population density, provided details of 2,128 domestic noise complaints covering 2,624 sources. The types of noise source reported are shown in Table 4.4. Amplified music and barking dogs together accounted for two-thirds of all noise complaints. Amplified music was the dominant source of noise complaint from people in flats and in noisy areas, and EHOs were much more likely to consider such noise a nuisance than noises from other sources. Dogs were the dominant source of noise complaint for people in detached houses.

Motor vehicle noise

Although a BRE survey shows that the proportion of people bothered by road traffic has now been overtaken by the proportion bothered by noise from neighbours and other people nearby, the most widespread environmental noise source is road traffic. Noise offences can be dealt with by prosecution, by the issuing of written warnings by the police for alleged offences, or (since October 1986) by the issue of fixed penalty notices. In October 1986 most police forces implemented Vehicle Defect Registration Schemes (VDRS) and by April 1987 all forces had done so. These schemes allow a motorist to remedy vehicle defects, or to scrap the vehicle, as an alternative to being reported for prosecution.

Table 4.5 shows that the number of convictions for noise offences relating to motor vehicles has fallen by 28 per cent between 1986 and 1989. The number of written warnings for alleged noise offences fell by about 50 per cent over the same period. With the introduction of fixed penalties for alleged noise offences in October 1986, the total number of actual or alleged offences dealt with by conviction, written warnings or fixed penalty notices fell from 11,400 in 1986 to 8,800 in 1987, probably as a result of the introduction of the VDRS, and to 8,200 in 1988 but rose to 8,600 in 1989.

Aircraft noise

Noise levels at various points around major airports have been recorded over a number of years. Table 4.6 gives data for Heathrow, Gatwick and Luton Airports showing the area affected by and the population exposed to three distinct levels of noise (see also Figure 4.2). At Heathrow both the population and area affected in 1988 were well below those in 1978 even though air transport movements increased by more than 20 per cent over the period. At Gatwick, the number of air passengers almost trebled and air transport movements almost doubled over the same period; this was associated with smaller proportionate increases in both the area and the population affected. At Luton, both the population and area affected in 1989 were well below 1979 levels although air transport movements increased by 60 per cent over the period. Since 1986 all aircraft on the UK register have had to

4.5 Noise offences[1,2] relating to motor vehicles: by region

England and Wales Number of offences

Region	Findings of guilt at Magistrates' Courts				Written warnings issued for alleged offences[3]				Fixed Penalty Notices[4]			
	1986	1987	1988	1989	1986	1987	1988	1989	1986	1987	1988	1989
Northern	527	356	198	240	227	80	63	59	35	64	56	59
Yorks and Humberside	473	399	446	452	331	154	93	94	62	145	101	95
East Midlands	761	835	682	747	123	184	235	208	22	55	73	92
East Anglia	467	488	386	410	72	45	27	35	58	133	147	160
South East												
Greater London	1,067	367	261	230	496	49	47	322	19	42	53	101
Rest of South East	1,760	1,558	1,747	1,579	514	321	249	226	245	574	377	488
South West	908	575	569	623	285	76	68	85	37	100	64	118
West Midlands	786	512	542	498	154	63	42	44	60	215	155	138
North West	743	454	619	596	171	77	79	87	93	228	155	158
England	7,492	5,544	5,450	5,375	2,373	1,049	903	1,160	631	1,556	1,181	1,409
Wales	654	487	558	509	197	53	58	56	75	127	89	66
England and Wales	8,146	6,031	6,008	5,884	2,570	1,102	961	1,216	706	1,683	1,270	1,475

[1] Offences relating to excessive noise while using a vehicle. For the years up to 1986 it is known that about 90 per cent of these involved faulty silencers. From 1987 the information collected does not distinguish the various offences relating to excessive noise while using a vehicle.
[2] Excludes alleged offences dealt with by Vehicle Defect Registration Schemes (VDRS).
[3] Written warnings may be issued by the police instead of instituting court proceedings.

Source: *Offences Relating to Motor Vehicles, England and Wales, Home Office*

[4] Since October 1986, fixed penalty notices may be issued by the police for some alleged noise offences, instead of instituting court proceedings.

have a noise certificate and this should have a beneficial effect around UK airports.

Table 4.7 shows the number of complaints arising from exposure to aircraft noise at four airports in England since 1979. At Heathrow, the number of complaints was much higher in the 1970s (around 4,000 a year) than it was at the end of the 1980s, when complaints numbered around 1,400. At Gatwick, complaints since 1986 have been higher than in the first half of the decade,

although 1989 saw the lowest number of complaints since 1985. Complaints at Manchester rose steadily over the 1980s with a tenfold increase between 1980 and 1988. The sharp rise in 1989 illustrates the effect of an unsuccessful campaign by local residents, in an attempt to have the airport registered as a noise control area under the Civil Aviation Authority Act 1982. Luton has experienced more than a fourfold increase in complaints since 1979, with a sharp increase in 1988, when the number of complaints doubled in a single year to over 1,200.

4.6 Aircraft noise: air traffic, passengers, area and population affected by noise around Heathrow, Gatwick and Luton

	1979	1980	1981	1982	1983	1984	1985	1986	1987[1]	1988[1]	1989[1]
London - Heathrow:											
Passengers (millions)	28.0	27.5	26.4	26.4	26.7	29.2	31.3	31.3	35.1	37.8	..
Air transport movements (thousands)[2]	276.2	276.7	250.4	254.9	265.0	278.0	288.3	293.9	308.0	330.4	..
Area (sq km) within:											
35 NNI contour	699	573	476	540	507	443	408	378	324	317	..
45 NNI contour	157	132	118	115	101	110	111	98	92	90	..
55 NNI contour	47	39	34	34	34	32	34	32	31	31	..
Population (thousands)[3] within:											
35 NNI contour	1,610	944	837	1,028	1,060	776	658	695	554	538	..
45 NNI contour	311	240	204	204	198	190	177	162	143	144	..
55 NNI contour	73	39	27	37	39	28	25	34	20	24	..
London - Gatwick:											
Passengers (million)	8.7	9.7	10.8	11.2	12.5	14.0	14.8	16.3	17.6	20.8	..
Air transport movements (thousands)[2]	114.9	123.4	125.0	134.5	137.4	143.1	150.2	157.7	173.8	182.5	..
Area (sq km) within:											
35 NNI contour	190	226	222	212	212	225	299	288	243	229	..
45 NNI contour	44	48	45	45	48	49	66	62	57	54	..
55 NNI contour	12	12	12	12	14	14	17	15	14	14	..
Population (thousands)[3] within:											
35 NNI contour	31	38	39	34	37	41	87	63	55	50	..
45 NNI contour	3	3	4	3	4	5	8	6	6	4	..
55 NNI contour	1	1	1	1	1	1	1	1	1	1	..
Luton:											
Air transport movements (thousands)[2]	23.8	26.4	27.2	27.5	28.6	30.4	27.9	27.6	33.0	35.7	38.4
Area (sq km) within:											
35 NNI contour	47.7	36.7	36.6	27.5	32.4	32.8	21.7	24.7	49.0	44.4	37.7
45 NNI contour	13.6	9.8	11.1	8.3	9.2	9.6	6.2	7.1	13.2	12.0	10.2
55 NNI contour	4.3	2.6	2.9	2.1	2.3	2.6	1.4	2.0	3.6	3.6	3.0
Population (thousands)[3] within:											
35 NNI contour	24.7	16.1	15.1	12.1	11.3	14.5	9.5	10.5	20.6	19.0	14.5
45 NNI contour	5.4	3.3	3.8	3.1	2.5	4.3	1.3	1.7	5.9	5.9	3.0
55 NNI contour	0.3	-	-	-	0.1	-	-	-	0.1	-	-

[1] For Luton, including "start-of-role" noise affecting older designs of jet aircraft.

[2] Air transport movements are landings or take-offs of aircraft engaged on the transport of passengers or cargo on commercial terms. All scheduled service movements, whether loaded or empty and charter movements transporting passengers or cargo and air taxi movements are included.

[3] The population figures shown for Heathrow and Gatwick for 1978-80 are based on the 1971 Census and those for 1981-8 on the 1981 Census. The area and population within an enumeration district (ED) were assigned to the noise contour within which the geocentre of the ED fell.

[4] Air transport movements figures were obtained from the Civil Aviation Authority, passenger figures from BAA plc.

Source: *Department of Transport;[4] CAA; Luton Borough Council; Bedfordshire CC; Hertfordshire CC*

Notes:

NNI - the Noise and Number Index, an index of air traffic noise. For a number of aircraft, N, heard in a day (normally 08.00 to 18.00 hours GMT, mid-June to mid-September), NNI is given by:

$$NNI = (\log) \text{ average peak perceived noise level(PNdB)} + 15 \log N - 80.$$

35 NNI represents a low annoyance rating, 45 NNI a moderate rating and 55 NNI a high rating. The NNI is an assessment of community response to aircraft noise but it is recognised that the reaction of different individuals to aircraft noise can vary considerably. These contours are affected by the modal split at the airport which depends upon meteorological conditions.

Figure 4.2 Noise: population affected by aircraft noise

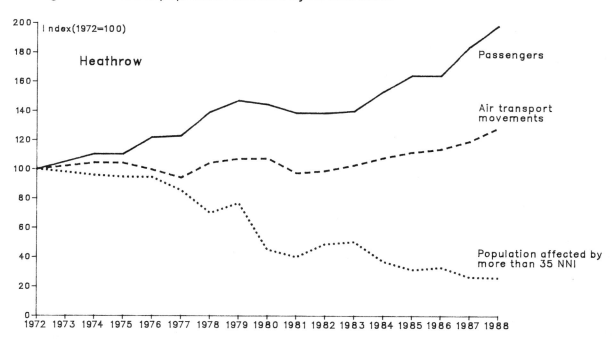

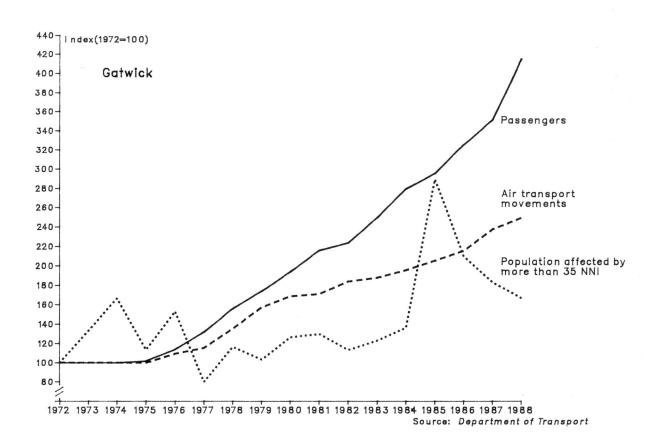

Source: *Department of Transport*

4.7 Aircraft noise: number of complaints received at Heathrow, Gatwick, Manchester and Luton: 1979-89

	Heathrow	Gatwick	Manchester	Luton
1979	2,520	870	80	290
1980	1,890	820	70	470
1981	900	590	80	370
1982	1,080	570	180	200
1983	1,000	480	200	320
1984	1,720[1]	860	180	210
1985	1,570	760	170	120
1986	1,400	1,260	310	190
1987	1,250	2,010	480	630
1988	1,100	1,080	700	1,240
1989	1,370	1,010	2,040	1,380

Source: *Department of Transport; Manchester International Airport Authority; Borough of Luton*

[1] A "Noiseline" was opened in July 1984 for the public to leave complaints about aircraft and helicopter noise in London. These complaints are then forwarded to the Department of Transport for recording and attention.

In 1988, air transport movements were 330,000 at Heathrow, 183,000 at Gatwick, 112,000 at Manchester and 36,000 at Luton.

Survey of noise levels outside dwellings

Trends in complaints about noise provide an indication of changes in levels of noise for sources which bother people but do not provide any information about changes in ambient noise levels. To provide an indication of current noise levels in the UK, the Department of the Environment has funded, since 1985, a survey of noise measurements by students of the Open University (OU) which forms part of their course.

Comparison of these results with those from a national survey of noise levels in 1972[3] indicate that there has been little change in overall mean noise levels over the past 16 years. The current survey runs until 1991,

allowing trends in noise levels to be monitored over a seven year period. However, the results for the four years so far covered are very similar to one another and show no significant changes in mean ambient noise over that time. The analysis below is based on all the data available to 1988, ie, the measurements of about 150 students in 1985 and just under 400 in each of the other three years.

Noise is measured in decibels on the A-scale - a measure of sound level modified to take account of the response of the ear to different frequencies. An increase of 10 dB(A) corresponds approximately to doubling the loudness. Because the noise level varies from moment to moment, it is helpful to use three measures of noise level - L_{A90}, L_{Aeq} and L_{A10}, which are normally in ascending order of magnitude. L_{Aeq} measures the average noise level; L_{A90}, the level exceeded by 90 per cent of the individual observations, measures the background noise persisting when intermittent sounds are not heard; L_{A10}, the level exceeded by only 10 per cent of the individual observations, measures the louder end of the noise range. In this survey, the measurements took place over a 5-minute period. Table 4.8 shows the distribution of these three measures, with an indication of the sort of noise level corresponding to each band of dB(A).

The participants were asked to describe the noise level outside their homes as "very noisy", "noisy", "quiet" or "very quiet". The replies were converted into a "perceived noise score", counting 4 for "very noisy" down to 1 for "very quiet". The mean score was 2.0, ie, "quiet". There was a fairly consistent relationship between the three measurements of noise and the perceived noise level.

As might be expected noise levels varied during the course of a day and between weekdays and weekends. On weekdays the average noise level, L_{Aeq}, was lowest in the late evening. Mean noise measurements were slightly lower at weekends than at the same time of day during the week. Noise measurements and perceived

4.8 External noise levels

Percentages and adjusted[1] dB(A)

Typical sound		dB(A)	*Percentages of measured levels in range*		
			L_{A90}	L_{Aeq}	L_{A10}
30 dB(A)	country lane	30-39	*25[2]*	*1*	*1*
40 dB(A)	residential area at night	40-49	*51*	*38*	*22*
50 dB(A)	quiet urban area	50-59	*19*	*40*	*44*
60 dB(A)	noisy office	60-69	*4*	*19*	*23*
70 dB(A)	alongside busy main road	70-79	*-*	*3*	*10*
80 dB(A)	alarm clock at 2 feet	80-89	*-*	*-*	*-*
		Total	*100*	*100*	*100*
		Average dB(A)	45	53	57
		n = 100%	1,188	1,335	1,191

[1] Adjusted for population density and time of day.
[2] Probably includes levels below 30 dB(A) because that was the minimum level on the meter.

Source: *Department of the Environment*

4.9 Main noise source identified: by average noise level[1]

Adjusted[2] dB(A) and scores and *percentages*

Main noise source identified	Sample size	% of mentions as main source	L_{A90}[3]	L_{Aeq}[3]	L_{A10}[3]	Noise score[3]	% of mentions as a source
Traffic	745	64	46	55	59	2.2	91
People and children	159	14	43	51	55	1.9	73
Wind or leaves	75	6	43	50	52	1.5	10
Birds	43	4	(39)	(47)	(49)	(1.5)	10
Aircraft	36	3	(42)	(52)	(55)	(1.7)	32
Mowers	34	3	(43)	(51)	(54)	(2.0)	13
Animals	24	2	(41)	(48)	(53)	(1.8)	35
Other sources	17	1	(42)	(48)	(50)	(1.5)	8
Construction	10	1	(43)	(51)	(58)	(2.2)	4
Industry	7	1	(43)	(52)	(53)	(2.1)	15
Railway	6	1	(37)	(51)	(51)	(1.9)	3

[1] Average noise level for students in the sample who identified each source or the main source of noise.
[2] Adjusted for population density and time of day.
[3] ( ) indicates sample size was less than 50.

Source: *Department of the Environment*

noise scores have been adjusted accordingly, to a standard time of 6 pm on a weekday evening. Noise levels also rose as population density increased. The results have been adjusted for the tendency of OU students on this course to live in less densely populated areas by standardising to the distribution of ward population densities in the 1981 census in England and Wales. The combined effect of these adjustments has been to increase mean L_{Aeq} by just over 1 dB(A) and the noise scores by less than 0.1.

Table 4.9 shows the average and perceived noise levels for the main sources of noise, together with the percentage of students reporting each main noise source. It also gives the percentage of students who reported each noise source as contributing to the ambient noise level, not just as the main source. About 64 per cent of students reported "traffic" as the main noise source and almost 90 per cent said it was a source of noise. Only 14 per cent reported "people and children" as the main noise source but it was one of the sources of noise for three-quarters of the students. The other main noise sources tended to be mentioned most often by students living in quieter areas. The survey also showed that noise levels were at their highest by A-roads, dual carriageways and bus routes, and lowest in sparsely populated rural areas and in cul-de-sacs. BRE carried out a national survey of noise measurements in 1990 and results will be included when they are available.

[1] *This Common Inheritance: Britain's Environmental Strategy*, Environment White Paper, 1990.
[2] *Report of the Noise Review Working Party 1990*, Department of the Environment, 1990.
[3] *Noise and Road Traffic outside Homes in England*, Harland and Abbott, TRRL Laboratory Report 770, 1977.

Chapter 5 Waste and recycling

The disposal of *industrial*, *household*, and *commercial* wastes is regulated in Great Britain under the Control of Pollution Act 1974 (CoPA). *Controlled* waste, as defined by CoPA, specifically excludes mine and quarry waste, wastes from premises used for agriculture, some sewage sludge and radioactive waste. Similar legislative provisions exist in Northern Ireland based on the same definitions and control requirements. Farm wastes should be disposed of to accord with the MAFF *Code of Good Agricultural Practice* (this is being updated and will be published later in 1991). Mine and quarry wastes are partly controlled through conditions attached to planning permissions for exploitation. Disposal of radioactive waste is controlled through the Radioactive Substances Act 1960.

Any controlled waste which consists of, or contains substances which are "dangerous to life" is classed as a *special* waste and its disposal is regulated under the Control of Pollution (Special Waste) Regulations 1980. "Dangerous to life" is defined in detail in the regulations and substances which meet this definition are listed in the regulations. Wastes containing drugs available on prescription only are classed as special waste.

This chapter concerns itself with controlled wastes including special wastes and recycling. Information about *sewage sludges* and *dredged spoil* is given in Chapter 2. Information on *radioactive* waste is given in Chapter 3.

The mechanism for regulating disposal of controlled wastes is through a licensing system. Persons wishing to operate disposal facilities or treatment plants have to apply for a licence from the Waste Disposal Authority (WDA). WDAs, which in due course will become Waste Regulation Authorities under the Environmental Protection Act 1990 (EPA), can impose conditions in the licences and have powers to require that the operations are carried out satisfactorily. Licence conditions are designed primarily to prevent damage to the environment, with incidental benefits for health and safety. An additional control system is used for special wastes. The movement and disposal of special waste must be notified and recorded by a system of consignment notes.

The Hazardous Waste Inspectorate was set up in August 1983 to examine the management of hazardous waste, to advise authorities and industry on their duties, and to use its influence towards the attainment of adequate and consistent standards of hazardous waste management across England and Wales. In its three annual reports[1,2,3] the Inspectorate revealed widely disparate attitudes amongst waste producers, waste disposal contractors and waste disposal authorities regarding this important aspect of industrial activity. In April 1987 the Inspectorate became part of Her Majesty's Inspectorate of Pollution (HMIP); the second annual report of HMIP was published in 1990.[4] The same duties are discharged by the Hazardous Waste Inspectorate of the Scottish Development Department and by the Department of the Environment for Northern Ireland.

The Environmental Protection Act 1990 makes waste reduction at source a central aim of waste policy and strengthens the powers of both HMIP and local authorities to control pollution. Waste minimisation will be achieved through the system of Integrated Pollution Control (IPC),[5] which is one of the most important features of the EPA, by requiring HMIP and local authorities to set emission standards in the authorisations which industry will require to operate. The act will replace CoPA as the principal means of controlling waste collection and disposal.

The European Community (EC) also plays a role in setting standards for waste disposal. Environmental rules governing how wastes should be disposed of are aligned at community level through community law. The key EC directives are the Framework Directive (75/442/EEC); the Toxic and Dangerous Wastes Directive (78/319/EEC), which is to be replaced by a new Hazardous Waste Directive; and the Transfrontier Shipment of Hazardous Wastes Directive (84/631/EEC) as amended which is to be replaced by a new regulation implementing the Basel Convention.

Information on waste arisings and disposal is available on an annual basis in a few cases only, eg, sewage sludges. Only year-on-year data can be used to deduce trends. Most of the information presented in this chapter does not refer to a specific year but provides a snapshot of the situation with regard to wastes in the UK and will be a reasonable guide to the situation in recent years. Non year-specific figures and totals derived from them should not be compared with previously published figures which were not produced on the same basis.

Waste arisings

Total waste arisings in the United Kingdom each year are currently estimated to be about 700 million tonnes. Figure 5.1 shows the proportion of waste arising from the main sources. Most of the data used in preparation of this figure are not based on regular surveys, but are estimates synthesised from information from a variety

Figure 5.1 Estimated total annual waste arisings in the UK in late 1980s

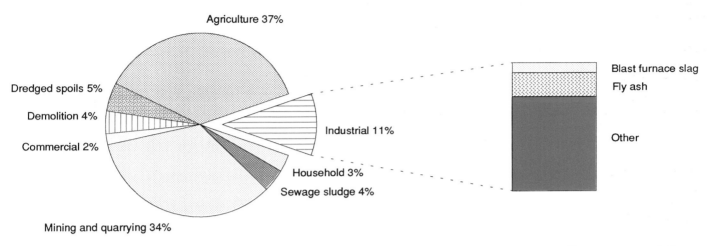

Total arisings = 700 million tonnes

Source: Department of the Environment / HMIP

of sources and interpreted using expert knowledge and may be regarded as valid for any 12-month period in recent years. The figure for agricultural wastes (about 40 per cent of all waste arisings) is a very broad estimate and is quite old, but is the best estimate currently available. Estimates made on these bases, and used to prepare Figure 5.1, have been rounded to the nearest million tonnes, except where figures exceed 50 million tonnes when they have been rounded to the nearest 10 million tonnes. Of the total waste arisings about 20 per cent or 140 million tonnes are subject to CoPA Regulations, ie, controlled wastes.

Special waste arisings in the UK are estimated at between 2.0-2.5 million tonnes in 1989/90. Table 5.1 presents estimates of special waste arisings in each of the countries of the UK. Figures for England and Wales are collected by WDAs and collated by HMIP. Although figures refer to specific years they should be regarded as estimates because of the incompleteness of the data. In 1987/8 many authorities in England and Wales found it impossible to provide figures. The previous years'

5.1 Special waste arisings: 1986/7-89/90

United Kingdom				Thousand tonnes
Year	England	Wales	Scotland	N. Ireland
1986/7	1,500	94	30	5
1987/8	2,070	..	59	12
1988/9	1,762	60	66	17
1989/90	2,146	80	71	18

Source: *Department of the Environment/HMIP; Scottish Development Department; Department of the Environment (N Ireland)*

figures for English local authorities not providing data were used and the resulting estimate is likely to have an error of at least 10 per cent. It was not possible to provide a figure for Wales in 1987/8. Reported special waste arisings have more than doubled over the last four years in Scotland and more than trebled in Northern Ireland. These figures do not include special wastes dealt with in-house as they do not have to be reported to the WDA. In Northern Ireland an annual reporting cycle was introduced in 1989 to improve monitoring performance.

Waste Disposal

Table 5.2 shows the number of licensed disposal facilities in the United Kingdom. The figures provide a reasonably up-to-date snapshot of the position, although it is probable that a number of these facilities will no longer be operating. Figure 5.2 shows the disposal route for all controlled wastes in the UK. Landfill continues to be the primary disposal route for most controlled wastes (86 per cent). Others include approximately four million tonnes of power station ash used in construction, about five million tonnes of blast furnace slag used in construction and road building and about one million tonnes of material recycled from municipal waste. Sewage sludge accounts for about five million tonnes of landfilled material and approximately two million tonnes of incinerated wastes. Only when disposed of in these ways is sewage sludge classed as controlled waste.

Table 5.3 shows the main disposal routes for municipal wastes. Again landfill is the predominant method of

5.2 Number of disposal facilities: by type and wastes accepted

United Kingdom

Type of disposal facility	No. of disposal licences	Licences for putrescible wastes[1]	Licences for clinical wastes[1,2]
England			
Landfill	3,309	712	91
Civic amenity[3]	411	121	4
Transfer[4]	631	162	30
Storage[5]	217	8	-
Treatment[6]	118	38	5
Incineration	151	78	52
Miscellaneous[7]	106	3	-
Wales			
Landfill	242	63	4
Civic amenity[3]	14	5	-
Transfer[4]	9	2	-
Storage[5]	6	1	-
Treatment[6]	13	4	-
Incineration	15	5	8
Miscellaneous[7]	7	-	-
Scotland			
Landfill	478	175	3
Civic amenity[3]	25	8	-
Transfer[4]	35	15	2
Storage[5]	3	-	-
Treatment[6]	23	14	-
Incineration	18	7	4
Miscellaneous[7]	6	1	-
Northern Ireland			
Landfill	80	34	3
Civic amenity[3]	54	26	-
Transfer[4]	5	2	-
Storage[5]	-	-	-
Treatment[6]	3	-	-
Incineration	3	-	1
Miscellaneous[7]	-	-	-

Source: *Department of the Environment/HMIP, Department of the Environment (N Ireland)*

[1] Putrescible includes household but not most commercial or industrial wastes, even those which are biodegradable. Although clinical waste includes putrescibles, it has been excluded from this category.
[2] Clinical wastes includes veterinary wastes.
[3] Refuse disposal amenity facilities.
[4] Transfer facilities are those licensed for the receipt, sorting, consolidation and onward movement of wastes. Facilities where such activities are incidental to a disposal activity are not included.
[5] Storage facilities are those licensed principally for storing waste remotely from final disposal. They do not include facilities where storage is an inevitable consequence of disposal or transfer.
[6] Treatment includes physical, chemical and biological treatment and licensable waste recovery facilities.
[7] Miscellaneous includes licensable scrapyards. At the time of preparation, the data for scrapyards facilities were incomplete, and amounts to a small number of the total in this category.

final disposal. Approximately 90 per cent of municipal waste in Scotland and England and nearly all municipal waste in Northern Ireland and Wales is destined to be landfilled. In Scotland approximately 25

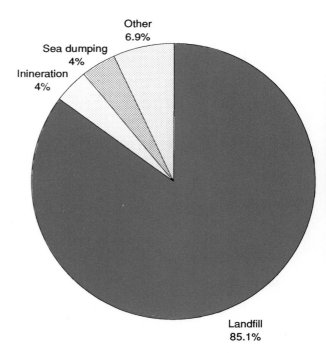

Figure 5.2 Annual waste disposal in the UK

Total disposed of = 140 million tonnes

per cent of municipal waste receives some form of processing before being landfilled. This processing is usually to reduce the bulk of the waste. The amount of waste processed by the shire counties of England, in Northern Ireland and in Wales is small by comparison. Approximately 2.0-2.5 million tonnes of municipal waste is incinerated in the UK, about one million tonnes with energy recovery.

5.3 Municipal waste disposal: 1986/7

United Kingdom *Percentage*

	England[1]	Wales	Scotland	N. Ireland[2]
Direct landfill[3]	82	94	63	88
Compacting[4]	7	4	8	-
Shredding[4]	1	-	-	-
Baling[4]	1	-	10	5
Pulverisation[4]	-	-	4	-
Transfer to loading station[4]	-	-	5	5
Incineration	5	-	6	1
Reclamation[5]	3	1	-	<1
Other	<1	<1	3[6]	-

Source: *Chartered Institute of Public Finance and Accountancy, Scottish Development Department, Department of the Environment (N Ireland)*

[1] Non-metropolitan counties only.
[2] 1989/90.
[3] Includes waste collected at civic amenity sites and landfilled.
[4] Followed by landfilling.
[5] Includes remainder of waste collected at civic amenity sites and not landfilled.
[6] "Other" includes an element of recycled waste.

Figure 5.3 Disposal of special wastes in the UK

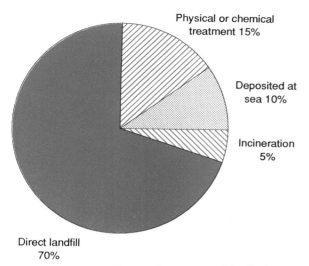

Source: Department of the Environment;
Scottish Office;
Department of the Environment
(Northern Ireland)

Figure 5.3 provides a rough estimate of the way special waste is disposed of in United Kingdom. This breakdown is based on estimates made for 1988 when approximately 1.9 million tonnes was disposed of and is probably typical for any 12-month period in recent years. Landfill is the main method of disposal for special wastes. Approximately 15 per cent of special waste receives some form of physical or chemical treatment designed to render them harmless or less harmful before being landfilled.

Hazardous waste imports

As well as the waste arising in the UK some *hazardous* waste is imported for treatment and disposal. Hazardous waste is not defined in present UK legislation, but is generally used to mean waste capable of harming living organisms or the environment. Assembling an accurate picture of hazardous waste imports has been difficult in past years and the figures previously reported in Digest no 12 are subject to a significant margin of error.

The Transfrontier Shipment of Hazardous Waste Regulations, 1988, implements EC Directives controlling the international trade in hazardous waste. Under the regulations, shipments of hazardous waste must receive prior written consent before they start and the shipment must be accompanied by a consignment note giving details of source, destination and nature of waste. This applies to shipments to or from non-EC states as well as those between member states. From October 1988 full details of imports to the UK are available and the partial data for 1988/9 has been used

to revise estimates of imported wastes in this year to 40,000 tonnes. Information on imported hazardous wastes is collected by HMIP from the WDAs who give consents to imports in the UK. The UK has signed the Basel Convention on the control of Transboundary Shipments of Hazardous Waste. It will be ratified by a new EC law.

1989/90 is the first year for which complete data are available. Total imports amounted to almost 35,000 tonnes. the wastes originated from 23 countries and from the Channel Islands. Those countries from which more than 500 tonnes of waste was imported are shown in Table 5.4. Almost 80 per cent of imports came from four countries: The Netherlands, Belgium, Switzerland and the USA, 30 per cent of imports coming from the Netherlands alone. Inorganic materials, miscellaneous wastes, filter sludges, and interceptor wastes accounted for more than half of all imports of hazardous wastes. Scrap refractories from the USA, and polychlorinated biphenyls (PCBs) and PCB-contaminated material each accounted for a further 10 per cent.

Table 5.5 shows imports of hazardous waste by port of entry and destination WDA. Fifty per cent of imports arrived through just two ports, Immingham and Felixstowe, and a further 40 per cent arrived through Dover, Flixborough, Ramsgate, Newport and Dartford. Ninety-five per cent of imports went to just four WDAs for disposal: Greater Manchester (43 per cent), West Midlands (22 per cent), Torfaen BC (18 per cent), and Humberside (12 per cent).

In 1988 about 450 tonnes of hazardous waste was imported into Scotland from Sweden and Ireland. This was mostly solvents and contaminated methylated spirits destined for recycling. In 1989 480 tonnes were imported from Eire, mostly through Stranraer and occasionally through Ardrossan.

There were no exports of hazardous waste from the UK in 1989/90.

Table 5.6 shows the disposal routes for imported waste. In general the UK shares the EC view that waste should be dealt with as close to its source as is practicable and that waste should not be regarded as a tradeable commodity. Waste should only be exported if it requires special treatment to ensure its safe disposal and that treatment is for some reason not available in the country of origin. Accordingly importation of waste into the UK for direct landfilling is discouraged. Only 140 tonnes of imported waste was sent direct to landfill in 1989/90. Most imported wastes (60 per cent) were physically or chemically treated at specialist facilities before being disposed of. About one-quarter of imported waste was incinerated and almost half that amount was PCBs.

5.4 Imports of hazardous waste: by country of origin: 1989/90[1]

England and Wales   Tonnes

	Neths.	Belgium	Switz.	USA	Italy	Ireland	Sweden	Germany	Norway	Canada	Other	Total
Inorganic and organic acids	1	2	44	-	-	6	-	-	-	-	-	53
Alkalis	5	1	98	-	-	262	-	39	-	-	50	455
Toxic metal compounds	285	180	4	-	-	323	-	-	-	-	8	800
Non-toxic metal compounds	-	166	-	-	-	1	-	-	-	-	-	167
Metals	-	-	-	4,237[2]	-	-	-	-	-	-	-	4,237
Metal oxides	1,597	-	6	-	-	177	-	-	-	-	41	1,821
Inorganic compounds	337	18	15	-	-	140	28	-	25	-	27	590
Inorganic compounds not defined	147	-	4,801	-	-	18	-	516	92	-	30	5,604
Organic materials (excl PCBs)	197	1,182	1	-	395	284	95	-	-	-	37	2,191
PCBs/PCB-contaminated waste	97	309	216	-	339	25	1,065	185	-	568	683	3,487
Polymeric materials and percursors	31	112	16	-	6	3	-	-	-	-	-	168
Fuels, oils and greases	20	366	-	-	20	5	-	-	-	-	-	411
Fine chemicals and biocides	1	54	361	-	80	85	-	77	-	-	59	717
Miscellaneous chemical wastes	504	343	20	-	133	319	30	69	-	-	56	1,474
Filter materials: sludge and rubbish	2,080	2,331	9	-	-	8	-	-	-	-	16	4,444
Interceptor wastes	1,656	443	143	-	880	-	23	-	498	-	-	3,643
Miscellaneous wastes	3,649	229	-	-	-	50	-	-	-	-	-	3,928
Animal and food wastes	61	21	-	-	-	-	-	-	-	-	-	82
Total	10,668	5,757	5,734	4,237	1,853	1,706	1,241	886	615	568	1,007	34,272

[1] Financial year 1 April 1989-31 March 1990.
[2] Scrap refractories contaminated with hazardous metals.

Source: *Department of the Environment/HMIP*

5.5 Imports of hazardous waste: by port of entry: 1989/90[1]

England and Wales   Tonnes

Port of entry	Destination WDA								
	Greater Manchester	West Midlands	Torfaen BC	Humberside CC	Hampsire CC	Essex CC	Cheshire CC	Other	Total
Immingham	6,738	41	1,860	-	72	-	-	41	8,752
Felixstowe	1,345	5,422	1,272	-	235	444	-	-	8,718
Dover	4,778	-	382	-	-	-	-	-	5,160
Flixborough	-	-	-	4,237[2]	-	-	-	-	4,237
Ramsgate	23	1,854	-	-	-	-	-	-	1,877
Newport	372	-	779	-	125	-	-	70	1,346
Dartford	23	-	666	-	448	-	-	-	1,137
Liverpool	182	77	495	-	-	-	-	-	754
Heysham	640	51	33	-	-	-	-	-	724
Chatham	182	-	227	-	-	-	-	-	409
Middlesbrough	203	-	-	-	-	-	-	-	203
Ipswich	-	-	185	-	-	-	-	-	185
Holyhead	92	-	10	-	-	-	54	-	156
Fleetwood	44	-	-	-	-	-	110	-	154
Harwich	35	-	100	-	-	15	-	-	150
Other	98	8	120	-	-	51	-	33	310
Total	14,755	7,453	6,129	4,237	880	510	164	144	34,272

[1] Financial year 1 April 1989-31 March 1990.
[2] Scrap refractories contaminated with hazardous metal.

Source: *Department of the Environment/HMIP*

5.6 Imports of hazardous waste: disposal methods: 1989/90[1]

England and Wales Tonnes

	Physical/ chemical treatment	Incineration	Other	Total
Inorganic and organic acids	7	46	-	53
Alkalis	400	54	-	454
Toxic metal compounds	800	-	-	800
Non-toxic metal compounds	133	34	-	167
Metals	-	-	4,237[2]	4,237
Metal oxides	1,820	-	-	1,820
Inorganic compounds	389	200	-	589
Inorganic compounds not defined	5,611	-	30[3]	5,641
Organic materials (excl PCBs)	264	1,927	-	2,191
PCBs/PCB-contaminated waste	-	3,500	-	3,500
Polymeric materials and precursors	110	38	20[4]	168
Fuels, oils and greases	409	2	-	411
Fine chemicals and biocides	109	607	-	716
Miscellaneous chemical wastes	638	837	-	1,475
Filter materials: sludge and rubbish	4,367	60	-	4,427
Interceptor wastes	2,154	1,501	-	3,655
Miscellaneous wastes	3,644	68	177[5]	3,889
Animal and food wastes	21	60	-	81
Total	20,876	8,934	4,464	34,272

[1] Financial year 1 April 1989-31 March 1990.
[2] Scrap refractories, contaminated with hazardous metals, all recycled.
[3] Landfill.
[4] Solidification.
[5] Landfill, 109 tonnes; solidification, 67 tonnes.

Source: *Department of the Environment/HMIP*

Resource recovery and recycling of materials from waste streams

Many waste streams contain useful materials that can be reclaimed and recycled. Reclamation and recycling of selected materials that would otherwise be thrown away can be justified on both environmental and economic grounds. Recycling reduces the amount of waste that needs to be disposed of, reducing demand for landfill void space and on incineration plant and cutting industry's disposal costs. Use of recycled material in production processes can also help to conserve energy and natural resources, and reduce pollution. For example, the production of aluminium from its ore, bauxite, causes environmental pollution when the ore is extracted from open cast mines and requires high energy inputs to convert the ore to pure aluminium. Recycling an aluminium can uses about 5 per cent of the energy needed to make one from the raw material.

Some sectors of industry already recycle significant amounts of process scrap in-house, or sell it to other industries as a raw material. Britain is particularly successful at recovering scrap metal from industrial processes: industry re-uses approximately 82 per cent of ferrous metal process scrap, 74 per cent of copper process scrap, and 66 per cent of lead. Britain has been less successful at recycling material from household waste, although it is estimated that 50 per cent of the waste, by weight is readily recyclable. In recent years, a large number of waste collection and waste disposal authorities have made arrangements for separate collection of valuable materials from the domestic waste stream, including glass, waste paper and metals.

Table 5.7 shows, for selected materials, the weight of recycled scrap and its proportion of the total consumed in manufacture. A greater weight of ferrous metal is recycled in the UK than all the other materials combined. The British Scrap Federation estimates that the ferrous scrap reclamation industry handles about 10 million tonnes of ferrous scrap annually and that significant tonnages are extracted from domestic waste at civic amenity sites and waste transfer stations. Included in this figure are approximately two million obsolete or crashed vehicles, and six million units of "white goods" (washing machines, cooker, freezers, refrigerators). Recycling of steel cans makes a substantial contribution to the amount of ferrous metals reclaimed in the UK. Over 1,000 million cans are recycled each year and are collected mainly by magnetic extraction from household waste. Consumer-collection is an important part in steel can recycling where magnetic extraction is not available. The *Save-a-Can* scheme operates over 250 can banks around the country.

The weight of ferrous metals recycled and its proportion of total consumption in manufacture in the UK has declined in the past 10 years due both to contraction and restructuring of the iron and steel industry. Since export controls were lifted in 1979 exports of scrap have increased and in 1989 amounted to 3.25 million tonnes.

5.7 Recycling of selected materials: weight and percentage of total consumption in manufacture

United Kingdom　　　　　　　　　　　　　　　　　　　　　　　　　　　　　　　　　　*Thousand tonnes and percentages*

	Weight of recycled scrap consumed in manufacture (thousand tonnes)						Recycled scrap as percentage of total consumption					
	1984	1985	1986	1987	1988	1989	*1984*	*1985*	*1986*	*1987*	*1988*	*1989*
Glass	155r	210	225r	245	275	310	*9*	*12*	*13*	*14*	*16*	*18*
Paper and board	2,003	2,067	2,147	2,310	2,417	2,578	*26*	*27*	*27*	*26*	*26*	*27*
Aluminium[1]	91r	81r	71r	80r	65[2]	45	*20r*	*19r*	*15r*	*17r*	*13*	*9*
Copper	200	193	199	206	207	200	*41*	*40*	*42*	*44*	*45*	*44*
Lead[3]	211	208	200	238	238	229	*67*	*69*	*65*	*73*	*70*	*68*
Tin[4]	7	7	6	5	6	7	*68*	*78*	*60*	*50*	*60*	*70*
Zinc	54	53	53	54	52	50	*23*	*25*	*23*	*22*	*21*	*20*
Ferrous metal[5]	9,619	8,369	7,826	8,203r	8,859	7,669	*58*	*49*	*50*	*48*	*44*	*41*

[1] Excludes aluminium scrap of approximately 30,000 tonnes a year which moves directly from the aluminium metal industry to other industries.
[2] It is estimated that a further 40,000 tonnes of recycled aluminium were used in 1988 in the production of aluminium ingots.
[3] The weight of recycled material refers to actual quantity recovered, not recycled scrap used in manufacture.
[4] Secondary refined consumption only.
[5] Includes in-house recycling of wastes but excludes exports.

Source: *Warren Spring Laboratory, Department of Trade and Industry; British Paper and Board Industry Federation; British Glass Manufacturers Confederation*

The weight of paper and board recycled in the UK increased steadily between 1983 and 1989 although its proportion of total consumption remained steady at around 26 per cent. The success of paper recycling depends on favourable market conditions, the capacity of mills to deal with reclaimed stocks and levels of cheap imports. There have been diffficulties in creating a stable market in the UK. The government is discussing with publishers and newsprint producers the possibility of increasing the proportion of recycled paper used in newspapers and magazines.

The weight and proportion of recycled copper and lead consumed in manufacture fell slightly in 1989 after increases in recent years. The weight and proportion of aluminium and zinc have both fallen since 1983. The fall in recycled aluminium has been particularly sharp and recycled aluminium accounted for only 9 per cent of consumption in 1989 compared with 20 per cent in 1983. In 1988 approximately 114,000 tonnes of aluminium, 125,000 tonnes of copper, 17,000 tonnes of lead and 25,000 tonnes of zinc scrap were exported.

The Aluminium Can Recycling Association now has a network of over 250 merchants willing to purchase used aluminium beverage cans and a new aluminium recycling plant is being built at Warrington with 50,000 tonnes per annum capacity. It is reported that there will not be enough indigenous material to service this plant and that it will depend on imported material.

Recycled glass (cullet) is important in the glass-making process. The British Glass Manufacturers Confederation reported a continuing increase in the amount of glass reclaimed from all sources, including industry. The amount of glass recycled doubled between 1984 and 1989 from 155,000 tonnes to 310,000 tonnes. In 1989 recycled glass accounted for 18 per cent of total glass consumed in manufacture.

The number of local authorities participating in the British Glass Manufacturers Confederation bottle bank scheme in Great Britain rose from 119 in 1980 to 431 in 1989 and the number of sites increased 10-fold over the same period from 433 to 4,330 (Figure 5.4). Table 5.8 shows that by the end of the first quarter of 1990 the number of bottle bank sites had risen to over 4,600 and that the amount of glass recovered in the financial year 1989/90 amounted to over 130,000 tonnes. Final 1990 figures have still to be confirmed but the number of bottle banks is known to have passed 5,000. In Northern Ireland glass collection figures continue to rise from the 500 tonnes recovered in 1988 when bottle banks were introduced to 1,200 tonnes in 1989/90. The recovery rate per capita was highest in Scotland and lowest in Northern Ireland.

5.8 Bottle bank sites and glass collected: 1989/90

United Kingdom

	Number of sites		Tonnage collected	Kilograms/ head
	Public	Commercial		
England	3,894	949	114,300	2.4
Wales[1]	137	10	2,000	1.8
Scotland	580	2,110	15,200	2.9
N. Ireland	37	24	1,200	0.8
Total	4,648	3,093	132,700	2.3

Source: *British Glass Manufacturers Confederation; Department of the Environment (N Ireland)*

[1] Figures for tonnage collected provided by only two-thirds of participating councils: estimate of amount collected per head based on reporting councils only.

Figure 5.4 Bottle bank scheme: number of sites and participating district councils in Great Britain

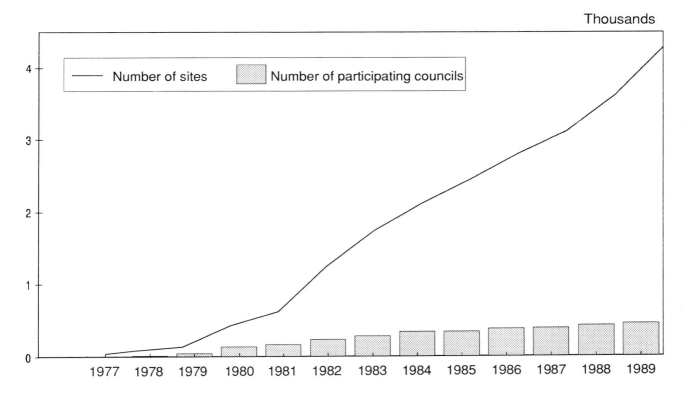

[1] *Hazardous Waste Management: an Overview. First Report*, The HazardousWaste Inspectorate, HMSO, 1984.
[2] *Hazardous Waste Management: "... Ramshackle & Antediluvian?" Second Report*, The Hazardous Waste Inspectorate, HMSO, 1986.
[3] *The Hazardous Waste Inspectorate: Third Report*, The Hazardous Waste Inspectorate, HMSO, 1988.
[4] *Second Annual Report, 1989-90*, Her Majesty's Inspectorate of Pollution, HMSO, 1990.
[5] *This Common Inheritance: Britain's Environmental Strategy*, Environment White Paper, HMSO, 1990.

Chapter 6   Land and nature conservation

Designated and protected areas

The primary purpose of the UK system for designating areas is to identify and protect the finest landscapes and the most important scientific sites throughout the country. Figure 6.1 shows the main protected areas and *national trails*. A new national trail, the Thames Path, was approved by the Secretary of State for the Environment in September 1985 and is currently being created.

The ten *National Parks* in England and Wales were designated in the 1950s by the National Parks Commission, the Countryside Commission's predecessor, to safeguard and secure public access to the most beautiful wilderness areas. They are exceptionally fine stretches of relatively wild countryside, such as the larger unspoilt areas of mountain, moor, heath and some of the coast. The National Parks cover 9 per cent of the total area of England and Wales and are mostly in private ownership. Planning functions are exercised by National Park Committees or Boards.

Although *The Broads* and the *New Forest* do not have National Park status, both areas have been given protection because of their unique features. The scenery of the Broads has long been acknowledged to be of national park quality, and in 1978 in recognition of the national importance of this area for landscape, nature conservation and recreation the eight local authorities concerned established the Broads Authority and delegated to it responsibility for planning, development control, recreation and amenity provision. The authority, however, did not have any responsibility for management of the water space. In April 1989 a new Broads Authority was established. This special statutory body took over the functions of the non-statutory Broads authority and has also powers to control navigation over most of the Broads river system. The area now has a status equivalent to a national park but with controls tailored to suit its special circumstances. The New Forest is an unenclosed area of woodland, heath and bog, once a Royal Forest, but now managed by the Forestry Commission who represent the rights of the Crown. Commoners have carefully defined rights over the area.

Thirty-eight *Areas of Outstanding Natural Beauty* (AONBs) have been designated by the Countryside Commission or its predecessor, the National Parks Commission, to protect other outstanding landscapes which are generally less suitable for large numbers of visitors. They cover 13 per cent of the total area in

6.1 Designated areas[1] at 31 March 1990: by region[2]

United Kingdom

Region	National Parks		Areas of Outstanding Natural Beauty[3]		Defined Heritage Coasts
	Area (sq km)	Percentage of total area in region	Area (sq km)	Percentage of total area in region	Length (km)
North	3,608	23	2,262	15	111
Yorkshire and Humberside	3,168	21	303	2	80
East Midlands	785	5	531	3	-
East Anglia	-	-	888	7	119
South East	-	-	6,395	23	73
South West	1,631	7	6,326	27	576
West Midlands	205	2	1,005	8	-
North West	155	2	782	11	-
England	9,550	7	18,492	14	959
Wales	4,098	20	832	4	501
England and Wales	13,648	9	19,324	13	1,460
Scotland	-	-	10,173	13	-
Northern Ireland	-	-	2,824	20	-

[1] Some areas may be in more than one category (see Figure 6.1).
[2] Estimated.
[3] National Scenic Areas in Scotland.

Source: *Countryside Commission, Countryside Commission for Scotland, Department of the Environment for Northern Ireland*

Figure 6.1 Protected areas in the United Kingdom

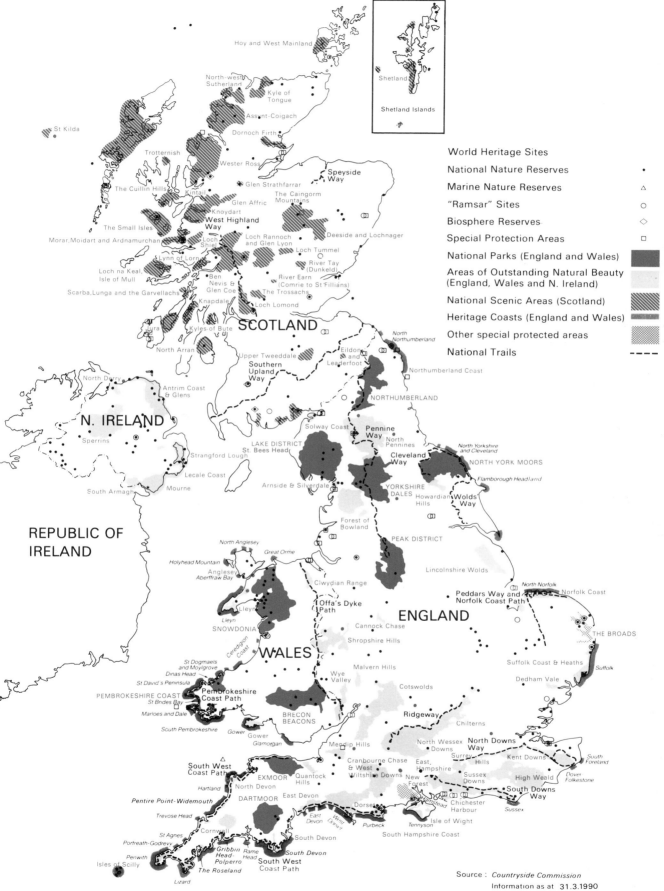

World Heritage Sites
National Nature Reserves •
Marine Nature Reserves △
"Ramsar" Sites ○
Biosphere Reserves ◇
Special Protection Areas ▢
National Parks (England and Wales)
Areas of Outstanding Natural Beauty (England, Wales and N. Ireland)
National Scenic Areas (Scotland)
Heritage Coasts (England and Wales)
Other special protected areas
National Trails - - - -

Source : *Countryside Commission*
Information as at 31.3.1990

England and Wales. AONBs are mostly in private ownership and include areas representing a wide range of nationally significant landscape including some lowland areas. The nine AONBs in Northern Ireland have been designated by the Department of the Environment for Northern Ireland, and cover about 20 per cent of the total area. A wide range of landscapes is covered by the designation, including fine stretches of relatively wild countryside. The AONBs are being reviewed and redesignated under the Nature Conservation and Amenity Lands (NI) Order 1985; to date three have been redesignated.

The 40 *National Scenic Areas* in Scotland cover 13 per cent of the total area and are areas of outstanding value and beauty in a national context which merit special protection measures. They were identified by the Countryside Commission for Scotland in 1978 and designated by the Secretary of State for Scotland. The land is mostly in private ownership. Planning authorities are responsible for development control in these areas in conjunction with the Commission, and for the introduction of suitable landscape conservation policies in structure and local plans. Also in Scotland four Regional Parks covering 718 sq km have been designated by Regional Councils and confirmed by the Secretary of State for Scotland.

Forty-three lengths of fine unspoilt coastline in England and Wales - 33 per cent of the total coastline of those countries - have been defined as *Heritage Coasts* by local authorities and the Countryside Commission. While the greater part of the Heritage Coasts is in private ownership, a substantial length is owned by the National Trust. In Scotland *preferred conservation zones* have been defined with a total length of 3,038 km covering nearly 80 per cent of Scotland's mainland coastline. Appropriate safeguards for them are indicated in local plans.

Table 6.1 shows the area of National Parks, AONBs, National Scenic Areas, and defined Heritage Coasts at 31 March 1990 by region. The Commission is currently working towards the designation of the Blackdown Hills and the Nidderdale Moors as AONBs and two proposed Heritage Coasts, the North Devon and Exmoor Heritage Coasts remain to be defined. In addition to these designated areas, which are established to reflect broader environmental aims, there are other categories of statutory protected area established for the protection of natural conservation features; the main ones are shown in Table 6.2.

National Nature Reserves (NNRs) are established to protect, through appropriate control and management, the most important areas of natural or semi-natural vegetation with their characteristic flora, fauna and environmental conditions, and notable geological and physiographic features. Under the National Parks and Access to the Countryside Act 1949 and the Wildlife and Countryside Act 1981, the Nature Conservancy

6.2 Statutory protected areas at 31 March 1990

United Kingdom

Status[1]	Number	Area (sq km)
National Nature Reserves	279	1,707
Local Nature Reserves[2]	197	167
Sites of Special Scientific Interest (SSSIs)[2]	5,435	17,138
- notified under 1981 Act	5,264	16,186
- subject to S15 management agreements	(a)	717
Areas of Scientific Interest[3]	47	740
Areas of Special Scientific Interest[3]	24	66
Special Protection Areas	33	1,273
Biosphere Reserves	13	443
"Ramsar" Wetland Sites	40	1,665
Environmentally Sensitive Areas	19	7,856

Source: *Nature Conservancy Council, Department of the Environment for Northern Ireland, Ministry of Agriculture, Fisheries and Food*

[1] Some areas may be included in more than one category. For example, in Great Britain NNRs, SPAs, Biosphere Reserves and Ramsar sites are all SSSIs (see also Figure 6.1).
[2] Great Britain only.
[3] Northern Ireland only.
(a) 1,759 agreements.

and its successor the Nature Conservancy Council (NCC) has the responsibility for establishing, managing and maintaining National Nature Reserves in Great Britain. These may be owned or leased by the NCC; or managed by the NCC through a Nature Reserve Agreement under section 16 of the 1949 Act; or managed by an approved voluntary body under section 35 of the Wildlife and Countryside Act 1981. There were 235 NNRs covering 1,663 sq km in Great Britain at 31 March 1990 and a further 44 NNRs in Northern Ireland covering 44 sq km. NNRs are protected through byelaws. The 44 NNRs in Northern Ireland have been designated by the Conservation Service of the Department of the Environment in Northern Ireland and are either owned or leased by the Department or managed in agreement with the owner. The service also manages eight country parks which are statutory protected areas. Similar powers relating to management agreements were granted to local authorities in Scotland and to the Countryside Commission for Scotland by the Countryside (Scotland) Act 1981.

Two statutory *Marine Nature Reserves* (MNRs) have been declared, Lundy in 1986 and Skomer in 1990. The purpose of marine nature reserves is both to conserve, and give opportunities for the study and research of, marine flora and fauna and geological and physiographic features of special interest. Activities within MNRs are regulated by a combination of NCC bylaws, local bylaws and a voluntary code of conduct. There are proposals for several more MNRs.

Local authorities have powers to establish *Local Nature Reserves* (LNRs), after consulting the NCC, under section 21 of the National Parks and Access to the Countryside Act 1949. The LNR sites include several SSSIs.

There are now 5,400 *Sites of Special Scientific Interest* (SSSIs) in Great Britain covering over 17,100 sq km. Under section 23 of the National Parks and Access to the Countryside Act 1949 the NCC, and its predecessor the Nature Conservancy, had a duty to notify local planning authorities of any area they considered to be of special interest by virtue of its flora, fauna, or geological or physiographic features. Under the Town and Country Planning and General Development Order 1950, now the 1988 Order, planning authorities are required to consult with the NCC before granting permission for developments on SSSIs. The Wildlife and Countryside Act 1981, as amended by the Wildlife and Countryside (Amendment) Act 1985, extended the protection afforded to SSSIs. The NCC is required to notify every owner and occupier of an SSSI of its special interest and operations that could damage that interest. Owners and occupiers are required to give notice to the NCC before carrying out any such operation and the operation may not then be undertaken for four months without the agreement of the NCC. This period is to allow the NCC to consider the likely effects of the operation and, if required, discuss how the proposal may be modified to protect the special interest. This requirement does not apply to operations authorised by planning permission or to emergency operations. If necessary, the NCC may negotiate for a management agreement to protect the site under section 15 of the Countryside Act 1968 or a Nature Reserve Agreement. On areas of national or international importance, the Secretary of State may make an order under section 29 of the 1981 Act to provide up to 12 months (or longer by agreement) for negotiations between the NCC and the owner or occupier. Table 6.3 shows the increase since 1981 in the areas notified under the 1981 Act and in those covered by section 15 management agreements. The latter has increased by a factor of 27 and now 4 per cent of the total area of SSSIs is subject to such agreements.

Since the Wildlife and Countryside Act 1981 habitat loss has declined from an estimated 6 per cent to 1 per cent. Table 6.4 shows that in 86 per cent of SSSIs reported as damaged in 1989/90, the damage was considered short-term from which the special interest could recover. The area of sites damaged was far exceeded by the additional area added to the SSSI network in that year. Table 6.4 shows that the most common cause of short-term damage in 1989/90 was agricultural activity. All the cases of damage expected to result in the denotification of part or all of the SSSI were caused in part by activities given planning permission.

6.3 Sites of Special Scientific Interest:[1] by type

Great Britain   Area (sq km)

	All SSSIs	Notified under 1981 Act	Subject to S15 Management agreement
1981	13,614	-	26
1982	13,669	8	30
1983	13,770	472	31
1984	13,884	2,298	46
1985	14,338	4,155	104
1986	14,309	6,902	167
1987	15,175	10,220	261
1988	16,268	11,902	384
1989	16,408	14,143	869
1990	17,138	16,186	717

Source: *Nature Conservancy Council*

[1] At 31 March of each year.

Areas of Scientific Interest (ASIs) in Northern Ireland are being replaced by Areas of Special Scientific Interest (ASSIs) and will be protected by legislation similar to that for SSSIs in Great Britain. Twenty-four ASSIs have now been designated covering a total area of 66 sq km.

The remaining categories of protected areas in Table 6.2 are the result of UK involvement with international conservation initiatives:

Special Protection Areas (SPAs) are established by member states of the EC to conserve bird species listed under Directive 79/409.

Biosphere Reserves were devised by UNESCO and are of particular value as standards for the measurement of long-term changes in the biosphere as a whole. They are protected areas of land and coastal environment representing significant examples of biomes throughout the world.

"Ramsar" Wetland Sites are designated in accordance with the provisions of the convention on Wetlands of International Importance, especially as waterfowl habitats, signed at Ramsar, Iran in 1971.

Environmentally Sensitive Areas (ESAs), designated under EC Regulation 797/85, are areas of outstanding beauty and historic wildlife interest where traditional farming is important for the protection of the environment. Farmers are encouraged to adopt or continue farming practices which will achieve conservation as well as agricultural objectives in return for annual incentive payments. Each farmer agrees to keep to conditions designed to protect natural habitats, particularly on grazing land and wet meadows, and to maintain landscape and archaeological features.

6.4 Sites of Special Scientific Interest: damage to existing and proposed sites: 1989/90

Great Britain

Site status	Short-term damage[1]	Long-term damage[2]	Partial or full loss[3]	Total
SSSIs notified or renotified under the 1981 Act	261	35	4	300
SSSIs awaiting renotification (1949 Act sites)	9	1	-	10
Proposed SSSIs	8	3	3	14
Total	278	39	7	324
Damage[4] caused by:				
Agricultural activities	129	18	2	149
Forestry activities	8	1	-	9
Activities given planning permission	8	10	7	25
Activities of statutory undertakers and other public bodies not included above	22	9	-	31
Recreational activities	53	5	-	58
Miscellaneous activities[5]	81	9	-	90
Insufficient management	68	-	-	68

[1] Damage from which the special interest could recover.
[2] Damage causing a lasting reduction in the special interest.
[3] Damage which will result in denotification of part or the whole SSSI.
[4] Some cases of damage caused by more than one activity; hence the sum by activity is greater than the total number of sites damaged.
[5] Including pollution, unauthorised tipping and burning.

Source: *Nature Conservancy Council*

The Wildlife and Countryside Act 1981 gave local planning authorities in England and Wales a power to make management agreements to conserve the natural beauty or amenity of the countryside. To date this has mainly been used for areas in National Parks, though some agreements have been made by local authorities elsewhere.

There are 15 separate *Green Belts* varying in size from 4,800 sq km around London to just 7 sq km at Burton-

6.5 Green belt areas: by region

England

Region	Green belt	Area (sq km)	
		1979	1989
Northern	Tyne and Wear	400	504
Yorkshire & Humberside	South & West Yorkshire	1,263	2,232
	York	-	248
East Midlands	Burton & Swadlincote	-	7
	Nottingham/Derby	-	608
Eastern	Cambridge	17	108
South East	London	3,068	4,847
	SW Hampshire/SE Dorset	-	856
	Oxford	251	349
South West	Avon	628	743
	Gloucester/Cheltenham	57	75
West Midlands	West Midlands	1,425	2,092
	Stoke-on-Trent	-	366
North West	Greater Manchester, Central Lancs[1]	15	2,451
England		7,125	15,485

[1] Including Lancaster and Fylde, Merseyside, Wirral; Lancaster and Fylde is a separate Green Belt.

Source: *Department of the Environment*

on-Trent and in total covering 15.5 thousand sq km, about 12 per cent of England (see Table 6.5). Green belts are established through development plans to check the unrestricted sprawl of large built-up areas; to safeguard the surrounding countryside from futher encroachment; to prevent neighbouring towns from merging into one another; to preserve the special character of historic towns; and to assist in urban regeneration. The area of Green Belts in England more than doubled between 1979 and 1989.

6.6 Non-statutory protected areas[1] at 31 March 1990: by protecting body

United Kingdom

Protecting body	Number	Area (sq km)
Royal Society for the Protection of Birds	118	747
Royal Society for Nature Conservation and Local Nature Conservation Trusts	2,000	674
National Trust[2]	88	129
Woodland Trust	414	53
Wildfowl and Wetlands Trust	9	17
Field Studies Council	2	14

Source: *Royal Society for the Protection of Birds, Royal Society for Nature Conservation, National Trust, Woodland Trust, Wildfowl and Wetlands Trust, Field Studies Council*

[1] Some areas may be included in more than one category and there is also overlap with the areas shown in Tables 6.1-6.3.
[2] Properties specifically managed as nature reserves.

Many agreements for managing land for nature conservation are non-statutory and conservation measures are not limited to designated areas. Many protected areas are owned or managed by voluntary bodies such as the Royal Society for the Protection of Birds (RSPB), Royal Society for Nature Conservation and the local Nature Conservation Trusts, Scottish Wildlife Trust, Wildfowl and Wetlands Trust, Woodland Trust, Field Studies Council and the National Trust. Some of these areas are SSSIs or include some NNRs. Table 6.6 shows the numbers and areas of sites owned or managed by some of these organisations. Also, 12 Forest Parks have been established and are managed by the Forestry Commission in Great Britain. These are large areas of forest, often with fine areas of mountain and other open country, where special provision has been made for public access and enjoyment.

Public interest in the environment has grown during the 1980s and it is now regarded as one of the most important issues the government should be dealing with.[1] The membership of selected voluntary conservation organisations is given Table 6.7. Between 1981 and 1989, membership of some smaller, newly established organisations, such as Friends of the Earth, the Woodland Trust and the Worldwide Fund for Nature, increased very rapidly indeed. The National Trust and the RSPB, which are larger well-established organisations, showed substantial increases of around 75 per cent.

People visit the countryside for a variety of reasons. A recent survey by the Countryside Commission of countryside recreation showed that, in 1989, 18 per cent of trips were to go on long walks, 17 per cent were for drives, outings and picnics, 13 per cent were to visit the coast (excluding resorts), 12 per cent were to visit historic houses, country and wildlife parks and nature

6.7 Membership of selected voluntary environmental organisations

United Kingdom   Thousands

Organisations	1971	1981	1987	1988	1989
Civic Trust[1]	214	..	240	249	293
Conservation Trust[2]	6	5	4	3[3]	3
Council for the Protection of Rural England	21	29	32	32	40
Friends of the Earth[4]	1	18	55	65	140
National Trust	278	1,046	1,545	1,634	1,865
National Trust for Scotland	37	110	160	179	197
Ramblers' Association	22	37	57	65	75
Royal Society for Nature Conservation[5]	64	143	184	204	210
Royal Society for the Protection of Birds[6]	98	441	561	540	771
Woodland Trust	..	20	58	62	66
Worldwide Fund for Nature	12	60	124	147	200

[1] Members of local amenity societies registered with the Civic Trust.
[2] In September 1987 the Conservation Society was absorbed by the Conservation Trust.
[3] 3,000 individual members plus about 500 organisations including schools and colleges.
[4] England and Wales only; Friends of the Earth (Scotland) is a separate organisation founded in 1978.
[5] Does not include members in junior organisation, WATCH, or clubs affiliated to WATCH.
[6] Includes members of the Young Ornothologists' Club.

Source: *Social Trends 1990*

reserves, 10 per cent were to visit friends and relatives and the remaining 30 per cent were mainly to take part or watch sporting and similar recreational activities. Membership of the Ramblers Association doubled between 1981 and 1989 and rights of way are the single most important means by which the public can enjoy the countryside. In 1988 The Countryside Commisssion carried out a survey[2] of the condition of rights of way in England and Wales. Seventy-six per cent of the 225,000 km of the rights of way network in England and Wales are footpaths and 20 per cent are bridleways. However only one-third of rights of way were signposted where they left the metalled road and a further third were both unsignposted and not easy to find. Walkers found 15 per cent of footpath links unusable with the most frequently encountered obstacles being crops, ploughed surfaces, fences, hedges and walls. The Countryside Commission has set the year 2000 as the target date by which the network should be legally defined, properly maintained and well-publicised.

Land cover

Information is regularly collected about land on agricultural holdings by the Ministry of Agriculture Fisheries and Food (MAFF) in the Agricultural Census, and about forestry and woodlands by the Forestry Commission in the Forestry Census. Table 6.8 shows the distribution of agricultural and forestry land use in 1989 for all countries in the UK.

Information on other land cover and uses is not so readily available. Following concern over the lack of reliable and consistent information about changes in land cover, a survey to monitor landscape change (MLC) was jointly commissioned by the Department of the Environment (DOE) and the Countryside Commission.[3] Air photography from around 1947, 1969 and 1980 was used to interpret and measure the extent of features at a sample of sites throughout England and Wales. Details and results were presented in Digest no 9.

Table 6.9 shows the distribution of broad categories of landscape features from the survey together with Agricultural and Forestry Census figures for the same dates. There are differences between the MLC survey and Census figures because of differences in methodology and classifications and because of the large standard errors for some classes in the MLC survey. Comparisons with Agricultural Census data are virtually impossible because of definitional differences. For example, land classified as rough grazing on agricultural holdings in the Agricultural Census was sometimes classified as semi-natural vegetation in the MLC survey. The main advantages of the MLC survey were that it covered all types of land cover, used consistent definitions and methodology for the three years and provided information about changes between land cover types. The MLC data show an increase in woodland, a small decrease in farmed land and a large decrease in semi-natural vegetation.

DOE also collects information about changes in land use in England drawing on the work of Ordnance Survey.[4] Table 6.10 shows changes between main land use categories recorded in 1989. Of the 260 sq km recorded as having a change of use just over one-third constituted a change from one rural use to another and just under one-third a change from one urban use to another. The remaining third were mainly changes from rural to urban uses. Under the Ordnance Survey map revision policy, changes involving physical development tend to be recorded relatively sooner than changes between other uses (for example, between agriculture and forestry), some of which may not be

6.8 Land: by agricultural and other uses: 1989

United Kingdom

Country	Percentage of country					Area (sq km)	
	Agricultural land			Forest and woodland[2]	Urban land and land not otherwise specified[3]	Total land (= 100%)	Inland water[4]
	Crops and fallow	Grass and rough grazing	Other[1]				
England	34	39	1	9	17	129,670	800
Wales	4	76	1	14	5	20,640	130
Scotland	8	66	1	15	10	77,080	1,700
Northern Ireland	5	73	2	6	14	13,480	640
United Kingdom	22	53	1	11	13	240,870	3,280

[1] Land on agricultural holdings comprising farm roads, yards, buildings, gardens, ponds, derelict land, etc.
[2] All forest land and private woodlands including woodland on agricultural holdings.
[3] Land which is neither agricultural nor wooded, ie, built-up areas, recreation areas etc.
[4] 1986 data - 1989 data not available.

Source: *Ministry of Agriculture, Fisheries and Food; Ordnance Survey*

6.9 Land cover and land use: 1947, 1969 and 1980

England and Wales

Percentage cover

	Monitoring landscape change survey[1]						Forestry Census	Agricultural Census
	Woodland	Semi-natural vegetation[2]	Farmed land[3]	Water and wetlands[4]	Other land[5]	Total	Forest and woodland[6]	Agricultural land[7]
1947	7.0	12.6	72.7	1.3	6.4	100.0	6.3	80.5
1969	7.9	10.1	72.1	1.1	8.8	100.0	7.2	78.5
1980	7.9	9.2	71.8	1.1	9.9	100.0	7.9	77.6

[1] Photographs were interpreted for a range of dates around those shown. Relative standard errors are approximately: woodland (7%), semi-natural vegetation (10%), farmed land (1.5%), water/wetland (17%), other land (5%).
[2] Includes heath, bracken, gorse, heather and grassland not included under farmed land.
[3] Cultivated land, and improved, neglected and rough pasture.
[4] Coastal and inland waters, freshwater marsh, salt marsh and peat bog.
[5] Includes built-up land, urban open space, major transport routes, bare rock, sand, shingle, mineral works and derelict land. Urban land can be defined in many ways. For example, Professor Best estimated that urban land defined as covering all land under

Source: *Department of the Environment; Forestry Commission; Ministry of Agriculture, Fisheries and Food*

urban uses covered the following proportion of England and Wales: 6.7% in 1930, 8.8% in 1950, 10.8% in 1970 and 11.6% in 1980. There is evidence to suggest the MLC survey underestimated urban land.
[6] All forest land and woodland including woodland on agricultural holdings.
[7] All agricultural land including crops, fallow, grasses, rough grazing, woodland and other land on farms, eg farm roads, yards, buildings, ponds, etc.

recorded for some years. For this reason the relative picture for recorded rural change may not be fully representative of the pattern and extent of change occurring in 1989.

The MLC survey showed over the period 1947-80 that losses of farmed land to built-up land were mainly from improved grassland; gains to farmed land were mainly from semi-natural vegetation and broadleaved

6.10 Changes in land use: recorded during 1989[1]

England

Area (sq km)

Previous use	New use								All uses
	Rural				Urban				
	Agriculture	Forestry, open land[2] and water	Other rural[3]	Total rural	Residential	Non-residential[4]	Vacant	Total urban	
Rural									
Agriculture	20.0	13.8	20.9	54.7	31.4	29.2	1.2	61.8	116.5
Forestry, open land[2] and water	13.2	8.5	6.6	28.4	3.0	3.9	0.5	7.4	35.8
Other rural[3]	6.7	5.1	3.6	16.8	3.1	3.4	1.6	8.1	24.8
Total	39.9	27.4	32.6	99.9	37.5	36.5	3.3	77.2	177.1
Urban									
Residential	0.2	0.1	0.1	0.5	13.8	1.8	2.0	17.7	18.2
Non-residential[4]	1.6	0.6	0.4	2.7	6.8	5.1	8.1	31.2	33.9
Vacant	1.1	1.2	1.7	4.0	15.6	12.4	0.3	28.3	32.2
Total	3.0	2.0	2.2	7.2	36.2	30.6	10.3	77.1	84.3
All uses	42.9	29.3	34.8	107.0	73.7	67.1	13.6	154.4	261.4
Net changes in use (- indicates reduction)	-73.6	-6.5	10.0	-70.1	55.6	33.2	-18.6	70.1	

[1] The information relates only to map changes recorded by Ordnance surveyors in 1989. Many of these changes will have occurred prior to 1989 and some, particularly those involving rural uses, might have occurred many years before being recorded by Ordnance surveyors.
[2] Open land includes rough grassland, bracken, natural and semi-natural land.
[3] Minerals, landfill, outdoor recreation and defence.
[4] Transport, utilities, industry, commerce, community services.

Source: *Department of the Environment*

6.11 Woodlands: use of broadleaves for new planting and restocking

Great Britain *Percentage*

	1983/4	1984/5	1985/6	1986/7	1987/8	1988/9	1989/90
Private Woodland							
Conifer	91	91	90	87	83	84	60
Broadleaved	9	9	10	13	17	16	40
Forestry Commission							
Conifer	98	98	97	92	91	92	91
Broadleaved	2	2	3	8	9	8	9

Source: *Forestry Commission*

woodland; cultivated land increased mainly at the expense of improved grassland; and most new coniferous woodlands were previously broadleaved woodland or upland grass.

In 1985 the Government announced a new policy in relation to the maintenance and enhancement of broadleaved woodlands for timber production, landscape, recreation and nature conservation. The measures to be taken to achieve these policy aims included the introduction in 1985 of a Broadleaved Woodland Grant Scheme. The scheme was designed to encourage the rehabilitation of existing broadleaved woodlands, by natural regeneration or planting, and the establishment of new ones. These aims continued under the Woodland Grant Scheme which succeeded the Broadleaved Woodland Grant Scheme in 1988. Table 6.11 shows trends in the use of broadleaves for new planting and restocking by the Forestry Commission and in private woodlands before and after the announcement of the policy. These figures show that after 1985 there was a switch to planting broadleaves in both types of woodland and a major switch to broadleaves in 1989-90 in private woodlands.

Tree felling in Great Britain is controlled under the felling licensing provisions of the Forestry Act 1967. With certain exceptions, it is an offence to fell trees without first having obtained a felling licence from the Forestry Commission. Tree preservation orders (TPOs) are designed to protect individual trees and woodland

from wilful damage or destruction, uprooting, lopping, topping or felling without the consent of the local planning authority. Details of TPO confirmations and applications to lop, top, fell, etc over the period 1978-87 are given in Statistical Bulletin (91)1.

The linear features study in the MLC survey used a sample which was a subset of the area features sample. Changes in the distribution of linear features over the period 1947-85 are shown in Table 6.12. Hedgerows are by far the most important linear feature in terms of length, and the relative change in their length has been much greater than for other features. There was a substantial loss of hedgerows of about 4,000-5,000 km a year over the period. Other surveys have also covered hedgerow loss. Differences in survey methodology make comparisons difficult but all sources show that although new hedges have been planted there was a net loss of hedgerows in the early 1980s.

The MLC results provided the first objective data set for England and Wales on countryside change since the late 1940s. However they also demonstrated that change statistics alone, without adequate assessment of the quality of the features that have changed, fail to state the significance of change for wildlife habitat, landscape quality or management requirements. The 1990 Countryside Survey, funded mainly by the DOE and the Natural Environment Research Council (NERC), is based on detailed ground survey in order to provide a better guide of policy implications. This

6.12 Survey to monitor landscape change: length[1] of linear features: 1947, 1969, 1980 and 1985

England and Wales Thousand kilometres

	Hedgerows	Fences	Banks	Open ditches	Walls	Woodland fringe
1947[2]	796	185	151	122	117	241
1969[2]	703	193	140	116	114	241
1980[2]	653	199	132	111	111	243
1985	621	210	128	112	108	243

[1] Relative standard errors are approximately: fences (5%), hedgerows and woodland fringe (8%), banks (18%), walls (26%), open ditches (29%).

[2] Photographs were interpreted for a range of dates around this year.

Source: *Monitoring Landscape Change. Department of the Environment and Countryside Commission*

survey,carried out by the Institute of Terrestrial Ecology (ITE), has mapped land cover and vegetation species at over 500 one-kilometre square sites throughout Great Britain. Results available in 1992 will enable comparisons with those from similar ITE surveys in 1978 and 1984 and also with those from the MLC survey. Information will also be available for each site in the 1990 survey on freshwater invertebrates and soil composition. Funded by the Department of Trade and Industry, ITE are also producing a digital map of land cover from satellite remote sensing, providing the ability to explore the role of landscape pattern in the ecological process. These results should be available in 1992. In separate exercises, land cover maps for Scotland and the National Parks in England and Wales are being produced following recent comprehensive air photo surveys of these areas by the Scottish Office and the Countryside Commission respectively.

Derelict land and mineral workings

Derelict land has been a major problem in this country for many years. It is a wasted resource and affects the attractiveness of surrounding land. Grants are available to local authorities to help remove dereliction and encourage new uses for the land. There is no statutory definition of derelict land, but for grant purposes land is defined as being derelict if it is so damaged by industrial or other development that it is incapable of beneficial use without treatment.

The most recent survey of derelict land[5] in England, was carried out in 1988 by local authorities on behalf of the DOE. Earlier surveys were carried out in 1974 and 1982. The main results of the three surveys are summarised in Table 6.13. In 1988, 405 sq km of land were derelict (0.3 per cent of the total area of the country), of which 316 sq km (78 per cent) were considered to justify reclamation. Land not justifying reclamation includes unobtrusive sites in remote rural areas, and sites that are impractical to reclaim for technical or financial reasons. During 1982-88, 140 sq km of land were reclaimed compared with 170 sq km during 1974-82. In 1988 derelict spoil heaps were the most extensive type of derelict land accounting for nearly 30 per cent of the total. There was a decrease in all types of dereliction between 1974 and 1988 except for the 'other forms of dereliction' category (mainly general industrial dereliction).

In 1988 the three most northerly regions (North West, North and Yorkshire and Humberside) contained over half the derelict land. The North West contained the largest area of derelict land, almost all of it thought to justify reclamation, and was the region with the greatest proportion of its total area (1.2 per cent) classified as derelict. Over a quarter of all derelict land reclaimed between 1974 and 1988 was in this region. The amount of derelict land decreased in all regions between 1982 and 1988 except Yorkshire and Humberside where it increased by over 10 per cent.

Of the 140 sq km of derelict land reclaimed between 1982 and 1988, 126 sq km were in use by 1 April 1988. Forty-one per cent of this land was being used for public open space and sport and recreation, 22 per cent for

6.13 Derelict land: by type of dereliction and by region: at 1 April 1974, 1982 and 1988

England   Sq km

	Areas			Area justifying reclamation				Land reclaimed	
	1974	1982	1988	1974	1982	1988	% in 1988	1974-82	1982-8
Type of dereliction									
Spoil heaps	131	133	119	91	83	75	63	61	32
Excavations and pits	87	86	60	66	64	44	73	28	19
Military dereliction	38	30	26	31	25	21	80	15	14
Derelict railway land	91	82	64	64	60	50	79	20	20
Other forms of dereliction	86	125	136	78	111	127	93	45	54
All derelict land	433	457	405	331	343	316	78	170	140
Region									
North	94	73	59	78	56	47	80	37	25
Yorkshire and Humberside	55	54	61	46	41	50	82	22	21
East Midlands	52	52	44	47	48	43	98	20	16
East Anglia	18	8	6	13	6	3	50	3	2
Greater London (GL)	3	20	14	3	16	12	86	4	5
South East (excl GL)	20	25	18	12	20	14	78	4	6
South West	64	66	58	18	14	14	24	4	7
West Midlands	47	58	56	42	52	49	88	34	23
North West	80	100	88	72	90	85	97	39	37
England	433	457	405	331	343	316	78	170	140

Source: *Derelict Land Surveys in 1974, 1982, 1988, Department of the Environment*

6.14 Mineral workings: area permitted and reclaimed: by mineral type: 1982 and 1988

England

Sq km

Mineral type	Land permitted for mineral working		Land covered by satisfactory reclamation conditions		Land reclaimed satisfactorily	
	1982	1988	1982	1988	1974-82[1]	1982-8[2]
Sand and gravel	321	292	236	226	113	88
Coal	202	197	131	140	100	65
Ironstone	158	145	151	107	10	5
Clay/shale	131	104	74	62	20	12
Limestone	129	123	52	47	7	6
Other minerals	291	281	22	97	18	19
Total	1,231	1,141	665	679	268	195

[1] Excludes Hampshire.
[2] Excludes Oxfordshire and North Yorkshire.

Source: *Survey of Land for Mineral Working in England, 1988, Department of the Environment (in press)*

agriculture and forestry, 27 per cent was in industrial, commercial or residential use, the remaining 10 per cent in miscellaneous use.

About half of all dereliction recorded in the 1988 derelict land survey was a result of former mineral workings. Dereliction has resulted mainly from sites worked under old planning permissions which had no provisions for reclamation. Another less widespread cause of minerals dereliction has been where provisions for reclamation were unfulfilled or reclamation conditions were unenforceable. The 1981 Minerals Act provided for mineral planning authorities to review mineral sites in their area and to update existing permissions to modern standards. Orders modifying permissions can however give rise to a liability for compensation.

Surveys of the land affected by mineral workings are carried out periodically by mineral planning authorities for the DOE. The most recent survey[6] was conducted in 1988, updating earlier surveys of 1982 and 1974. Table 6.14 shows the area of land in 1982 and 1988 with planning permissions for surface mineral workings and for the surface disposal of mineral working deposits (ie, spoil tips). A total area of 1,141 sq kms had planning permission for either surface mineral working or spoil tips, a decrease of over 7 per ecnt since 1982. Permissions for surface mineral workings covered 961 sq km and for spoil tips 180 sq km. Of the total, 58 per cent have been or were being worked. The remainder had not yet been worked. Permissions for sand and gravel extraction were the most extensive, covering 292 sq km, over 25 per cent of the total permitted area for all mineral.

Almost 60 per cent of the total permitted area was covered by reclamation conditions which were considered by mineral planning authorities to be adequate to ensure satisfactory reclamation after the extraction had finished. A further 17 per cent had reclamation conditions which were considered to be unsatisfactory and 22 per cent had no provisions for reclamation. A total of 206 sq km were reclaimed between 1982 and 1988, of which 195 sq km (95 per cent) was reclaimed to a satisfactory standard. Over 80 per cent of the reclamation was a result of reclamation conditions attached to the relevant planning permissions. The remainder was reclaimed either by Derelict Land Grant or as a result of planning permissions for subsequent development on the sites.

Forest health surveys

Within the context of international assessments, forest health is characterised by crown density (the amount of light passing through the crown) and needle or leaf discolouration. Both reflect the general condition of the tree, but neither has an exclusive cause. Besides air pollution, other factors such as frost, drought, wind and nutrient deficiencies can cause discolouration and reductions in crown density, as can a variety of fungi and insect pests. Two surveys of forest health are undertaken annually by the Forestry Commission and the results of these are presented below.

In the main survey, 7,644 trees were assessed in 1990. Figure 6.2 compares tree crown density results between 1987 and 1990. The figures presented for 1987 to 1989 may differ slightly from those published in Digest no 12 due to changes in the numbers of trees sampled. Sitka spruce generally improved in 1990 mainly as a result of increased needle mass following the defoliation caused by the green spruce aphid in 1988-9. The crown densities of oak also improved during 1990 whereas Norway spruce and Scots pine showed little change. Some of the more marked changes in 1990 occurred in beech trees which appear to have suffered most from the summer droughts of 1989 and 1990.

The second survey, as part of a European Community survey, is much smaller with 1,700 trees assessed in 1990. Consequently results from the two surveys are not strictly comparable. Figure 6.3 shows the results

Figure 6.2 Forest health survey: crown density 1987-90

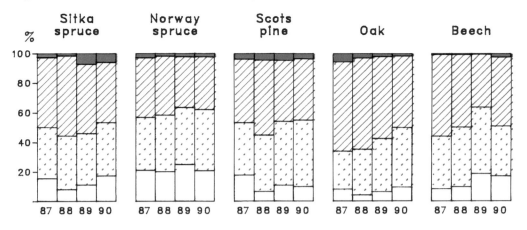

Figure 6.3 EC Grid survey for the UK: crown density 1987-90

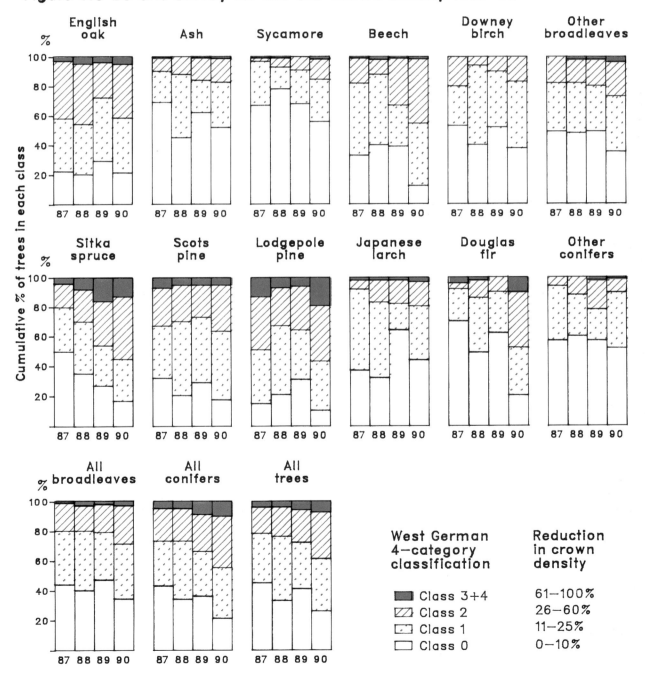

West German 4-category classification	Reduction in crown density
■ Class 3+4	61-100%
▨ Class 2	26-60%
⊡ Class 1	11-25%
□ Class 0	0-10%

Source *Forestry Commission*

covering a number of both broadleaf and conifer species. The results indicate a deterioration in crown densities in 1990 for most species with beech and Douglas fir particularly affected. The differences in the results from the two surveys reflect differences in the sample size, the age distribution of the trees and the spatial distribution of the plots.

Analysis of data from the past few years indicate that the condition of individual trees can vary markedly from one year to the next.[7] Trees with very high levels of defoliation are capable of recovery and the recovery may occur quite rapidly. Consequently, the limitations of overall figures of forest condition should be recognised.

Wildlife protection

The NCC use a classification devised by the International Union for the Conservation of Nature (IUCN) to compile Red Data books on the status of rare and endangered species in the UK. Table 6.15 shows the latest assessment of the minimum number of species thought to be endangered, vulnerable or rare. Many species have become extinct or declined during this century. For example, 14 of the 1,425 species of native seed-bearing plants have become extinct since 1930; the distribution of 117 of the 317 species of plants

considered to be rare in Britain has declined by one-third or more in the same period; insects have suffered substantial falls in their populations; 3 of our 43 species of dragonflies have become extinct since 1953 and a further 12 are vulnerable or declining; and most of our 55 resident species of butterfly have declined significantly since 1950 and one, the large blue, died out in Britain but has since been re-introduced on a small scale.

Within Great Britain the 1981 Wildlife and Countryside Act provides specific protection for a number of species of wild animals, as well as broad protection for wild birds, by making it an offence intentionally to kill, injure or take them, or offer them for sale. Only under licence is it legal to take protected species. Details of wild birds taken under licence between 1988 and 1990 are given in Statistical Bulletin (91)1. Sixty-two of Britain's rarest wild flowers are also protected from intentional destruction, picking, uprooting or sale. Similar legislation applies in Northern Ireland. The NCC, which advises Government on the species of wild animals and plants which should receive protection, is required by the 1981 Act to carry out a review of protected species every five years and advise on additions and deletions to existing lists. The first such review was carried out in 1986 and the NCC advised that protection should be extended to

6.15 Native species at risk: 1990

Great Britain

Species group	Number of native species	Number endangered[1]	Number vulnerable[2]	Number rare[3]
Animals				
Mammals	76	2	12	5
Birds	519	61	2	12
Reptiles	11	2	-	-
Amphibians	6	1	1	-
Freshwater fish[4]	34	3	4	2
Marine fish[5]	310	-	-	-
Dragonflies/damselflies	41	4	2	3
Grasshoppers/crickets	30	3	2	1
Beetles	3,900	142	84	266
Butterflies/moths	2,400	27	22	55
Spiders[6]	622	22	31	26
Crustaceans[6]	2,742	2	1	3
Bryozoans[6]	280	-	-	1
Molluscs[6]	1,044	10	7	13
Worms/leeches[6]	837	-	-	1
Cnidarians[6]	374	1	-	1
Plants				
Seed plants	1,425	51	93	154
Ferns etc[7]	69	3	2	3
Liverworts/mosses	1,000	30	66	118
Stoneworts	30	4	7	4
Lichens	1,500	57	67	190

IUCN categories have been adopted to fit a national context:

[1] IUCN category defining species in danger of extinction and whose survival is unlikely, if the causal factors continue operating.

[2] IUCN category defining species believed likely to move into endangered category in the near future, if the causal factors continue operating.

[3] IUCN category defining species with small world populations that are not at present endangered or vulnerable but are at risk.

Source: *Nature Conservancy Council*

[4] Includes fish which leave the sea to breed in freshwater, eg, salmon.

[5] Includes fish which leave freshwater to breed in the sea, eg, eels.

[6] Numbers at risk relate to terrestrial, freshwater and brackish species only.

[7] Includes clubmosses and horsetails.

about a further 50 species of animals. These included the dormouse, pine marten, wild cat and all previously unprotected species of whales and dolphins in British waters. In addition, the NCC advised that a further 31 species of wild plants needed protection, but that the chequered skipper butterfly be removed from the fully protected list, because of the discovery of more breeding sites than had been previously known, as well as two snails. Changes to the lists of protected species were made in 1988, as shown in Table 6.16 and 22 species of butterfly were given "sale licensing" protection in 1989.

The UK is a party to the Convention on International Trade in Endangered Species of wild fauna and flora (CITES) which aims to conserve wildlife threatened by overexploitation by controlling the import and export of rare animals and plants, and products made from them such as fur coats, ivory and skins. This has been implemented by the EC since 1984. The UK is also a party to the Ramsar convention on Wetlands of International Importance (1971), the Bern Convention on conservation of European and natural habitats (1982) and the Bonn convention on conservation of migratory species (1985).

Wildlife monitoring

National recording schemes for wildlife are organised by several organisations and often receive the help of thousands of amateur and professional naturalists. The DOE commissioned the University of York to investigate and report on data collected and held by public and voluntary organisations. Its report[8] covered hundreds of datasets for species and habitats providing the most comprehensive British inventory of biological monitoring and surveying activity currently available. The research identified about a dozen datasets which could be used to produce wildlife statistics at a national level:

bird monitoring (five schemes)	British Trust for Ornithology
wildfowl counts	Wildfowl and Wetlands Trusts
rare bird breeding success	Rare Breeding Birds Panel
squirrel distribution	Forestry Commission
butterfly monitoring scheme	Institute of Terrestrial Ecology
moths dataset	Rothamsted Insect Survey
otter counts	Vincent Wildlife Trust and Nature Conservancy Council
Red Data Books for plants	Nature Conservancy Council

The researchers are currently examining each dataset with the aim of producing a bulletin of wildlife statistics describing the current abundance and distribution of certain species of British wildlife together with recent changes and trends. Summaries from their examination of counts of wintering populations of wildfowl and waders and of the distribution of red and grey squirrels in Crown Forests are given below together with information recently published on breeding birds and seals.

6.16 Protected native species

Great Britain

Species group	Number of protected species					
	Fully protected			Partially protected		
	1980	1981-7	1988-90	1980	1981-7	1988-90
Plants[1]	21	62	93	a	a	a
Non-marine molluscs	-	3	2	-	-	-
Insects	2	14	16	-	-	22[2]
Spiders	-	2	2	-	-	-
Other invertebrates	-	-	8	-	-	1
Freshwater fish	-	1	3	b	b	b
Amphibians	1	2	2	-	4	4
Reptiles	2	2	c	-	3	3
Birds	d	d	d	34	36	36
Mammals breeding on land[3]	3	e	f	10	19	16
Cetaceans	-	3	g	g	h	-

a The remainder of plants are protected from unauthorised uprooting.
b All fish species breeding in fresh water, as well as eel.
c Four species of terrestrial reptiles as well as all marine turtles which have occurred or may occur in British territorial waters.
d All species which have occurred or may occur in Britain except those specifically listed as partially protected.
e Two species as well as all horseshoe bats and typical bats which have occurred or may occur in Britain.
f Six species as well as all horseshoe bats and typical bats which have occurred or may occur in Britain.

Source: *Nature Conservancy Council*

g All cetaceans (whales, dolphins and porpoises) which have occurred or may occur in GB territorial waters.
h All cetaceans (whales, dolphins and porpoises) which have occurred or may occur in GB territorial waters except bottle-nosed dolphin, common dolphin and harbour porpoise.
[1] Flowering plants, ferns and others.
[2] Added in 1989.
[3] Including seals but excluding cetaceans.

The RSPB have identified[9] over 100 bird species of conservation importance in Britain and collectively summarised the main threats to them. In defining conservation importance a broad view was taken to include species that were rare, very localised or rapidly declining, or for whom Britain has international responsibility. The NCC and RSPB publication *Red Data Birds in Britain,*[10] in a series of detailed texts for 117 species, summarised their conservation importance, legal status, ecology, distribution, threats and conservation action necessary to address those threats. The RSPB are embarking on a programme to prepare Species Action Plans for all these species, giving priority to the 43 most threatened.

Table 6.17 shows NCC estimates of the abundance of 228 species of British breeding birds. The most abundant species, with over three million breeding pairs, are the chaffinch, blackbird, house sparrow, starling, robin, blue tit, wren and pheasant. The table also shows the abundance of British breeding Red Data birds by category. There are three species in the most threatened category which have internationally important numbers breeding in Britain (more than 20 per cent of the population of Western Europe): the roseate tern (about 300 pairs), the golden eagle (about 400 pairs) and the red grouse (over 200,000 pairs).

In 1990 the British Trust for Ornithology (BTO) and the NCC published a comprehensive report on *Population Trends in British Breeding Birds*[11] based mainly on data from the *Common Birds Census* and the *Waterways Bird Survey*. Counting birds in the breeding season is an efficient way of keeping track of the overall population both of resident birds and of those birds only here for the summer because breeding birds are relatively stationary while their eggs are hatching whereas winter flocks for some species tend to be more mobile. The *Common Birds Census* is the main scheme by which populations of common breeding birds are monitored in the UK. It measures changes in bird populations between years by means of annual censuses of target species holding territory on particular plots of land. Between 200 and 300 plots are covered each year and more than 40,000 territories are mapped. The *Waterways Bird Survey* covers rivers, streams and canals and surveys populations of waterside birds using similar methods.

The use of map-based techniques makes it possible to relate changes in bird populations to changes in their habitats. Declining trends in a wide array of species can be associated with the changing pattern of lowland agriculture (eg, lapwing, skylark, green woodpecker); the shift from spring to autumn sowing (eg mistle thrush, linnet); increased use of herbicides (eg, greenfinch); loss of traditional farm buildings (eg, swallow, barn owl); and increased drainage (eg snipe, redshank).

Pollution in rivers is suggested as a cause of the current decline in kingfishers. Increasing trends are also associated with human activities. For example, the spread of great crested grebes associated with new water environments such as gravel pits; of magpies which benefit from tree-planting in towns; and of coal tits and goldcrests which have probably benefitted from conifer plantations. Climate also affects population trends. Several species, especially small birds such as the wren, goldcrest and long-tailed tit, increased in the generally mild winter conditions of the late 1960s to early 1970s but declined in the following period of more frequent cold winters.

6.17 Abundance of British breeding birds: by Red Data status

British Isles

Number of species

Number of pairs[1]	British breeding birds	Red Data bird species breeding in Britain[2]				Threatened mainly by extreme rarity as breeding species in Britain[5,6]	Non-threatened	Total
		Most threatened		Other threatened				
		Internationally important[3] numbers breeding in Britain	Other	Internationally important[3] numbers breeding in Britain	Other[4]			
500,000-5 million	27	-	-	1	-	-	-	1
50,000-500,000	49	1	1	4	-	-	1[3]	7
5,000-50,000	45	-	4	4	3	-	1[3]	12
500-5,000	35	-	8	3	4	-	2	17
50-500	32	2	8	1	8	-	8	27
0-50	40	-	11	-	4	21	2	38
Total	228	3	32	13	19[4]	21[6]	14	102[4,6]

[1] Territories or breeding females are the units used where these are more appropriate to a species' breeding biology.
[2] Where species are listed under more than one category they have been included in the more threatened category.
[3] Internationally important: more than 20% of population of western Europe.
[4] Excludes crane.

Source: *British Trust for Ornithology; Nature Conservancy Council; Royal Society for the Protection of Birds*

[5] None of international importance
[6] Excludes bee-eater.

6.18 Net change in abundance of wildfowl and waders: by Red Data status

British Isles

Net change	Wildfowl (1965/6-1988/9)		Waders (1971-89)
	Red Data status	Other	Red Data status
Reduction	Scaup[1]		
Little change	Pochard[3]* Goldeneye	European white-fronted goose Mallard	Dunlin[1]* Knot[1]* Redshank[1]* Curlew[2]* Sanderling[2]*
Smaller increase	Shelduck[2]* Whooper swan[2]* Wigeon[3]*	Mute swan	Bar-tailed godwit[1]* Ringed plover[2]* Turnstone[3]*
Larger increase	Pintail[1]* Dark-bellied Brent goose[1,2]* Bewick's swan[2]* Teal[2]* Shoveler[2] Gadwall[3]*	Canada goose Goosander Red-breasted merganser Tufted duck	Grey plover[2]* Oystercatcher[2]*

1 Most threatened.
2 Other threatened.
3 Non-threatened.
* Internationally important (more than 20% of population in western Europe) numbers wintering in Britain.

Source: *Wildfowl and Wetlands Trust; British Trust for Ornithology*

The UK provides a major wintering ground for many species of wildfowl and waders. In addition to the UK breeding populations, large numbers of these birds migrate from countries further north and east to winter on UK wetlands. Wildfowl, for example ducks, geese and swans, are found on wetlands throughout the UK. Waders, for example the oyster catcher, dunlin and curlew, are found on estuaries around the UK coast. During winter months wildfowl are counted at up to 2,000 wetland sites by the National Wildfowl Counts organised by the Wildfowl and Wetlands Trust and waders are counted at 112 estuarine sites by the Birds of Estuaries Enquiry organised by the BTO. The most comprehensive counts for both schemes are usually achieved in January to coincide with counts organised for international purposes.

Indices of abundance for both sets of counts are published annually by the Wildfowl and Wetlands Trust[12] and, as shown in Table 6.18, currently cover 19 species of wildfowl and 10 species of waders. Twelve species of wildfowl are included in the Red Data book, nine of whose numbers are internationally important wintering species (more than 20 per cent of the population of western Europe). All wader species listed in this table are included in the Red Data book and all numbers wintering in Britain are internationally important.

Only one of these species, the scaup, has declined in the last couple of decades and all other species have either shown little net change or increased. Most of the UK scaup population used to be found feeding around effluent from sewage works in the Firth of Forth but this population largely disappeared when their food source was removed following modernisation of the works. Reasons for increases in abundance include successful breeding seasons (Bewick's swan, dark-bellied Brent goose, grey plover), increased protection in Great Britain and other countries (dark-bellied Brent goose) and ability to occupy habitats unsuitable for most other wildfowl (Canada goose).

Cold weather is a common cause of fluctuations in annual abundance of wintering wildfowl and waders in this country. Many species increase in numbers during cold winters when they come further south and west than usual to avoid harsh conditions on the continent. Similarly populations of pochard and teal fall in the UK when winters are cold because they leave for Southern Europe. Other birds, for example the redshank and shoveler, are particularly likely to die in cold weather. For birds that breed in or near the Arctic, adverse breeding conditions can cause UK wintering populations to fall.

The monitoring of mammals has a shorter history and is less intensive than for birds. The best data are for squirrels, red deer, otters and sea mammals. Results from surveys of squirrels and seals are presented below.

Two species of squirrel occur in the British Isles: the native red squirrel and the grey squirrel which was introduced from North America from 1876. During this century the red squirrel has declined and is now found mainly in Cumbria, Northumberland and Scotland

Figure 6.4 Distribution of red and grey squirrels: 1973-89

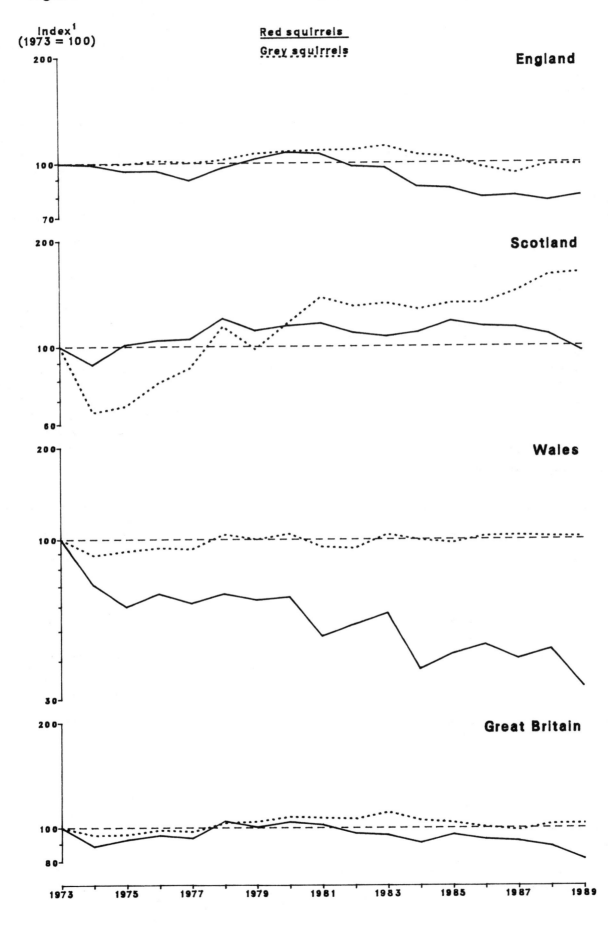

Index[1]
(1973 = 100)

Red squirrels

Grey squirrels

England

Scotland

Wales

Great Britain

[1]Log scale

Source: Department of the Environment using Forestry Commission surveys.

with small numbers in East Anglia, Wales and the Isle of Wight. Grey squirrels are found mainly in England and Wales but are slowly expanding into red squirrel strongholds in the lowland belt of Scotland and Kintyre.

The Forestry Commission carries out an annual survey of squirrels present on Forestry Commission land.[13] Distribution maps on a 10 km National Grid square basis have been compared for pairs of consecutive years and a series of index numbers for each species has been constructed by the University of York. These reflect yearly changes in the numbers of 10 km squares in which squirrels have been recorded as present. It is important to note that the series reflect changes in distribution and not abundance. Also coverage of the survey is restricted to Forestry Commission land. This results in a slightly uneven coverage across Great Britain, with the greatest gaps in low-lying areas of north west and eastern England. Figure 6.4 shows recent trends in the distribution of red and grey squirrels in each country and in Great Britain as a whole. The index numbers have been plotted on a logarithmic scale so that the shape of the series is independent of tthe base year chosen. The figure shows that the distribution of red squirrels has shrunk rapidly in Wales and to a lesser extent in England but remained steady in Scotland. The grey squirrel has spread in Scotland and remained steady in England and Wales where it already has higher coverage and there is virtually no scope for expansion.

Changes in the size and status of stocks of grey seals and common seals in Britain are monitored by the Sea Mammal Research Unit (SMRU) of NERC through a programme of regular survey and assessment to provide information as required by the Conservation of Seals Act 1970. For most of the year grey seals are dispersed widely around and beyond the coasts of Britain and it is impossible to count them. However, during the autumn they breed in colonies on a relatively small number of sites. The pups stay ashore for about three weeks until they are weaned; at this time they can readily be counted from the ground or by using aerial photographs. Each year the SMRU surveys all the major grey seal breeding colonies in Great Britain and estimates the number of pups born in each colony. Smaller colonies are surveyed every three to six years. These survey results are then used to estimate the size of grey seal populations in different parts of the country. Common seal populations are also counted when resources permit, but surveys are concentrated at the time of the moult when the largest numbers are hauled out. Fixed-wing aircraft are used in estuarine areas, but helicopter surveys using a thermal imager allow accurate counts on rocky coasts.

Estimates by SMRU[14] of the size of different seal stocks for the period 1986-9 are shown in Table 6.19. The largest grey seal stocks are in the Outer Hebrides and Orkney. At most colonies pup production increased in 1987, remained constant or fell in 1988 and rose again in 1989. In all areas numbers of pups produced in 1988

6.19 Status of grey seals and common seals

Great Britain

	Survey Date	Inner Hebrides	Outer Hebrides/ N. Rona	Orkney	Shetland	Farne Islands	Isle of May	South west Britain
Grey seals								
Estimated pup production[1]	1986	1,700	9,100	6,000	1,000[2]	910	950	800-900[3]
	1987	2,000	9,600	6,900	..	930	870	..
	1988	2,000	9,600	6,100	..	810	690	..
	1989	..	10,400	7,200	..	890	940	..
Equivalent all-age population	1986	..	← 55,500 →		3,500[2]	← 6,700 →		3,000[3]
	1987	7,000	← 59,000 →		..	← 7,000 →		..
	1988	..	← 62,000 →		..	← 7,400 →		..
	1989	..	← 65,000 →		..	← 7,600 →		..

	Survey Date	Inner Hebrides/ W. Scotland	Outer Hebrides	Orkney	Shetland	East coast	Wash
Common seals							
Peak count	1988	5,900[4]	1,300[5]	6,600[6]	4,700[7]	1,100-1,400[8]	3,900
	1989	..	..	7,100	..	1,000[8]	2,000

[1] 95% confidence interval for air surveys are estimated at 20% for Inner Hebrides, Outer Hebrides and North Rona and Orkney and 30% for Shetland and south west Britain. Counts on Farne Islands and Isle of May are done from the ground.
[2] 1983
[3] 1982
[4] 1980
[5] 1974
[6] 1985
[7] 1984
[8] Surveys conducted by Aberdeen University and the Department of Agriculture and Fisheries for Scotland.

Source: *Sea Mammal Research Unit*

6.20 Pesticide poisoning of animals: 1985-9

Great Britain

	Number of incidents investigated[1]			Incidents where pesticides were detected					
				Number			*Percentage*		
	1985-7[2]	1988	1989	1985-7[2]	1988	1989	1985-7[2]	1988	1989
Vertebrate wildlife[3]	541	277	343	199	71	97	*37*	*26*	*28*
Livestock[4]	102	47	56	17	5	7	*17*	*11*	*12*
Companion animals[5]	327	206	200	118	69	65	*36*	*34*	*32*
Exotic species[6]	15	13	6	2	1	-	*13*	*8*	*-*
Beneficial insects[7]	188	108	109	135	60	59	*72*	*56*	*54*
Aquatic insects and fish	1	2	1	-	-	-	*-*	*-*	*-*
Suspected poison baits without animals affected	45	24	38	24	13	22	*53*	*54*	*58*
Total[1]	1,182	641	736	447	216	234	*38*	*34*	*32*

[1] Animals from more than one category may be involved in a single incident.
[2] October 1985-December 1987 ($2\frac{1}{4}$ years).
[3] Birds and mammals.
[4] Cattle, sheep, pigs, poultry.

Source: *Ministry of Agriculture, Fisheries and Food*

[5] Cats, dogs, horses.
[6] Eg, aviary birds.
[7] Honeybees, bumblebees.

were lower than was expected from the estimated population of breeding females. Figures given for common seals, which are mainly found around the coast of Scotland and in the Wash, are estimates of the minimum number in each region. More than 3,000 seals were found dead around the UK coasts in the second half of 1988. A high proportion were common seals which appeared to have died as a result of infection with a distemper virus. The worst affected area was the Wash where numbers of common seals halved between 1988 and 1989.

Pesticide poisoning of animals

When an animal is reported dead or ill and pesticide poisoning is suspected, the case is investigated by MAFF in England and Wales or by the Department of Agriculture and Fisheries for Scotland. In most cases a field investigation by a biologist is followed by post-mortem examination of carcasses and analysis for the presence of pesticide residues. Generally, mortality is only attributed to a pesticide if residues of the chemical or its derivatives are detected above levels believed to represent lethal exposure. The results of the investigations are reported[15] to the Environmental Panel of the Advisory Committee on pesticides and used to evaluate pesticide approvals.

Table 6.20 provides a summary of incidents investigated since October 1985. In 1989 pesticides were found to be involved in 234 out of 736 cases, many of the remainder being attributable to disease, starvation or physical trauma. Most cases were caused by misuse or abuse of pesticides unlike earlier decades when most cases were attributable to the approved use of pesticides. For wildlife, and for cats and dogs, the most frequent cause of mortality was deliberate illegal

abuse of pesticides (chiefly three chemicals - strychnine, mevinphos and alphachloralose) in attempts to kill predators of game or livestock. In contrast, most cases involving livestock or honeybees arose from careless misuse or from approved use of pesticides.

[1] Public attitudes to the Environment, *Digest of Environmental Protection and Water Statistics*, no 12.
[2] *National Rights of Way Condition Survey 1988*, CCP 284. Countryside Commission,1990.
[3] *Monitoring Landscape Change*. Hunting Surveys and Consultants Limited,1986.
[4] *Land Use Change in England*. DOE Statistical Bulletin (90)5.
[5] *Survey of Derelict Land in 1988*. Department of the Environment (in press).
[6] *Survey of Land for Mineral Working in England, 1988*. Department of the Environment (in press).
[7] J L Innes and R C Boswell, "Reliability, presentation and relationships among data from inventories of forest condition", *Canadian Journal of Forest Research*, vol 20,1990.
[8] T J Crawford, R Toy and M B Usher, *Key Indicators for British Wildlife (Stage 1)*. (Unpublished report for the Department of the Environment,1989); summary in *National Perspectives in Biological Recording in the UK*, edited by G Stansfield and P T Harding. National Federation for Biological Recording, 1990.
[9] C Bibby, S Housden, R Porter and G Thomas, "Towards a bird conservation strategy", *RSPB Conservation Review*, vol 3, 4-8,1989.
[10] *Red Data Birds in Britain*. Nature Conservancy Council and Royal Society for the Protection of Birds (in press).
[11] *Population Trends in British Breeding Birds*. British Trust for Ornithology,1990.
[12] D G Salmon, R P Prys-Jones and J S Kirby, *Wildfowl and Wader Counts 1988-9*. The Wildfowl and Wetlands Trust,1989. (Similar reports for earlier years.)
[13] H W Pepper, *Squirrel Questionnaire 1988 Report*. Forestry Commission, 1989. (Similar reports for earlier years.)
[14] J Harwood, A R Hiby, D Thompson and A Ward, "Seal stocks in Great Britain: surveys conducted between 1986 and 1989", *NERC News*,1991.
[15] P W Greig-Smith, M R Fletcher, K Hunter, M P Quick, A D Ruthven and I C Shaw, *Pesticide Poisoning of Animals 1988: Investigations of Suspected Incidents in Great Britain*. Ministry of Agriculture, Fisheries and Food, 1990.

Chapter 7 Water supply and use

Abstractions of both surface water and groundwater in England and Wales are licensed under powers derived from the Water Resources Act 1963 as amended by the Water Act 1989. Licence holders include not only the public water supply undertakers but also the electricity generating companies and other industrial concerns as well as individual farmers and others. The statutory companies abstract for general water supply - the mains system which serves cities, towns, and most rural areas with piped water. Almost all (99.2 per cent) of the population of England and Wales is served by the public water supply.

Table 7.1 and Figure 7.1 show annual abstractions of water by purpose in England and Wales. The data exclude water abstracted by industry from tidal sources. Total abstractions fell by about 12 per cent over the period 1979-85, but thereafter increased by 8 per cent between 1985 and 1987, rising from 31,500 to 34,000 megalitres (Ml) per day. Total abstractions fell by over 1,600 Ml per day in 1988, but increased by 1,000 Ml per day in 1989. The fall in abstractions in 1988 by over 1,600 Ml per day is almost all accounted for by the redefinition of some Manchester Ship Canal abstractions in the North West Water area as tidal.

Since 1979, there has been a long term decline in abstractions by industry, other than companies generating electricity; abstractions fell by almost 58 per cent over the period 1979-89. The main causes of this sustained decline were more efficient use of water by industry, including recycling, and changes in industrial structure, including the contraction of some of the major water-using industries. The large fall in industrial abstractions between 1979 and 1980 may have been due, in part, to the inclusion of some abstractions for hydro-electricity in data for earlier years, although it may also have been affected by changes in economic activity. Figure 7.1 shows there was a similar fall between 1973 and 1974.

Abstractions by the electricity generating companies fell by 2,000 Ml per day between 1979-85, but returned to 1979 levels in 1987. Three-quarters of the increase in abstractions between 1985 and 1987 is accounted for by the increased demand for water for hydro-electric power generation in Wales, abstractions rising from 3,600 Ml per day in 1985 to 5,500 Ml per day in 1987. There have, though, been considerable year to year fluctuations in total abstractions by the electricity generating companies since 1979.

Abstractions for water supply, mainly by the former water authorities and water companies, have increased by 10 per cent since 1979, and most of the increase has occurred since 1984. Abstractions for water supply in 1989 were almost 290 Ml per day more than in 1988. Since the early 1980s abstractions for water supply have accounted for half of all abstractions.

7.1 Abstractions from surface water and groundwater: by purpose

England and Wales
                                                            Megalitres a day

	Water supply[1]	Agriculture		Industry		Total quantity abstracted
		Spray irrigation[2]	Other	Electricity generating companies[3]	Other[4]	
1979	16,268	106	140	12,710	6,773	35,997
1980	16,115	92	133	13,088	4,634	34,062
1981	16,039	116	111	12,208	4,972	33,446
1982	16,331	139	117	11,587	4,729	32,903
1983	16,360	170	119	12,179	4,095	32,923
1984	16,394	199	122	11,757	3,893	32,365
1985	16,685	102	121	10,710	3,920	31,538
1986	16,617	169	123	12,744	4,099	33,752
1987	17,240	101	121	12,806	3,702	33,970
1988	17,597[5]	133	114	11,787	2,692	32,323
1989[6]	17,884	281	117	12,189	2,862	33,333

[1] Water supply (ie piped mains water) includes abstractions by water service companies, water companies and small private abstractions.
[2] Includes small amounts for non-agricultural spray irrigation.
[3] Excludes tidal water but includes water used for water power.
[4] Excludes tidal water and water used for water power and fish farming.

Source: *National Rivers Authority; Department of the Environment*

[5] Using 1987 data for former South West Water Authority.
[6] Using 1988 data for Southern region and South-West region.

Figure 7.1 Surface water and groundwater combined: annual abstractions by purpose

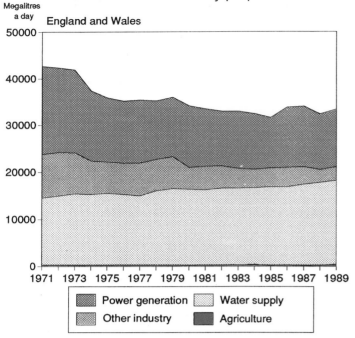

Source: *Department of the Environment*

water used in this way is lost to the atmosphere or ground. Water abstracted for other purposes is at least partially returned to rivers and can be used again. Abstractions for other agricultural uses show some evidence of a decline.

Table 7.2 shows abstractions by purpose for the National Rivers Authority (NRA) regions. Total abstractions increased in all regions except Severn Trent and Yorkshire. Public water supply was the main purpose for abstractions in all but the Welsh and Severn Trent water regions, where the electricity generating companies were the main abstractors, taking 75 per cent and 51 per cent of all abstractions respectively. Abstractions by the electricity generating companies and other industry showed a small increase in 1989. Abstractions for spray irrigation increased almost threefold in the Anglian and Severn Trent regions.

Table 7.2 shows the extent to which water is abstracted from surface and groundwater sources. Abstractions from groundwater in England and Wales in 1989 accounted on average for 20 per cent of all abstractions. The percentage of abstractions from groundwater varied by less than 2 per cent from 1988 in all authorities except South West, which showed a 3 per cent decline, and Wessex, where there was a 2 per cent increase.

The amount of water derived from groundwater sources varied widely between NRA regions, ranging from 74 per cent in Southern, to 1 per cent in Wales. These variations are explained by a number of factors. The presence of groundwater requires particular geological formations which occur only in certain parts of the

Abstractions for spray irrigation have fluctuated between 1979-89 being to some extent dependent on the weather. In 1988 and 1989 the amount of water abstacted increased by 32 Ml per day and 148 Ml per day respectively. This was due to hot dry weather during the summer months. Although relatively small in total, abstractions for spray irrigation may have a significant impact on available resources as they tend to be highest in periods of hot dry weather when water resources may be already stretched, and almost all the

7.2 Abstractions from surface water and groundwater: by purpose and by NRA region: 1989

England and Wales
Megalitres a day

NRA region	Water supply[1]	Agriculture		Industry		Total quantity abstracted	Percentage of total abstractions that were from groundwater
		Spray irrigation[2]	Other	Electricity generating companies	Other[3]		
Anglian	1,798	145	17	2	295	2,257	*49*
Northumbria	1,186	-	-	-	40	1,226	*10*
North West	1,930	3	5	56	791[4]	2,785	*17*
Severn Trent	2,421	73	8	3,007	442	5,951	*19*
Southern[5]	1,156	7	11	-	144	1,318	*74*
South West	711	3	29	201	121	1,065	*12*
Thames	4,008	11	13	105	219	4,356	*42*
Welsh	2,351	6	12	8,047	287	10,704	*1*
Wessex	837	11	9	-	145	1,002	*49*
Yorkshire	1,486	21	12	772	378	2,669	*12*
England and Wales	17,884	281	117	12,189	2,862	33,333	*20*

[1] Water supply (ie, piped mains water) includes abstractions by water services companies, water companies and small private abstractions.

[2] Includes small amounts for non-agricultural spray irrigation.

[3] Excludes tidal water and water used for water power and fish farming.

Source: *National Rivers Authority*

[4] Certain abstractions from Manchester Ship Canal have been redefined as tidal.

[5] Figures not available for 1989. Figures given are for 1988.

7.3 Estimated total abstractions from surface and groundwater sources: by NRA regions:[1] 1980, 1988 and 1989; and percentage change

NRA region	Thousand Ml a year			% change	
	1980	1988	1989	1980-8	1980-9
North West	1,854	1,173	1,130	-36.7	-39.1
Yorkshire	1,549	1,148	1,065	-25.8	-31.2
Severn Trent	3,205	2,530	2,345	-21.1	-36.7
Northumbria	415	354	450	-14.7	8.4
Thames	1,599	1,618	1,659	1.2	3.8
South West	828[2]	851	980	2.8[3]	18.4
Wessex	355	381	422	7.3	18.9
Anglian	700	768	835	9.7	19.3
Southern	498	594	..	19.3	19.3
Welsh	2,750	3,786	3,944	37.7	..
England and Wales	13,753	13,203	13,426	-4.0	-2.4

Source: *Department of the Environment (1980 and 1988); National Rivers Authority (1989)*

[1] Previously water authority areas.
[2] 1985.
[3] % change 1985-8.

country; groundwater may be difficult to extract because of the nature of rock formations or faulting; and, groundwater reservoirs may be too far from the main areas of demand to make abstraction and distribution economic. In times of drought, areas which have a large proportion of abstractions from groundwater are usually affected less than areas with a large proportion of abstractions from surface water. However, many of the areas most seriously affected by drought in 1990 were those largely dependent on groundwater, low rainfall in the winter of 1989-90 not allowing adequate recharge of aquifers.

Table 7.3 shows that there was a 4 per cent decline in total water abstractions for England and Wales between 1980 and 1988. This trend was reversed in 1989. The decline has been concentrated in the north of England, where abstractions fell in all regions between 1980 and 1988. In 1989 the decline in abstractions in the north and west midlands continued, with the exception of Northumbria where abstractions increased sharply; after a fall of almost 15 per cent between 1980-8, abstractions in Northumbria showed an 27 per cent increase in 1989. In other regions of England and Wales

7.4 Water put into public water supply:[1] by water service company area and country

a)   By water service company area in England and Wales

Megalitres a day

	Metered						Unmetered[2]					
	1984	1985	1986	1987	1988	1989/90	1984	1985	1986	1987	1988	1989/90
Anglian	506	508	525	536	540	492	1,151	1,164	1,226	1,198	1,236	1,277
Northumbria	494	503	498	510	530	529	525	525	525	526	528	547
North West	760	750	732	591	591	732	1,765	1,840	1,875	1,855	1,823	1,755
Severn Trent	612	617	549	627	634	654	1,737	1,719	1,809	1,690	1,689	1,730
Southern	327	315	329	335	337	333	936	925	927	946	1,000	989
South West	101	104	108	115	116	117	327	348	359	366	367	364
Thames	729	739	743	733	760	743	3,090	3,083	3,175	3,222	3,199	3,331
Welsh	371	361	376	381	393	410	779	801	815	824	837	836
Wessex	304	299	304	306	309	308	575	571	581	589	595	607
Yorkshire	349	345	385	384	413	398	1,061	1,060	1,119	1,105	1,091	1,059
Total	4,553	4,541	4,549	4,518	4,623	4,716	11,946	12,036	12,411	12,321	12,365	12,495

b)   By country

Megalitres a day

	1979	1980	1981	1982	1983	1984	1985	1986	1987	1988	1989/90
England and Wales											
metered	5,147	4,790	4,591	4,667	4,495	4,552	4,541	4,550	4,518	4,623	4,716
unmetered[2]	10,961	11,118	11,223	11,551	11,765	11,946	12,036	12,411	12,321	12,365	12,495
Scotland											
metered	806	704r	674	678	632	662	658	642	641r	629r	677
unmetered[2]	1,495	1,533r	1,588	1,568	1,601	1,537	1,540	1,602	1,553	1,576r	1,571
Northern Ireland											
metered	199	188	161	147	132	153	169	168	165	151	161
unmetered[2]	486	498	502	540	559	529	509	513	505	509	505

[1] Includes water supplied by water companies.
[2] Unmetered water includes leakage from mains and water used in fire fighting.

Source: *Department of the Environment (1979-88); Scottish Development Department; Department of the Environment for Northern Ireland; Water Services Association (1989/90); Water Companies' Association*

there has been a sustained increase in abstractions over the period. The very large increase in abstractions in the Welsh region is due to increases in demand for water by the electricity generating industry for hydro-electric power generation.

Table 7.4 shows water put into public water supply (metered and unmetered) by each of the statutory water undertakers.The use of unmetered water, which is supplied mainly to domestic and commercial users, has increased steadily in England and Wales rising from over 10,000 Ml per day in 1979 to over 12,000 Ml per day in recent years. In contrast, the use of metered water, which is supplied mainly to industry, fell from a peak of over 5,100 Ml per day in 1979 to under 4,500 Ml per day in 1983. Since then the metered supply has increased slightly, reaching over 4,700 Ml per day in 1989. Although the number of metered commercial and domestic users has been increasing, this factor has been more than offset by the long-term downward trend in water used by industry. About 27 per cent of water used from public supply in England and Wales in 1989 was metered.

Rateable values (RVs) will cease to be used for water charging from April 2000. In order to help the water industry and interested parties make decisions about future charging methods, national water metering trials were started in 1989. Trials are taking place on the Isle of Wight and 11 small-scale trial areas (see Figure 7.2) and the trials are expected to last for a further 18 months.

The trials indicate that metering is a feasible proposition for 95 per cent of households although there are a number of technical problems and social issues to be resolved. In the small-scale trial areas 65 per cent of households are paying the same or less than their previous RV bills. Although it is too soon to draw firm conclusions, there has been an overall average reduction in demand for water of 10 per cent across the trial areas.

Average domestic consumption in 1989 was about 136 litres per person per day. Figure 7.3 shows how this can be broken down for the average household. Estimates from studies by the water industry give the litres of water used per use by various domestic appliances as follows; automatic washing machine, 110; dishwasher, 55; WC, 9.5; bath, 80; and shower 35. The water industry brochure published in 1989 gave typical figures for industrial water use. For example, it takes about 30,000 litres to build the average car and 8 pints to brew a pint of beer.

Drought orders in England may be made by the Secretary of State for the Environment under sections (S) 131 or 132 of the Water Act 1989 to meet deficiencies in water supplies resulting only from an exceptional shortage of rain. He can do so only on application by either a water undertaker or the

Figure 7.2   Metering trial sites

Source: Water Research Centre

National Rivers Authority and can approve orders under S 131 only if he is satisfied that due to an exceptional shortage of rain a serious deficiency of supplies of water in any area exsists or is threatened. For orders under S 132, which are in practice very rare, he must be satisfied that the deficiency is likely to impair the economic or social well-being of people in the area.

Drought orders may include various powers, the most common of which are the varying of conditions of abstraction, the reduction of compensation flows, the taking or discharge of water and the prohibition of types of water use. From 1979 to 1990, 238 orders, including extensions of expired orders, were approved by the Secretary of State. Mostly these occurred in 1984 (82), 1989 (76) and 1990 (60).

Fluoridation of water supplies began in the early 1960s following the successful completion of trials which showed a substantial improvement in the condition of the teeth of young children. Water companies' powers to add fluoride to water supplies were clarified with the

Figure 7.3 Average household water use in England and Wales

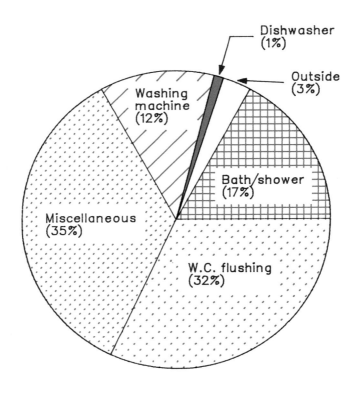

Source : *Water Services Association*

passing of the Water (Fluoridation) Act 1985. Section 1(1) of the Act makes provision for a water company to increase the fluoride content of water supplied within a specified area on receipt of a written request from a health authority. Section 1(5) of the Act requires a health authority making such arrangements with a water company to ensure that the concentration of fluoride in the water supplied is, so far as is reasonably practicable, maintained at 1.0 mg/l.

Figure 7.4 has been compiled from data supplied by water companies and shows the concentration of fluoride in public water supplies in England and Wales at 1 September 1990. It distinguishes between areas supplied with water to which fluoride has been added at treatment works (fluoridation) and areas supplied with water in which fluoride occurs naturally. The map shows areas supplied with water which has been fluoridated at the optimum concentration of 0.9 to 1.1 mg/l and areas where the operation of the water distribution system results in fluoridated water mixing with unfluoridated water to give a fluoride concentration below 0.9 mg/l.

Figure 7.4 provides a general guide to the fluoride concentrations in water supplies. However, in some complex water distribution systems the boundaries of the areas receiving a particular water supply can change. Also fluoridation has been suspended temporarily at a few treatment works to enable equipment to be renovated or replaced. Fluoridation will continue as soon as practicable and these areas have been included on the map as receiving fluoridated water. Information on the fluoride concentration of the water supply to a particular location can be obtained from the appropriate water company.

Figure 7.4 Fluoride concentrations in water supplies

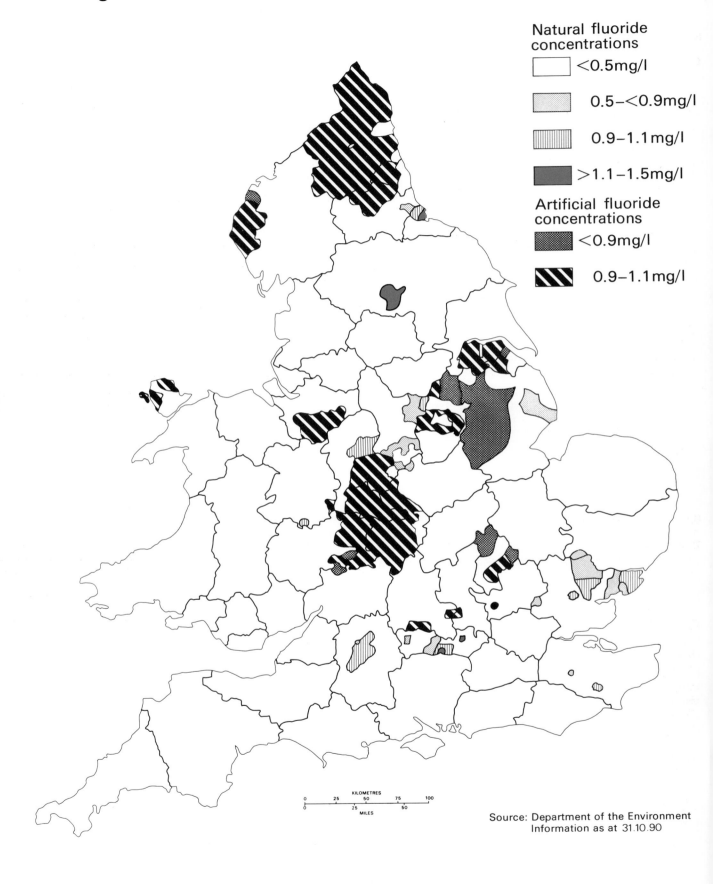

Natural fluoride concentrations

- <0.5mg/l
- 0.5–<0.9mg/l
- 0.9–1.1mg/l
- >1.1–1.5mg/l

Artificial fluoride concentrations

- <0.9mg/l
- 0.9–1.1mg/l

KILOMETRES
0 25 50 75 100

MILES
0 25 50

Source: Department of the Environment
Information as at 31.10.90

Chapter 8 Supplementary

8.1 Home population[1] and population density: by region and country

United Kingdom   Thousands

Region	1961	1971	1981	1984	1985	1986	1987	1988	1989	Area[2] (sq km)	No of persons per sq km in 1989
North	3,113	3,152	3,117r	3,093	3,086	3,080	3,077	3,071	3,073	15,401	200
Yorkshire and Humberside	4,677	4,902	4,918	4,904	4,903	4,899	4,900	4,913	4,940	15,420	320
East Midlands	3,330	3,652	3,853	3,874	3,897	3,920	3,942	3,970	3,999	15,630	256
East Anglia	1,489	1,688	1,895	1,940	1,965	1,992	2,014	2,034	2,045	12,573	163
South East	16,071	17,125	17,011r	17,112	17,192	17,265	17,318	17,344	17,384	27,222	639
Greater London	7,977	7,529	6,806	6,756	6,768	6,775	6,770	6,735	6,756	1,579	4,279
Rest of South East	8,094	9,596	10,205r	10,356	10,424	10,489	10,547	10,609	10,628	25,643	414
South West	3,712	4,112	4,381r	4,461	4,501	4,543	4,588	4,634	4,652	23,850	195
West Midlands	4,762	5,146	5,187r	5,176	5,183	5,181	5,198	5,207	5,216	13,013	401
North West	6,407	6,634	6,460	6,396	6,386	6,374	6,370	6,364	6,380	7,331	870
England	43,561	46,412	46,821	46,956	47,112	47,254	47,407	47,536	47,689	130,440	366
Wales	2,635	2,740	2,814	2,807	2,812	2,821	2,836	2,857	2,873	20,768	138
Scotland	5,184	5,217	5,180	5,146	5,137	5,121	5,112	5,094	5,091	77,167	66
Northern Ireland	1,427	1,538	1,564	1,579	1,558	1,567	1,575	1,578	1,583	14,120	112
United Kingdom	52,807	55,907	56,379	56,488	56,619	56,763	56,930	57,065	57,236	242,495	236

[1] Home population includes members of British, Commonwealth and foreign armed forces in the United Kingdom. Figures relate to 30 June each year. No adjustment is made for visitors in the summer months. Figures may not add to totals due to independent rounding.

[2] Excluding inland and tidal water and foreshore in Scotland.

Source: *Office of Population Censuses and Surveys; General Register Offices of Scotland and Northern Ireland; Department of the Environment*

8.2 Home population:[1] by Water Service Company[2] area

England and Wales   Thousands

Water Service Company	1980	1981	1982	1983	1984	1985	1986	1987	1988	1989	Estimated area[3] (thousand sq km)
North West	6,902	6,925	6,899	6,879	6,864	6,856	6,846	6,843	6,839	6,861	14
Northumbria	2,634	2,658	2,647	2,639	2,639	2,624	2,616	2,613	2,605	2,605	9
Severn Trent	8,187	8,273	8,258	8,259	9,269	8,288	8,298	8,321	8,342	8,370	22
Yorkshire	4,523	4,558	4,553	4,550	4,547	4,546	4,543	4,546	4,557	4,582	14
Anglian	4,921	5,015	5,044	5,077	5,115	5,169	5,233	5,297	5,356	5,387	27
Thames	11,541	11,540	11,513	11,526	11,561	11,601	11,629	11,630	11,607	11,632	13
Southern	3,821	3,883	3,897	3,907	3,926	3,950	4,006	4,039	4,046	4,046	11
Wessex	2,300	2,318	2,329	2,344	2,364	2,385	2,404	2,425	2,444	2,447	10
South West	1,399	1,411	1,416	1,424	1,437	1,451	1,467	1,483	1,502	1,514	11
Welsh	3,017	3,053	3,046	3,046	3,047	3,053	3,062	3,079	3,102	3,116	21
England and Wales	49,244	49,632	49,602	49,651	49,762	49,923	50,073	50,243	50,393	50,560	152

[1] Home population includes members of British, Commonwealth and foreign armed forces in the United Kingdom. Figures relate to 30 June each year. No adjustment is made for visitors in the summer months. The estimated home populations within the Water Service Company areas as defined for administrative purposes are different from the populations served by the Water Service Companies both because the boundaries for the various functions (such as water supply and sewerage) of Water Service Companies are not identical and because supply lines cross Water Service Companies boundaries.

Source: *Office of Population Censuses and Surveys; Department of the Environment*

[2] The Water Service Companies were set up in 1989, and replaced the water authorities.

[3] The areas of the Water Service Companies have been estimated from maps and are approximate (these areas include inland water).

8.3 Mean daily air temperature at sea level

United Kingdom Degrees celsius[1]

	Average 1951-80	1979	1980	1981	1982	1983	1984	1985	1986	1987	1988	1989
England and Wales												
Annual mean	9.8	9.3	9.9	9.7	10.4	10.5	10.0	9.2	9.1	9.5	10.2	10.9
January	4.0	0.9	3.1	5.2	3.6	7.0	3.8	1.3	4.1	1.4	5.8	6.7
February	4.1	1.9	6.3	3.7	5.5	2.6	3.5	2.8	-0.4	4.1	5.2	6.4
March	5.9	5.3	5.4	8.3	6.6	7.0	4.6	5.0	5.4	4.6	6.6	7.8
April	8.2	8.1	9.0	8.2	8.9	7.3	8.5	8.7	6.1	10.3	8.5	6.9
May	11.3	10.3	11.3	11.6	11.9	10.6	10.1	11.0	11.3	10.3	12.0	13.2
June	14.3	14.3	14.3	13.8	15.7	14.6	14.7	12.9	14.8	13.1	14.6	14.7
July	16.0	16.5	15.0	16.0	16.8	19.2	16.6	16.4	16.1	16.2	15.1	18.3
August	15.9	15.4	16.3	16.6	16.4	17.6	17.8	15.0	14.1	16.0	15.7	17.0
September	14.0	13.9	15.2	15.1	14.8	14.2	14.1	14.9	11.9	14.2	13.8	15.1
October	11.0	11.8	9.6	8.9	10.7	11.0	11.7	11.4	11.4	10.3	11.1	12.3
November	7.1	7.3	7.0	8.1	8.5	8.1	8.6	4.7	8.3	7.2	6.2	7.2
December	5.1	6.3	6.0	1.4	4.9	6.3	5.7	6.7	6.4	6.1	7.7	5.5
Scotland												
Annual mean	8.5	7.9	8.7	8.4	8.9	9.1	8.3	7.6	7.9	8.2	9.0	9.1
January	3.5	0.8	2.8	4.3	2.9	5.6	1.5	1.6	2.9	2.0	4.2	7.3
February	3.4	1.9	4.9	3.9	5.5	2.7	2.8	3.4	0.5	3.5	4.5	5.2
March	5.1	3.6	4.2	6.0	5.6	6.2	4.1	4.2	5.0	3.8	5.0	5.7
April	7.1	6.7	8.3	7.3	8.2	5.8	7.2	7.2	5.2	8.5	7.2	6.0
May	9.9	8.3	10.4	10.6	9.9	9.0	9.1	9.7	9.9	9.3	10.5	10.7
June	12.7	12.8	12.7	12.9	12.8	12.2	12.5	11.4	13.0	11.0	13.6	12.5
July	13.9	13.9	13.5	13.9	15.1	16.0	14.6	14.1	13.8	14.3	13.7	15.6
August	13.9	13.2	14.1	14.7	14.3	15.5	15.5	13.2	12.1	13.8	13.9	14.1
September	12.2	11.9	13.3	13.1	12.2	13.3	11.8	11.9	10.7	11.9	12.3	12.0
October	9.8	10.6	8.1	6.7	9.6	9.4	9.8	10.3	9.8	8.2	9.3	10.4
November	6.0	5.9	6.3	6.3	6.6	7.2	7.4	3.4	7.1	6.4	6.0	6.3
December	4.5	4.7	5.5	0.8	3.9	6.1	5.6	4.9	4.7	5.2	7.3	3.2
Northern Ireland												
Annual mean	9.0	8.4	9.2	9.2	9.4	9.8	8.4	8.6	8.3	8.9	9.4	9.7
January	4.0	0.9	2.7	5.6	4.0	5.8	2.2	1.3	3.6	3.2	4.5	7.0
February	4.2	2.6	5.4	4.4	5.6	3.2	2.3	4.2	1.3	4.2	4.8	5.6
March	5.7	4.3	4.9	7.3	6.2	7.0	4.5	5.0	5.4	4.9	6.4	6.3
April	7.7	6.9	8.7	8.2	9.0	6.0	7.3	8.3	5.4	9.3	8.5	6.1
May	10.3	8.6	11.3	10.9	10.8	9.8	8.5	9.8	10.0	10.7	10.7	11.2
June	13.1	13.1	12.8	13.1	14.1	13.2	12.9	12.0	13.8	11.6	14.2	13.3
July	14.4	15.0	13.8	14.5	15.6	17.5	14.7	14.5	14.3	15.1	13.8	17.0
August	14.3	13.8	15.1	15.4	12.9	16.7	16.1	13.3	12.1	14.8	14.0	14.7
September	12.6	12.4	13.9	13.6	12.9	14.5	12.6	13.6	11.3	12.2	12.5	12.6
October	10.2	10.9	8.9	7.2	10.3	10.1	10.0	10.7	10.1	8.3	9.9	11.2
November	6.4	6.9	6.7	7.5	6.5	7.8	6.3	4.3	7.1	7.0	6.0	6.6
December	5.1	4.9	5.7	2.2	4.4	6.8	5.4	5.9	5.5	6.1	7.8	4.2

[1] To convert degrees celsius into degrees fahrenheit: multiply by 9, divide by 5, and add 32.

Source: *CSO Annual Abstract of Statistics, based on data supplied by Meteorological Office*

8.4 Rainfall

United Kingdom

Millimetres[1]

	Average 1951-80	1979	1980	1981	1982	1983	1984	1985	1986	1987	1988	1989
England and Wales												
Annual mean	912	1,001	978	999	973	879	899	885	992	919	923	814
January	86	85	79	58	72	92	144	72	120	30	154	47
February	65	65	93	53	44	42	57	29	17	58	63	88
March	59	125	103	153	101	67	59	66	80	89	102	92
April	58	70	19	64	23	108	11	70	84	66	42	83
May	67	123	32	91	46	117	59	65	85	48	60	21
June	61	41	126	49	129	37	43	94	43	105	37	55
July	73	34	72	55	39	40	27	73	54	73	129	38
August	90	95	96	48	90	33	57	117	117	67	85	58
September	83	39	67	141	78	101	116	46	27	67	66	41
October	83	78	131	124	125	78	100	48	98	166	92	98
November	97	87	87	69	126	53	145	77	124	85	49	61
December	90	159	71	94	100	111	81	128	143	65	44	134
Scotland												
Annual mean	1,431	1,531	1,551	1,522	1,675	1,456	1,473	1,505	1,642	1,345	1,608	1,496
January	137	118	119	156	154	220	223	85	192	70	202	206
February	104	39	102	91	107	59	111	47	21	88	140	240
March	92	183	116	152	153	149	103	95	169	153	171	178
April	90	97	20	33	46	74	60	111	80	68	77	63
May	91	102	28	87	92	115	24	73	176	74	55	53
June	92	77	149	103	72	86	66	84	63	98	33	76
July	112	103	125	92	57	43	55	167	87	109	190	49
August	129	139	146	52	158	51	50	224	120	120	171	184
September	137	118	172	235	200	172	166	200	66	150	150	96
October	149	152	187	218	196	230	216	85	159	161	170	187
November	142	204	181	216	229	49	233	141	232	113	99	60
December	156	199	206	87	213	208	166	193	277	141	150	96
Northern Ireland												
Annual mean	1,095	1,137	1,157	1,214	1,165	952	1,037	1,114	1,173	964	1,188	963
January	104	95	115	101	107	117	180	76	155	49	167	74
February	75	29	99	68	90	51	111	38	5	63	112	100
March	70	95	113	128	112	113	72	86	115	104	138	121
April	68	82	19	47	24	59	30	76	106	47	42	104
May	73	94	37	141	65	83	22	74	124	42	43	34
June	79	56	117	88	123	53	57	74	46	94	46	59
July	93	51	85	78	21	20	49	118	74	72	127	42
August	103	135	84	43	92	35	71	183	141	120	122	115
September	107	76	118	175	99	111	104	156	10	88	104	52
October	107	136	148	158	126	132	112	49	106	136	141	143
November	102	163	88	94	167	39	114	86	131	83	54	49
December	114	125	134	93	139	139	115	98	160	66	92	72

[1] 1 millimetre = 0.0394 inches.

Source: *CSO Annual Abstract of Statistics, based on data supplied by Meteorological Office*

8.5 Retail Price Index[1]

United Kingdom

	1974	1975	1976	1977	1978	1979	1980	1981	1982	1983	1984	1985	1986	1987	1987	1988	1989
January	100.0	119.9	147.9	172.4	189.5	207.2	245.3	277.3	310.6	325.9	342.6	359.8	379.7	394.5	100.0	103.3	111.0
February	101.7	121.9	149.8	174.1	190.6	208.9	248.8	279.8	310.7	327.3	344.0	362.7	381.1		100.4	103.7	111.8
March	102.6	124.3	150.6	175.8	191.8	210.6	252.2	284.0	313.4	327.9	345.1	366.1	381.6		100.6	104.1	112.3
April	106.1	129.1	153.5	180.3	194.6	214.2	260.8	292.2	319.7	332.5	349.7	373.9	385.3		101.8	105.8	114.3
May	107.6	134.5	155.2	181.7	195.7	215.9	263.2	294.1	322.0	333.9	351.0	375.6	386.0		101.9	106.2	115.0
June	108.7	137.1	156.0	183.6	197.2	219.6	265.7	295.8	322.9	334.7	351.9	376.4	385.8		101.9	106.6	115.4
July	109.7	138.5	156.3	183.8	198.1	229.1	267.9	297.1	323.0	336.5	351.5	375.7	384.7		101.8	106.7	115.5
August	109.8	139.3	158.5	184.7	199.4	230.9	268.5	299.3	323.1	338.0	354.8	376.7	385.9		102.1	107.9	115.8
September	110.0	140.5	160.6	185.7	202.2	233.2	270.2	301.0	322.9	339.5	355.5	376.5	387.8		102.4	108.4	116.6
October	113.2	142.5	163.5	186.5	201.1	235.6	271.9	303.7	324.5	340.7	357.7	377.1	388.4		102.9	109.5	117.5
November	115.2	144.2	165.8	187.4	202.5	237.7	274.1	306.9	326.1	341.9	358.8	378.4	391.7		103.4	110.0	
December	116.9	146.0	168.0	188.4	202.4	239.4	275.6	308.8	325.5	342.8	358.5	378.9	393.0		103.3	110.3	

[1] Figures up to the end of 1986 based on January 1974 = 100; figures thereafter based on January 1987 = 100

Source: *CSO, Economic Trends, Annual Supplement, 1990*

8.6 Gross domestic product: at current and constant prices

£ million

	1979	1980	1981	1982	1983	1984	1985	1986	1987	1988	1989
Gross domestic product at current market prices	198,262	231,852	254,934	278,974	304,448	325,266	356,216	383,154	421,160	470,117	513,242
Gross domestic product at 1985 market prices	330,600	323,535	319,301	324,727	336,769	343,945	356,216	370,020	387,305	405,263	414,076
Index (1985 = 100) of GDP at 1985 market prices	92.8	90.8	89.6	91.2	94.5	96.6	100.0	103.9	108.7	113.8	116.2

Source: *CSO, UK National Accounts, 1990*

8.7 Road traffic: by type of vehicle[1]

Great Britain

Billion vehicle kilometres

	1979	1980	1981	1982	1983	1984	1985	1986	1987	1988	1989[2]
Cars and taxis[3]	201.45	215.17	219.62	227.50	231.45	244.30	250.46	264.44	284.63	305.41	326.99
Motor cycles etc	6.39	7.69	8.90	9.25	8.31	8.16	7.37	7.07	6.71	6.03	6.32
Large buses and coaches	3.33	3.50	3.47	3.49	3.65	3.81	3.66	3.69	4.08	4.33	4.46
Goods vehicles											
Light vans[4]	22.38	23.14	23.39	23.18	23.15	24.48	25.17	26.49	28.98	32.06	35.12
Heavy goods											
2 axles	13.24	13.10	12.56	12.11	12.37	13.06	13.33	13.51	14.55	15.46	15.94
3 axles rigid	1.85	1.69	1.49	1.42	1.39	1.32	1.35	1.41	1.49	1.51	1.74
4 axles rigid	1.20	1.24	1.27	1.24	1.24	1.17	1.24	1.38	1.58	1.68	1.81
3 axles artic	1.01	0.97	0.84	0.77	0.77	0.75	0.70	0.68	0.71	0.67	0.68
4 axles artic	5.02	4.92	4.80	4.92	5.20	4.72	4.41	4.15	4.50	4.48	4.35
5 or more axles artic					0.48	1.30	1.90	2.40	3.23	4.08	5.11
All	22.32	21.93	20.95	20.46	21.45	22.33	22.94	23.53	26.06	27.90	29.70
All motor vehicles	255.87	271.42	276.33	283.88	288.02	303.07	309.59	325.23	350.47	375.71	402.59
Pedal cycles	4.58	5.10	5.46	6.41	6.40	6.41	6.08	5.48	5.74	5.24	5.17

[1] Traffic (vehicle kilometres) estimates are derived from the lengths of the road network in place each year.
[2] Provisional estimates.
[3] Includes three-wheeled cars, excludes all vans whether licensed for private or commercial use.
[4] Not exceeding 1,525 kg unladen weight.

Source: *Transport Statistics Great Britain 1989*

8.8 Energy consumption by final users

United Kingdom   Million therms

	1985	1986	1987	1988	1989
Industry	16,517	16,233	16,609	16,846	16,461
Transport	15,284	16,257	16,940	18,002	18,836
Domestic	16,698	17,348	17,253	16,737	16,073
Public administration	3,540	3,547	3,408	3,287	3,051
Agriculture	564	565	544	536	502
Miscellaneous	3,714	3,895	3,921	4,067	4,155
Total supplied to final consumers	56,319	57,845	58,677	59,475	59,078

Source: *Digest of UK Energy Statistics, 1990*

Calendar of events

1982

June — Adoption of Sveso Directive on major accident hazards of certain industrial activities.

Stockholm Conference on Acidification of the Environment.

July — White paper on Radioactive Waste Management; policies for the major categories of wastes.

September — Ringing and registration of protected birds under the Wildlife and Countryside Act 1981.

December — Adoption of EC Directive on air quality standards for lead.

1983

January — Opening of public inquiry into CEGB's application to construct pressurised water reactor at Sizewell.

February — Implementation of Sections 32 and 41 Wildlife and Countryside Act 1981 imposing new duties on Agriculture Ministers, Nature Conservancy Council and National Park Authorities with regard to Sites of Special Scientific Interest and National Parks.

Environment Council approved the general approach of the Community's Third Environment Action Programme (1982-6).

May — Miscellaneous Financial Provisions Act converted Development Commission into a full grant-in-aid body.

June — First meeting of the Executive Body for the UN/ECE Convention on Long-Range Transboundary Air Pollution.

The Wood Inquiry on *Heavy Lorries in London* published; recommended night time ban on lorries in London.

August — The Health and Safety (Emissions into the Atmosphere) Regulations 1983 came into operation.

Hazardous Waste Inspectorate formed.
Asbestos: guidelines to local authorities published following major review.

September — Government set target date of December 1989 for completion of main programme of remedial measures to reduce lead in drinking water.

Bonn agreement on co-operation in dealing with pollution of the North Sea by oil and other harmful substances.

October — Two-year EC ban on commercial import of Harp and Hooded sealpup skins and products implemented.

Dissolution of Water Space Amenity Commission.

Nirex announced initial choice of sites for examination as potential disposal facilities - Elstow and Billingham.

December — Radioactive waste disposal at sea suspended, pending independent review of the scientific evidence.

Asbestos: advice to householders published.

1984

January — EC CITES Regulations imposing community controls on the import, and sale of endangered species (and their products) implemented.

March — Miners strike began resulting in a decline of coal consumption by the CEGB and a corresponding shift to the use of oil fired power stations.

Ottawa Conference on Acid Rain.

UNEP Working Group on export of banned or severely restricted chemicals (Netherlands).

April — *Nature Conservation in Great Britain* published by the Nature Conservancy Council.

25-year DOE Programme (supported by EC regional fund) commenced to improve the Mersey Basin.

June — Asbestos: central/local Government working party set up.

High level OECD Conference on Environment and Economics (Paris).

Munich multilateral conference on damage to forests and waters by air pollution in Europe.

Adoption of EC industrial air pollution "framework" Directive.

July — Parts of Control of Pollution Act 1974 Part II implemented.

September — Publication of House of Commons Environment Committee report on acid rain.

October — First North Sea Conference (Bremen).

December — EC Directive to control transfrontier shipment of hazardous wastes.

Disposal facilities on land for low and intermediate-level radioactive wastes: principles for the protection of the human environment published by DOE.

Publication of Holliday Report which found no scientific evidence that sea disposal of radioactive waste was hazardous.

1985

January — Completion of implementation of major provisions of Part II Control of Pollution Act 1974.

Variation to liquid waste authorisation at Sellafield came into force, reflecting reductions that had been achieved and tightening controls on discharges.

Secretary of State announced that Nirex would be requested to carry out geological investigations at at least three possible sites for each type of disposal facility.

February — Agreement reached with the Paintmakers' Association to stop the addition of lead-based driers to a wide range of paints and varnishes by July 1987.

March	Adoption of EC Directive on lead content of petrol. Adoption of EC Directive on air standards for nitrogen dioxide. Commissioning of new waste treatment plant at Sellafield. End of coalminers' strike (began March 1984).
April	Groundwork Foundation set up to promote and guide development at Groundwork Trusts throughout country.
May	UK signed Vienna Convention for the Protection of the Ozone Layer.
June	Adoption of Environmental Impact Assessment Directive on the effects of certain public and private projects on the environment. EC Directive on containers of liquids for human consumption.
July	Implementation of EC directive relating to quality of water intended for human consumption. The Food and Environmental Protection Act came into effect. Bonn Convention on conservation of migratory species ratified by UK. "30% club" protocol signed by 21 countries at third meeting of the executive body for the UN/ECE Convention on Long-Range Transboundary Air Pollution in Helsinki. Announcement of discovery by British Antarctic Survey of a large spring time depletion of stratospheric ozone over Antarctica.
August	Amendments introduced to Wildlife and Countryside Act 1981 increasing protection for sites of special scientific interest and badgers. UK ratified European Monitoring and Evaluation Programme (EMEP) long-term financing protocol.
September	Launch by Countryside Commission of "Watch over the National Parks" campaign.
December	Amount of lead permitted in petrol reduced from 0.40 grams/litre to 0.15 grams/litre.

1986

January	Accession to Spain and Portugal to EC. Night-time and weekend ban on Heavy Goods Vehicles over 16 tonnes gross weight in London. Anti-fouling paint regulations published.
February	White paper on the Privatisation of the Water Authorities in England and Wales. Announcement by UK Nirex Ltd of four shallow sites for geological investigation.
March	Publication of BPEO Report (DOE) on disposal of radioactive waste.
April	Accident and fire at Chernobyl. Government's consultative proposals (the Water Environment: The Next Steps) for environmental protection under a privatised water industry published.
May	*Conservation and Development* - the Government's response to the World Conservation Strategy - published.

June	Adoption of EC Directive on protection of soil when sewage sludge is used in agriculture. Control of Pollution (Supply and Use of Injurious Substances) Regulations (PCBs). EC Council Directive amending 1984 directive on supervision and control of transfrontier shipments of hazardous wastes.
July	New authorisations came into force at Sellafield, setting tighter limits.
August	*Asbestos Materials in Building* guide published.
September	Announcement of decision to retrofit the flue gas desulphurisation (FGD) equipment to three CEGB power stations. Conservation and Business Sponsorship initiative re-launched by DOE and the World Wildlife Fund. Export of banned or severely restricted chemicals: provisional notification scheme implemented by UK.
October	The Control of Pesticides Regulations came into force.
November	Sandoz chemical spillage on the Rhine. First Marine Nature Reserve declared at Lundy.
December	Adoption of EC amending Directive on the disposal of waste oils. HSE report on the safety audit at Sellafield published.

1987

January	Layfield report on Sizewell B published. Statement by Environment Minister on radon gas levels in houses and action needed.
February	London guidelines agreed on export of banned or severely restricted chemicals.
March	Beginning of European Year of the Environment. Nature Conservancy Council reached target of re-notifying 80 per cent of the Sites Special Scientific Interest under Section 28 of the Wildlife and Countryside Act 1981. Publication by Countryside Commission of *New Opportunities for the Countryside*. Designation of first Environmentally Sensitive Areas took effect. Adoption of EC Directive on the prevention and reduction of environmental pollution by asbestos. Secretary of State's decision on the Sizewell B Inquiry.
April	Her Majesty's Inspectorate of Pollution established - a unified pollution Inspectorate within DOE. Report of World Commission on Environment and Development, "The Brundtland Report", launched in London. DOE's Environmental Protection Technology Scheme, to stimulate private sector research, announced.
May	Announcement of decision to retrofit low nitrogen oxide (NOx) burners to all major coal-fired power stations.

Announcement that low and intermediate level radioactive waste to be placed in a multi-purpose deep facility; UK Nirex Ltd withdrew from geological investigations at the four shallow sites.

June — Prime Minister announced framework of a contingency plan to cater specifically for the consequences to the UK of nuclear accidents outside the UK.

July — Amendment to Treaty of Rome (the Single European Act) containing an environment chapter entered into force.

Regulations introduced banning the use of organotins in anti-fouling paints for small vessels.

Publication of Government proposals for creating a National Rivers Authority.

EC Environment Council agreed new measures for controlling vehicle emissions.

Government designated all anti-fouling paints as pesticides.

September — UK signed Montreal Protocol for substances that deplete the ozone layer.

Publication by Countryside Commission of *Recreation 2000 - Enjoying the Countryside*.

October — Hurricane force winds (16th) caused massive damage to trees in southern England. Government gave special help for replacement of amenity trees.

November — UK hosted second international Ministerial conference on protection of the North Sea.

December — EC Regulation on export of banned or severely restricted chemicals.

1988

January — Publication of Government proposals for implementing the National Response Plan and the RIMNET radiation monitoring system for handling overseas nuclear incidents.

EC Resolution agreed on action programme on cadmium.

February — UK issued national guidance on implementation of the decisions reached at the North Sea Conference, November 1987.

March — Control of Asbestos at Work Regulations 1987 came into force.

UK hosted a preliminary meeting of the North Sea Task Force.

End of European Year of the Environment.

Royal assent given to the Norfolk and Suffolk Broads Act establishing a new authority for the Broads.

April — Merger of COSIRA and the Development Commission to form the Rural Development Commission.

May — Sections 12-14 of the Control of Pollution Act 1974 implemented. Clarification of requirements for disposal licences for deposit of waste on land.

EC agreed measures to ratify and implement the Montreal Protocol.

June — Secretary of State announced conclusions following consultations on waste disposal law amendments.

Launch of Environmental Protection Technology (EPT) scheme: first invitation for research proposals.

EC Directive (88/436/EEC) on vehicle emissions.

July — Government announced the establishment of the Interim Advisory Committee on Introductions (IACI), set up to advise the DOE on the ecological implications of the release of genetically manipulated or non-indigenous organisms into the environment.

Publication of *Our Common Future* (with a foreword by the Prime Minister): the government's response to the Bruntland report.

September — Regulations laid to implement EC Directive on the transfrontier shipment of hazardous waste.

House of Lords Report on Radioactive Waste Management published. This advised the deep burial of low and intermediate level nuclear waste and continuance of the THORP project at Sellafield.

October — Ministerial opening of the first phase of the RIMNET radiation monitoring network.

November — Government implemented EC Directive on transfrontier shipment of hazardous waste.

UK signed Sofia protocol to freeze the level of emissions of nitrogen oxides at 1987 levels by 1994 and by 1996 to agree further reductions based upon the critical loads approach.

EC Directive (88/609/EEC) on emissions from large combustion plants.

December — Government policy proposals on the National River Authority published.

1989

January — Waste management paper on landfill gas published by DOE.

February — UK Nirex report recommended that low level nuclear waste should be placed with intermediate waste in a deep repository.

March — *Environment in Trust*, a series of leaflets setting out the Governments's environmental record, launched by the Secretary of State.

London International conference on Saving the Ozone Layer opened by the Prime Minister.
House of Commons Environment Committee report on toxic waste policy published.

Budget proposals included a further reduction in the price of unleaded petrol which became 10p per gallon cheaper than leaded.

Full operation of the National Radioactivity Monitoring Network (RIMNET) announced by DOE.

Nirex report recommendations on radioactive waste disposal accepted by Government which said that detailed geological surveys would be carried out near Sellafield and Dounreay.

UK signed UNEP global declaration on hazardous wastes.

April — Consultation paper on *Cost Recovery Charging for Integrated Pollution Control* published.

The Prime Minister hosted a seminar at 10 Downing Street on climate change.

May	The Secretary of the State for the Environment attended the first meeting of the parties to the Vienna Convention and the Montreal Protocol on the protection of the ozone layer. Sir Cripin Tickell, UK ambassador to the United Nations, addressed UN General Assembly on global climate change. The Minister of Agriculture announced that the Government was setting up pilot zones, called Nitrate Sensitive Areas (NSAs), where the use of nitrates and other agrichemicals would be restricted.
June	World Environment Day: Lord Caithness, environment minister, addressed a seminar on climate change organised by the UK committee for UNEP. EC Directive (89/427/EEC) on air quality limit values and guide values for sulphur dioxide and suspended particulates. UK banned all imports of ivory. Second plenary session of the Inter-governmental Panel on climate change held in Nairobi.
July	Water Act 1989, which set up water and sewerage business in England and Wales and created National Rivers Authority, received Royal assent. Government announced intention to reorganise the Nature Conservancy Council to reflect more closely the differing needs of England, Scotland and Wales. House of Commons Energy Select Committee reported on the energy policy implications of the greenhouse effect. "Forests for the Community" to promote the creation of multi-purpose forests on the fringes of major towns and cities, launched by DOE. EC Directive (89/458/EEC) on emissions from motor vehicles.
August	DOE discussion paper on environmental labelling issued. House of Lords select committee report on nitrates in water published. Pearce report on sustainable development launched at a DOE press conference. Consultation paper on *Integrated Pollution Control and Local Authority Air Pollution Control: Public Access to Information* published.
September	Vesting day for water privatisation. National Rivers Authority comes into being. Progress report on the implementation of the Bruntland Commission report produced as a contribution to the UK's Awareness Raising and Public Participation seminar at Selsdon Park. The first of four preparatory workshops prior to the Bergen Ministerial Conference in 1990. CLEAR lead free petrol week and the national lead free petrol week. Commonwealth Secretariat report on *Climate Change: Meeting the Challenge* launched.
October	The Convention on International Trade in Endangered Species (CITES) agreed to further measures to protect the African elephant.

	UK signed the UNEP Basle convention on the Control of Transboundary Movements of Hazardous Waste and their Disposal. The Secretary of the State for the Environment, speaking at the Conservative Party conference, said that the Government would produce a white paper on environmental policies as well as a forthcoming "Green Bill". He also set a target that within 10 years, at least half of recyclable household waste should be recycled (the present figure is 6 per cent). Sofia Conference on Security and Co-operation in Europe (CSCE) proposed action for the prevention and control of the transboundary effects of industrial accidents, the management of hazardous chemicals and the pollution of transboundary watercourses and international lakes. Langkawi declaration of Commonwealth heads of government called for co-ordinated effort to tackle global environmental problems.
November	Leaflet on *Global Climate Change*, explaining the facts about climate change and the measures being taken to deal with them, launched by DOE. UK signs international declaration at Noordwijk recognising the need for stabilisation of CO_2 emissions by the year 2000. The Prime Minister's speech on environmental protection to the United Nations General Assembly proposed aid to developing countries to enable them to preserve tropical rain forests.
1990	
January	EC Directive (90/35/EEC) on dangerous preparations adopted. Drinking Water Inspectorate established and new monitoring regime for for public water supplies came into operation. Consultation paper on *Special Waste and the Control of its Disposal* published.
March	The Secretary of State for the Environment announced, to coincide with the third North Sea Conference, that the UK would cease the dumping of sewage sludge in the North Sea by 1998, while significant discharges of sewage to coastal and estuarial waters would in future receive treatment at sewage treatment works. The Minister of Agriculture also announced the government's decision to end the dumping of industrial waste at sea by 1993 at the latest, while incineration of toxic waste in the North Sea would cease by the end of 1990. North Sea Conference in The Hague ends with agreement to destroy,in an environmentally acceptable manner, all identifiable polychlorinated biphenyls (PCBs) by 1999 and reduce the flow into the sea of nutrients such as phosphates and nitrates. There will also be further reductions in the amount of hazardous substances and pesticides allowed to enter the sea via rivers and the atmosphere. The conference also agreed measures to reduce operational discharges from shipping and offshore platforms to help protect marine wildlife species.
April	Limit set on release of asbestos to air (SI 1990 no 556). The Minister of Agriculture designated 10 Nitrate Sensitive Areas (for the control of nitrates released to watercourses from agriculture), and nine advisory areas.

May	EC Environment Council adopted regulation to set up European Environment Agency.

EC Directive (90/219/EEC) on the contained use of genetically modified micro-organisms (GMOs), and EC Directive (990/220/EEC) on the deliberate release into the environment of GMOs were adopted.

Declaration issued by the 34-nation Bergen Conference on Sustainable Development. The declaration endorsed the precautionary principle, which recognises the need to prevent serious environmental damage even when full scientific understanding does not exist. The Conference also agreed to provide help for developing countries in tackling environmental problems and restated international commitment to the Inter-governmental Panel on Climate Change (IPCC) and the need for a climate change convention.

Prime Minister opened Hadley Centre for Climate Prediction and Research.

June Maximum permitted sulphur content of gas oil and motor fuel reduced to 0.3 per cent by weight (SI 1990 nos 1096 and 1097).

EC Directive (90/313/EEC) on the freedom of access to information on the environment adopted.

Second meeting of parties to the Montreal Protocol on substances that deplete the ozone layer, chaired by the Secretary of State for the Environment, agreed to strengthen the Protocol and establish a financial mechanism to assist developing countries to comply with its terms.

July Wide-ranging review of discharge consent system and compliance policy published by National Rivers Authority.

Second interim report on national water metering trials published.

Badenoch Report on cryptosporidium in water supplies published, together with government response.

August EC Directive (90/415/EEC) on dangerous substances in water adopted.

IPCC completed first report, which included UK-led working group report on science of climate change.

September *This Common Inheritance: Britain's Environment Strategy* (Cm 1200), the government's environment white paper, published.

New leaflet on heritage (in the Environment in Trust series) issued.

The government issued a draft plan for the implementation of the Large Combustion Plants Directive (88/609/EEC) which set out the UK's proposals for emission reductions for sulphur dioxide and oxides of nitrogen from exsisting plant.

Implemention of EC Directive (90/476/EEC) on interim measures applicable after the unification of Germany in anticipation of the adoption of transitional measures by the council in co-operation with the parliament.

October DOE published *Report of the Noise Review Working Party, 1990* (Batho Report).

NRA published report on occurrences of toxic blue-green algae in freshwater.

The government ratified the NO_x Protocol signed in Sofia in November 1988. It commits the UK to reduce overall emissions of oxides of nitrogen to 1987 levels by 1994 from all sources and to develop programmes for further reductions based on the critical loads approach.

The Secretary of State for the Environment announced a three-point plan to improve Britain's environment. This involves the creation of a midlands national forest, an initiative to help farmers and landowners protect areas of the countryside under pressure from visitors, and the provision of extra funds for the restoration of cathedrals and churches.

The government announced that air quality information would be given in weather bulletins from the Meteorological Office.

Second World Climate Conference held in Geneva. Scientific sessions endorse IPCC report; ministerial declaration calls for negotiations on framework convention on climate change by 1992, welcomed commitments made by many industrial countries to set targets to reduce greenhouse gas emissions and recognised need to assist developing countries to play their full part in the international response. EC member states agreed that, assuming other leading countries took similar action, they were willing to take action aimed at stabilising carbon dioxide emissions at 1990 levels by the year 2000 in the EC as a whole. Acknowledgement was made of UK target of returning carbon dioxide emissions to 1990 levels by the year 2005.

The DOE issued a consultation document proposing that companies will have to increase the amount of information they disclose on environmentally sensitive processes.

November Environmental Protection Act received Royal Assent.

The DOE issued draft regulations prescribing processes and substances for control from April 1991 under part 1 of the Environmental Protection Act.

Agreement at the London Dumping Convention to ban by 1995 the dumping of industrial waste by ships at sea.

Director General of Water Services published a consultation paper on *Paying for Water: a Time for Decisions*.

December DOE published a consultation paper which set out the basis on which it intended to implement the Control of Pollution (Amendment) Act 1989. The paper included a draft of the regulations necessary to give effect to the registration of waste carriers and the procedure under which a waste regulation authority may seize a vehicle used for fly-tipping.

Consultation paper on tree preservation, proposing to streamline Tree Preservation Orders and introduce Hedgerow Management Orders, issued by DOE.

EC agreed to cut CFC emissions by 85 per cent by mid-1995 and eliminate them by 1997. UK announced that it would ban CFCs at least six months earlier than its European partners. The production of halon gases would be phased out by 2000.

DOE issued invitation to voluntary groups to apply for project funding under the new environmental grant fund, proposed in the environment white paper published in September 1990.

Statistical Bulletin (91)1

The Statistical Bulletin may be purchased from the Department of the Environment, price £3. All tables cover the United Kingdom and the year 1989 unless otherwise stated.

Orders should be sent to:
DOE Publications Sales Unit
Victoria Road
South Ruislip
HA4 0NZ
Telephone: (081) 841 3425

Air quality

1 Smoke: estimated emissions from coal combustion: by source
2 Smoke and sulphur dioxide: derogation areas and breaches of limit values - Directive 80/779/EEC
3 Smoke and sulphur dioxide: average urban concentrations
4 Offences under Clean Air Acts: contraventions, prosecutions and convictions: England and Wales, and Northern Ireland
5 Lead: average airborne concentrations

Water quality

6 River water quality: annual average concentrations of selected determinands: by river location: Great Britain
7 Bathing waters survey

Radioactivity

8 Radioactive gaseous effluent: annual emissions: by site: Great Britain
9 Radioactive liquid effluent (radionuclides subject to separate limits in authorisation): annual discharges to surface and coastal waters: by site: Great Britain
10 Radioactive liquid effluent (radionuclides not subject to separate limits in authorisations): annual discharges to surface and coastal waters: by site: Great Britain
11 Isotopic composition of liquid effluent from CEGB stations: Great Britain
12 Radioactivity from world-wide fall out: annual concentrations of strontium-90 to calcium and concentrations of caesium-137 in milk
13 Radioactivity concentrations in some samples of fish and shellfish at selected sites: Great Britain
14 Raw drinking water: radiochemical and chemical analyses: England and Wales
15 Summary of maximum committed effective dose equivalents to a one-year old infant from milk consumption: licensed nuclear sites: England and Wales
16 Radioactive liquid effluent: estimated collective doses from consumption of fish and shellfish: United Kingdom and other European states

Land and nature conservation

17 Agricultural and forestry land use: England and Wales: 1947,1969 and 1980
18 Tree preservation orders: confirmation, applications and appeals: 1979-87: England
19 Protected bird species: licences issued and birds taken
20 Fertilisers: trends in deliveries to agriculture

DISCONTINUED TABLES

Tables that can be updated are included in the Digest or the Statistical Bulletin. Enquiries about discontinued tables should be addressed to: Department of the Environment, EPS, Room B241, Romney House, 43 Marsham Street, London SW1P 3PY; telephone (071) 276 8425.

ROYAL COMMISSION ON ENVIRONMENTAL POLLUTION - REPORTS

DOE responses are published in the pollution papers series - listed on pages 115-16 - and the relevant number is given in brackets below.

1st report	First Report. Cmnd 4585 February 1971
2nd report	Three Issues in Industrial Pollution. Cmnd 4894 March 1972
3rd report	Pollution in some British Estuaries and Coastal Waters. Cmnd 5054 September 1972
4th report	Pollution Control: Progress and Problems. Cmnd 5780 December 1974. (No 4)
5th report	Air Pollution Control: an Integrated Approach. Cmnd 6371 January 1976. (No 18)
6th report	Nuclear Power and the Environment. Cmnd 6618 September 1976
7th report	Agriculture and Pollution. Cmnd 7644 September 1979. (No 21)
8th report	Oil Pollution of the Sea. Cmnd 8358 October 1981. (No 20)
9th report	Lead in the Environment. Cmnd 8852 April 1983. (No 19)
10th report	Tackling Pollution - Experience and Prospects. Cmnd 9149 February 1984. (Nos 22 and 23)
11th report	Managing Waste: the Duty of Care. Cmnd 9675 December 1985. (No 24)
12th report	Best Practicable Environmental Option. Cm 310 February 1988
13th report	The Release of Genetically Engineered Organisms to the Environment. Cm 720 July 1989. £13.90

DOE Pollution Papers and Reports

This digest is no 30 of the Department's series of Pollution Reports (which complements the series of official papers issued as Pollution Papers). Titles already published as Pollution Reports and Pollution Papers are listed below:

Pollution Reports

1* The Monitoring of Environmental Pollution: Report of the First UK/USSR Monitoring Symposium (DOE, 1977).

2   Monitoring the Marine Environment of the United Kingdom: First Report of the Marine Pollution Monitoring Management Group 1975-6 (DOE, 1977). £1.55.

3   Elaboration of the Scientific Bases for Monitoring the Quality of Surface Water by Hydrobiological Indicators: Report of the first Anglo-Soviet Seminar (DOE, 1978).

4* Digest of Environmental Pollution Statistics No 1 (HMSO, 1978). £3.25.

5   Glossary of Air Pollution Terms: Air Pollution Monitoring Management Group (HMSO, 1979). £2.

6   Monitoring the Marine Environment 1979-83: The Way Ahead: Second Report of the Marine Pollution Monitoring Management Group 1977-8 (DOE, 1979). 70p.

7* Digest of Environmental Pollution Statistics No 2 (HMSO, 1979).

8   Elaboration of the Scientific Bases for Monitoring the Quality of Surface Water by Hydrobiological Indicators: Report of the Second Anglo-Soviet Seminar (DOE, 1980).

9* Digest of Environmental Pollution and Water Statistics No 3 (HMSO, 1980).

10 European Community Screening Programme for Lead: United Kingdom Results for 1979-80 (DOE, 1981). £3.85.

11 The Glasgow Duplicate Diet Study (1979-80): A Joint Survey for DOE and MAFF (DOE, 1982). £1.80.

12 Department of the Environment Sponsored Research on Radioactive Waste: Progress Report 1980 (DOE, 1981). £2.85.

13* Digest of Environmental Pollution and Water Statistics No 4 (HMSO, 1982). £5.95.

14 Monitoring the Marine Environment: Into the Eighties: The Third Report of the Marine Pollution Monitoring Management Group 1979-81 (DOE, 1982). £2.10.

15 Blood-lead Concentrations in Pre-school Children in Birmingham (DOE, 1982). £4.15.

16* Digest of Environmental Pollution and Water Statistics No 5 (HMSO, 1982). £6.95.

17 State of the Art Review of Radioactivity Monitoring Programmes in the United Kingdom (DOE, 1983). £6.05.

18 European Community Screening Programme for Lead: United Kingdom Results for 1981 (DOE, 1983). £4.70.

19* Digest of Environmental Protection and Water Statistics No 6 (HMSO, 1983). £7.50.

20 Digest of Environmental Protection and Water Statistics No 7 (HMSO, 1984). £7.85.

21 Digest of Environmental Protection and Water Statistics No 8 (HMSO, 1985). £7.80.

22 UK Blood Lead Monitoring Programme 1984-7: Results for 1984 (HMSO, 1986). £7.

23* Digest of Environmental Protection and Water Statistics No 9 (HMSO, 1987). £8.

24 UK Blood Lead Monitoring Programme 1984-7: Results for 1985 (HMSO, 1987). £7.

25 Digest of Environmental Protection and Water Statistics No 10 (HMSO, 1988). £8.

26 UK Blood Lead Monitoring Programme 1984-7: Results for 1986 (HMSO, 1988). £6.70.

27* Digest of Environmental Protection and Water Statistics No 11 (HMSO, 1989). £9.

28 UK Blood Lead Monitoring Programme 1984-7: Results for 1987 (HMSO, 1990). £15.

29* Digest of Environmental Protection and Water Statistics No 12 (HMSO, 1990). £10.80.

Pollution Papers

1   The Monitoring of the Environment in the United Kingdom (1974). £1.

2   Lead in the Environment and its Significance to Man (1974). £2.

3* The Non-Agricultural Uses of Pesticides in Great Britain (1974).

4* Controlling Pollution (1975).

5   Chlorofluorocarbons and their Effect on Stratospheric Ozone (1976). £2.50.

6   The Separation of Oil from Water for North Sea Oil Operations (1976). 75p.

7* Effects of Airborne Sulphur Compounds on Forests and Freshwaters (1976).

8   Accidental Oil Pollution of the Sea (1976). £3.

9* Pollution Control in Great Britain: How it Works (1976).

10 Environmental Mercury and Man (1977). £1.40.

11 Environmental Standards: A Description of UK Practice (1977). 75p.

12* Lead in Drinking Water (1977).

13 Tripartite Agreement on Stratospheric Monitoring Between France, the United Kingdom and the United States of America (1977). £2.75.

14 Lead Pollution in Birmingham (1978). £3.75.

15 Chlorofluorocarbons and their Effect on Stratospheric Ozone: Second Report (1979). £4.75.

16 The United Kingdom Environment 1979: Progress of Pollution Control (1979). £2.

17 Cadmium in the Environment and its Significance to Man (1980). £3.75.

18 Air Pollution Control (1982). £2.80.

19 Lead in the Environment (1983). £2.95.

20 Oil Pollution of the Sea (1983). £4.20.

21 Agriculture and Pollution (1983). £4.20.

22 Controlling Pollution: Principles and Prospects (1984). £3.80.

23 Public Access to Environmental Information (1986). £4.50.

24 Managing Waste - The Duty of Care (1986). £4.10.

25 Organotin in Antifouling Paints: Environmental Considerations (1986). £5.80.

26 Nitrate in Water (1986). £6.30.

27 Dioxins in the Environment (HMSO, 1989). £8.60.

---

* Out of print

OECD reports

Two new environmental reports were published by the Organisation for Economic Co-operation and Development (OECD) in January 1991 on the occasion of the OECD Meeting of Environment Ministers (Paris, 30-31 January 1991):

The OECD *State of the Environment* report: 298 pages, 121 tables, figures and insets. OECD Paris, January 1991. ISBN 92-64-13442-5;

OECD *Environmental Indicators*, issued as a supplement to the State of the Environment report: 79 pages, 50 tables and figures. OECD Paris, January 1991.

The third report on *The State of the Environment* reviews the progress achieved in OECD countries in attaining environmental objectives over the past two decades. The report also examines the agenda for the 1990s: global atmospheric issues, air, inland waters, the marine environment, land, forests, wildlife, solid waste and noise. Whilst focused on the relationships between the state of the environment, economic growth and structural change in OECD countries, the report places its analysis in the context of world ecological and economic interdependence and the need for sustainable development. The report also calls for improvements in the coverage and reliability of environmental information and its availability.

The *Environmental Indicators* supplement presents a preliminary set of indicators following the request of the G7 summits of Heads of States and Governments in Paris (July 1989) and Houston (July 1990).

The third report on *The State of the Environment* is priced at £22. The *Environmental Indicators* supplement is provided free with the report. Copies can be obtained at HMSO outlets or by post from OECD Publications and Information Centre, 2 rue André Pascal, 75775 Paris, Cedex 16.

Printed in the United Kingdom for HMSO.
Dd.0293145, 3/91, C18, 3390/3, 5673, 141874.